W9-BRB-095

Contents at a Glance

Find the online chapter and other helpful information on this book's website at http://informit.com/title/9780789759894.

Table of Contents

3 Automating Your Home Lighting   41

6   Automating Your Kitchen and Laundry   **135**

7 Automating Home Entertainment   153

Find the online chapter and other helpful information on this book's website at http://informit.com/title/9780789759894.

About the Author

Michael Miller is a popular and prolific writer of close to 200 non-fiction books, known for his ability to explain complex topics to everyday readers. He writes about a variety of topics, including technology, business, and music. His best-selling books for Que include *My iPad for Seniors*, *My Facebook for Seniors*, *My Social Media for Seniors*, *My Internet for Seniors*, *My Samsung Galaxy S7 for Seniors*, *My Windows 10 Computer for Seniors*, *Easy Computer Basics*, and *Computer Basics: Absolute Beginner's Guide*. Worldwide, his books have sold more than 1.5 million copies.

Find out more at the author's website: www.millerwriter.com

Follow the author on Twitter: molehillgroup

Dedication

To my six wonderful grandkids, who are all interested in smart technology (especially Amazon Alexa!): Collin, Alethia, Hayley, Judah, Lael, and Jackson.

Acknowledgments

A big thanks to everyone at Que Publishing and Pearson who helped to turn this idea into a book, including but not limited to Laura Norman, Charlotte Kughen, Greg Wiegand, and technical editor Jeri Usbay. Thanks also to all the people at all the companies who provided products for me to evaluate, including Nicol Addison (Google and Nest), Beth Brenner (Philips), Brigid Gorham (Ring), Andrew Hussey (TrackR), Carley Lassalette (Kwikset), Patrick Mahoney (Wink), Sean Miguad (Insteon), Josh Oppenheim-Rothschild (SimpliSafe), Evan Stein (iHome), and Callie Stephans (Revolar). In addition, a special thanks to Jodi Lipson and the other kind folks at AARP for adding even more to this project.

Photo Credits

Chapter 2

Insteon Hub and devices and Amazon Echo, Insteon Starter Kit (page 20); courtesy Insteon (www.insteon.com)

Apple iPhone and Home app (page 35); courtesy Apple Inc. (www.apple.com)

Amazon Echo (page 36); courtesy Amazon.com, Inc. (www.amazon.com)

Google Home (page 37); courtesy Google, Inc. (madeby.google.com/home/)

Chapter 3

Bedroom with smart lighting (page 40); courtesy Philips Lighting B.V. (www.meethue.com)

Chapter 4

Nest Learning Thermostat (page 70); courtesy Nest Labs (www.nest.com)

Carrier Cor Wi-Fi Thermostat (page 76); courtesy Carrier Corporation (www.carrier.com)

Ecobee4 (page 78); courtesy Ecobee, Inc. (www.ecobee.com)

Emerson Sensi Wi-Fi Thermostat (page 78); courtesy Emerson Electric Co. (www.sensicomfort.com)

Honeywell Lyric Wi-Fi Thermostat and Honeywell Wi-Fi Smart Thermostat (page 79); courtesy Honeywell International Inc. (yourhome.honeywell.com)

Chapter 5

August Doorbell Cam (page 102), August Smart Lock (page 109), and installing August Smart Lock (page 110) courtesy August Home (www.august.com)

Ring Video Doorbell (page 103) and Ring Chime Pro (page 105); courtesy Bot Home Automation (www.ring.com)

SkyBell HD Wi-Fi Video Doorbell (page 106); courtesy SkyBell Technologies, Inc. (www.skybell.com)

Kwikset Kevo (page 111) and Kwikset Premis Touchscreen Smart Lock (page 112); courtesy Spectrum Brands, Inc. (www.kwikset.com)

Schlage Connect (page 113) and Schlage Sense (page 114); courtesy Schlage (www.schlage.com)

Yale Assure Lock with Bluetooth (page 114); courtesy ASSA ALLOY (www.yalelock.com)

Arlo Q (page 117) and Arlo Pro (page 118); courtesy NETGEAR (www.arlo.com)

Canary Flex (page 119) and Canary (page 129); courtesy Canary Connect, Inc. (www.canary.is)

Nest Cam Indoor (page 120), Nest Cam Outdoor (page 121), and Nest Protect (page 125); courtesy Nest Labs (www.nest.com)

Birdi (page 123); courtesy Birdi (www.getbirdi.com)

Halo+ (page 124); courtesy Halo Smart Labs (www.halosmartlabs.com)

SmartThings Home Monitoring Kit (page 127); courtesy SmartThings, Inc. (www.smartthings.com)

Piper (page 130); courtesy Icontrol Networks (www.getpiper.com)

iSmartAlarm Preferred Package and smartphone app (page 131); courtesy iSmart Alarm Inc. (www.ismartalarm.com)

SimpliSafe Starter Home Security System (page 132); courtesy SimpliSafe, Inc. (www.simplisafe.com)

Chapter 6

GE Laundry smartphone app (page 134) and GE Wi-Fi Connect dishwasher (page 146); courtesy GE Appliances (www.geappliances.com)

Samsung Family Hub refrigerator (page 140), Samsung Wi-Fi gas range (page 144); courtesy Samsung (www.samsung.com)

Whirlpool Smart Cabrio washer and dryer (page 149); courtesy Whirlpool (www.whirlpool.com)

Chapter 7

Samsung Smart Hub screen (page 157); courtesy Samsung (www.samsung.com)

Roku Premiere (page 158) and Roku home screen (page 159); courtesy Roku, Inc. (www.roku.com)

Harmony Hub, Harmony Elite remote control, and smartphone app (page 163); courtesy Logitech (www.logitech.com)

Chapter 8

Chamberlain MyQ Garage Door Opener (page 168); courtesy The Chamberlain Group, Inc. (www.chamberlain.com)

Wemo Light Switch (page 168); courtesy Belkin International, Inc. (www.wemo.com)

Neato Botvac D3 Connected (page 168); courtesy Neato Robotics, Inc. (www.neatorobotics.com)

Nespresso Prodigio (page 168); courtesy Nestle Nespresso S.A. (www.nespresso.com)

iHome Smart Plug (page 170); courtesy SDI Technologies, Inc. (www.ihomeaudio.com)

Lutron Serena window coverings and remote control (page 173); courtesy Lutron Electronics Co., Inc. (www.lutron.com)

Samsung POWERbot Robot Vacuum (page 174); courtesy Samsung (www.samsung.com)

Mr. Coffee Smart Brew Optimal Brew coffeemaker and Wemo smartphone app (page 177); courtesy Sunbeam Products, Inc. (www.mrcoffee.com)

Automatic Pro car adapter and smartphone app (page 180); courtesy Automatic Labs (www.automatic.com)

Robomow (page 182); courtesy Robomow (www.robomow.com)

Chapter 9

Wink Hub2 (page 184); Wink Hub 2 and Wink Relay Touchscreen Controller (page 195); courtesy Wink Labs Inc. (www.wink.com)

Chapter 10

Apple iPad, iPhone, and iWatch (page 212); courtesy Apple Inc. (www.apple.com)

Chapter 11:

Amazon Echo and Echo Dot (page 234); courtesy Amazon.com Inc. (www.amazon.com)

Amazon Echo (page 237); courtesy Amazon.com Inc. (www.amazon.com)

Amazon Echo Dot (page 238); courtesy Amazon.com Inc. (www.amazon.com)

Amazon Echo Show (page 239); courtesy Amazon.com Inc. (www.amazon.com)

Chapter 12

Google Home (page 268); courtesy Google, Inc. (https://madeby.google.com/home/)

Google Home (page 270); courtesy Google, Inc. (https://madeby.google.com/home/)

Google Chromecast (page 282); courtesy Google, Inc. (https://madeby.google.com)

Chapter 13

Arlo Smart Security System (page 290); courtesy NETGEAR (www.arlo.com)

GMS Med-e-lert Automatic Pill Dispenser (page 296); courtesy Group Medical Supply, LLC (www.medelert.net)

Revolar personal safety device (page 301); courtesy Revolar (www.revolar.com)

TrackR Bravo (page 302); courtesy TrackR, Inc. (www.thetrackr.com)

About AARP

AARP is a nonprofit, nonpartisan organization, with a membership of nearly 38 million, that helps people turn their goals and dreams into *real possibilities*™, strengthens communities, and fights for the issues that matter most to families such as healthcare, employment and income security, retirement planning, affordable utilities, and protection from financial abuse. Learn more at aarp.org.

We Want to Hear from You!

As the reader of this book, you are our most important critic and commentator. We value your opinion and want to know what we're doing right, what we could do better, what areas you'd like to see us publish in, and any other words of wisdom you're willing to pass our way.

We welcome your comments. You can email or write to let us know what you did or didn't like about this book—as well as what we can do to make our books better.

Please note that we cannot help you with technical problems related to the topic of this book.

When you write, please be sure to include this book's title and author as well as your name and email address. We will carefully review your comments and share them with the author and editors who worked on the book.

Email: feedback@quepublishing.com

Mail: Que Publishing
ATTN: Reader Feedback
800 East 96th Street
Indianapolis, IN 46240 USA

Reader Services

Visit our website and register this book at www.informit.com/register for convenient access to any updates, downloads, or errata that might be available for this book.

Technology Note

Smart home technology is continuously and rapidly changing. The products and services discussed in this book were accurate at the time of writing, but it's likely that some things will have changed by the time you are reading this text. Always consult with device manufacturers for the latest models, features, and prices.

AARP Benefits

At the time this book went to publication, AARP members are able to take advantage of discounts on certain smart home devices. Check http://www.aarp.org/benefits-discounts/ for these and other discounts and benefits for AARP members.

Making Your Life Easier with Smart Home Technology

What if your home could turn your lights on or off by themselves, based on who's in the room? What if your washer and dishwasher could automatically start their cycles when you're asleep or away from home, to reduce noise and save water? What if your thermostat knew what temperature you liked in each room at any given time of day (or night)? What if you could see on your smartphone who's ringing your doorbell—even if you're away from home? What if you could control music playback in other rooms from your comfy chair in the living room? What if you could control all these operations—and more—with simple voice commands?

If you'd like your home to do any or all of the above, then you need to embrace smart home technology. A smart home automates these and other functions to make your home more efficient and easier to live in and with.

What Is a Smart Home?

You've no doubt heard about this thing called a *smart home*, even if you're a little vague on what a smart home is or does. That's okay; the whole notion of smart homes and smart home technology is a little fuzzy, or at least has been in the past. Let's see if I can clear things up.

At its most basic, a smart home is one that uses so-called "smart" technology to automate and operate important tasks and devices, including:

- Lighting
- Heating and cooling
- Door locks and doorbells
- Home security
- Home entertainment
- Kitchen and laundry appliances

Smart technology is technology that senses what's happening around a particular sensor or device and acts autonomously based on the information it collects. For example, a smart device might sense someone walking into a room and open the shades or turn off the lights or turn up the heat or whatever you've programmed it to do.

The goal with these devices is to make your home "smart" enough that you're not bothered by manually performing mundane operations. The theory is that these devices free up your valuable time for more important things.

Beyond this simple type of home automation of basic tasks, smart home technology can learn about the things you and your family do and use that information to make your home more efficient. We're talking about things like the following:

- Turning off the lights when no one's in the room, dimming them when you're watching TV, and turning them up all the way when you're reading, without you having to flip a single switch
- Running the air conditioner or furnace only when needed, or when electricity costs are at a minimum, so that you save on your gas and electric bills

- Automatically locking the doors and activating home security systems when you leave the house—and unlocking and deactivating them when you return home

- Monitoring your home's air quality, water usage, and more, alerting you—and proper authorities—if there's smoke, too much CO_2, a water leak, or anything else remotely out of whack

In addition, most of today's smart home devices not only let you program in various operating scenarios, but also control them via your smartphone whether you're at home or away. Not sure whether you turned off the lights or locked the front door when you left? Check the status and make adjustments from a smartphone app. Want to be alerted when somebody rings your doorbell? Activate a remote camera from your smartphone, even if you're halfway across the continent. Want to start your oven when you leave work so your dinner will be ready when you get home? There's an app for that, too.

>>>Go Further
THE SMART EVOLUTION

Up until just a few years ago, a smart home was considered one in which various electrical and electronic devices were hardwired to a central computerized control system. That definition has gone by the wayside as wireless technology replaced wired connections, and free or inexpensive controllers and apps replaced big and expensive computer systems.

Today, more and more of the "smarts" in a smart home installation have been offloaded to inconspicuous wireless controllers or to smartphone apps. We're no longer talking about expensive proprietary hardwired systems but rather lightweight and low-cost systems that can work independently or in conjunction with compatible systems from other manufacturers.

This new definition of the smart home, based on the evolution of various technologies, has opened up smart home technology to a larger consumer market. You no longer have to call an expensive home automation installer; you can now hook up your smart home one piece at a time, at a cost that doesn't put a huge dent in your pocketbook.

How Smart Home Technology Works

Smart lighting, smart thermostats, smart door locks—how do all these smart devices work? Well, it's all about using wireless technology and computer algorithms to add more functionality to traditional everyday devices. Here are some basics.

Smart Communications

Let's start with how various smart devices "talk" to one another. The first generation of home automation devices used hardwired connections, via Ethernet cable (or, in some cases, proprietary connectors), to connect to a central brain. This brain was either a traditional computer system (typically a large desktop model with lots of expansion capability) or some sort of controller box using proprietary technology. This central brain controlled all the connected devices, turning them on and off according to a preprogrammed schedule.

As you might suspect, it's difficult and costly to hard-wire all the rooms in even an average-sized house, so the second generation of home automation devices turned to wireless technology to connect everything. Unfortunately, proprietary technology still ruled, so one company's wireless devices couldn't connect to those from another company. You had to pick a company and a technology up front and then buy only those devices that worked with that technology. Buy something from another company and it simply wouldn't work with what you already had installed.

Fortunately, wiser heads prevailed over time, and the major smart device suppliers designed "hubs" that let devices from a variety of other companies work with each other. A single hub now supports multiple protocols, which makes it easy to connect whatever type of smart device you want. And most of these so-called smart hubs also connect to your home's Wi-Fi network to control any devices that may be connected via Wi-Fi.

It's Not All Good

Incompatible Technologies

While you can connect most smart home devices to your home Wi-Fi network, you could still run into compatibility issues between devices from different manufacturers. In short, not everything is compatible with everything else. For example, some devices might connect to Amazon's Echo hub but not to Apple's Home app. When you want to connect a given device to an existing hub or app, always check compatibility before you buy.

Smart Operations

As noted, you connect smart devices (either to each other or to a central control hub) via your home's Wi-Fi network. What happens next?

The thing that makes smart technology so useful is the ability to control those smart devices you've connected. In many instances, you can control a smart device via a smartphone app; this means you can control smart lighting, heating, etc., even when you're not at home, using your smartphone. You may control devices using the app supplied by the device's manufacturer, or via an app that consolidates control of multiple devices from a variety of manufacturers. (The best example of this is Apple's Home app.)

You can also use smart controllers to operate multiple smart devices. Many companies supply smart hubs and smartphone apps to control their own devices, or you can use a central controller (such as Amazon Echo or Google Home) to control multiple devices via voice commands. Just tell the controller or the app what you want to do, such as "turn on the living room lights" or "lock the front door," and the appropriate devices are activated.

You can also opt to program your smart control devices to turn on/off and do things according to the schedule you select. This may be the least "smart" aspect of your smart home, as you can currently set internal or external timers to control your thermostat, oven, irrigation system, and more; it's not anything that's remotely new. That said, it's still more advanced than turning things on or off manually, so there's that.

>>>Go Further

INTERNET OF THINGS

The concept of the smart home and smart devices is part of a larger technology trend called the Internet of Things (IoT). In the IoT, various smart devices connect with other smart devices, both inside and outside the home, to provide automated operation and decision-making.

Today, the IoT is beginning to permeate all aspects of our modern life, in the form of "smart" houses, cars, airplanes, hospitals, and even cities and states. Virtually any device that can incorporate some type of sensor and Wi-Fi transmitter can become part of the IoT, and thus enhance the command and control of related operations.

If you're interested, you can learn more about the IoT in my companion book, *The Internet of Things*, available wherever good books are sold.

Smart Interactivity

Smart devices get even smarter when they can communicate with and control each other. The information collected by one device can be shared with others to better automate their operation.

Let's say you have a smart lighting system and add a motion sensor—you know, a device that senses when someone is moving around in a room. With the motion sensor connected to the home lighting system, when the motion sensor senses motion it sends that data to your lighting system and then turns on the lights. If there's no motion sensed for a given period of time, the lighting system knows to dim or turn off the lights to save energy. That's useful.

Now connect that motion sensor to a smart home security system, or to a smart thermostat, and you see the true benefit of the smart home coming into focus. There are lots of things you want your home to do when you're away, and different things you want your home (or a particular room) to do when you're home. When your smart home knows whether you're there (thanks to a motion sensor or other smart sensor), your home gets a lot smarter.

Let's examine, for example, how various smart devices can work together when you leave the house. Via a smart tracking device or a smart garage door opener, your interconnected system recognizes that you've just left home. Great. This information is fed to various smart devices to make things happen. First, your home security system is activated, which probably involves multiple smart devices, such as door locks, motion sensors, and window sensors. Next, your smart lighting system kicks in and turns off all the lights you left on—unless you've programmed the system to turn lights on and off in various rooms to confuse any particular burglars while you're away. To conserve energy use, your smart thermostat adjusts the heat or the air conditioner, according to the season. And various smart appliances kick in as necessary; for example, your dryer may go into low heat mode (to avoid wrinkles) or the dishwasher may start, or whatever you've programmed. It's all about all your smart devices working together without any manual interaction needed on your part.

Even better, you can create different "scenes" or scenarios that involve multiple smart devices. Create a "movie" scene, tell your system to "play a movie," and then watch the lights dim, the automatic curtains close, your TV and sound system turn on and switch to movie playback, and your noisy dishwasher and washing machine switch off. Create a "party" scene and have your sound system switch to a particular streaming station, turn on speakers in selected rooms around the house, turn up lights and turn down air conditioning (because parties tend to heat things up), and maybe even turn on some outside lighting so the fun can go outdoors.

You see the possibilities here. There's a lot that smart home technology can do when the different smart devices start working together. (And there's even more benefit to come when your home devices start talking to other devices in your neighborhood or city or even around the world in the cloud—the sky's the limit!)

What Can Your Smart Home Control?

All this sounds intriguing, but let's get down into more details. What specific types of things can you control with smart home technology?

Smart Lighting

Smart lighting systems let you to control the lights inside and outside your house. Lights can be controlled on a preprogrammed time cycle, or you can configure them to automatically shut off when a room is unoccupied—but turn back on when someone walks into the room. You can also control individual lights via a smartphone app or smart hub.

These systems typically require the smart bulbs to be wirelessly connected to some sort of gateway device or to your home network. Alternatively, some smart lighting systems work by plugging an existing light into a so-called smart plug.

In either instance, you then connect the gateway device to a system remote control or a smartphone app and use that remote control or app to send the necessary commands to all connected bulbs. You can turn on or off individual lights or groups of lights, or, in some instances, you can dim the lights. For that matter, you can use the system's smartphone app and the Internet to control the lighting in your house while you're away.

Beyond simple on/off operation, some smart LED lights can be configured to output a specific brightness or color. This lets you provide different levels and types of lighting for different tasks.

LED Lighting

One of the advantages of LED lighting is that the individual LEDs in a bulb can be adjusted to different brightness levels and different colors. You can't do that with CFL or traditional incandescent bulbs.

A number of companies offer smart lights and smart lighting control systems, including Connected by TCP, Cree, GE, Hue by Philips, LIFX, Lutron, and WeMo by Belkin.

Learn More

Learn more about smart lighting in Chapter 3, "Automating Your Home Lighting."

>>>Go Further

SMART PLUGS AND SWITCHES

Sometimes you want to control a lamp or kitchen appliance or other thing that isn't inherently smart—that is, it doesn't have smart technology built in. In this instance, you can employ a smart plug or smart switch to do the work. The plug itself connects to a standard wall outlet, but it contains all the wireless smarts to control whatever is plugged into it.

So you plug in a smart plug and then connect the lamp or appliance or other device you want to control. The smart plug is connected (wirelessly) to your smart controller so that you can control whatever is connected to the smart plug from the plug's smartphone app or controller. Thus, you can connect that "dumb" device to your smart home network and control it as you would any smart device. It's kind of an ingenious way to add smart technology to existing devices.

In addition to smart plugs, you can install smart outlets that replace existing power outlets in your home. It's a little more work, but the result looks nicer.

You can find smart plugs, switches, and outlets from ConnectSense, D-Link, iDevices, iHome, Insteon, TP-Link, WeMo by Belkin, and other companies. Like most smart devices, you can find them at Home Depot, Lowe's, and other home stores, as well as online at Amazon.com and similar online retailers.

Smart Heating and Cooling

Whether you live in a house or apartment, you control your home's furnace and air conditioner with some sort of thermostat. Older thermostats were purely manual, letting you dial in the fixed temperature you wanted. Newer thermostats offer some degree of automatic operation, typically by setting desired daytime and nighttime temperatures, defined by time of day.

Today's smart thermostats take this automated operation several steps further, with the goals of more precisely controlling your home's temperature and lowering your heating and cooling bills. After you use the smart thermostat a bit, it knows that you turn up the heat when you wake up on a winter morning and turn down the air when it gets warm on summer afternoons. All it takes is a week or so and it knows all your habits—and adjusts itself accordingly. It even knows when you leave the house, so it can put itself into an energy-saving "away" mode.

The most advanced smart thermostats not only control your home's temperature but also interface with other smart devices in your home. For example, a smart garage door opener can connect to your smart thermostat to tell it when you've left the house, so it can activate "away" mode. When you're away, your smart thermostat can trigger your smart appliances to adapt their operation—for example, your dryer can use longer (that is, cooler) cycles to save energy and to keep your clothes tumbling so that they stay fresh and unwrinkled until you get home. It can also trigger your smart lighting system to automatically turn on or off lights throughout your house to make it look as if you're at home.

The best-selling smart thermostat today is the Nest Learning Thermostat from Google, which interfaces with a large number of other smart devices. Other major manufacturers, such as Ecobee and Honeywell, also offer their own smart thermostats.

Learn More

Learn more about smart thermostats in Chapter 4, "Automating Your Heating and Cooling."

Smart Home Security

Traditional home security systems incorporate a variety of motion sensors, prox-imity sensors, and door/window sensors that connect to a main control unit. When the system is switched on and one of the sensors is breached, a signal is sent to the control unit. This may sound an alarm, turn on some lights, or send another signal to the system's monitoring company. The company then places a 911 call to local police, and things really start jumping!

Smart home security systems do all these things and more—and often without a monthly service fee. Today's complete systems let you to activate security on a room-by-room or zone-by-zone basis, whether you're at home or away (via smartphone apps). Some systems also integrate with smoke alarms and carbon monoxide sensors to alert the monitoring company when there's a fire or deadly gas in the house.

Things get more interesting when you connect your smart home security system with other smart home devices. For example, pressing a single button might lock all outside doors, arm the alarm system, close the motorized curtains, turn on selective lighting, and turn down the furnace. Not that you need to install an entire whole-house system. Smart home technology makes it easy to purchase only those components you need.

One of the most popular smart security devices is the so-called *smart lock*. This is a type of lock that you install in place of your existing door lock, and connects to your home network via Bluetooth or Wi-Fi. You can operate the lock with a smart-phone app, which means you no longer need to fumble for your keys to open the front door. Smartphone operation also means you can lock or unlock your doors while you're away from home.

In addition, you can install a smart doorbell on your front door. This type of device not only rings a bell when somebody pushes a button, it also activates a small security camera that beams a picture of whomever is doing the ringing to an accompanying smartphone app—so you can see who's at your door even when you're away.

There are also all sorts of other smart monitors you can add to your smart home. We're talking smart smoke detectors, smart CO_2 detectors, smart air quality monitors, smart water leakage detectors, and so forth—all accessed and con-trolled via smartphone, and all connected to your smart hub and other smart devices.

Learn More

Learn more about smart home security systems in Chapter 5, "Automating Home Security."

Smart Appliances

The kitchen is ripe for automation. You have a lot of different appliances in your kitchen (and laundry room), and they're all pretty dumb today.

That's about to change, as more and more smart appliances, both large and small, become available. Some of these appliances have only rudimentary smarts; others promise significantly automated operation.

In terms of small appliances—those that sit on your kitchen counter—look for items that can be controlled via smartphone app or tied into larger smart home systems. For example, a smart crock pot can be turned on via smartphone app while you're still at work, or programmed to turn on X number of hours before you come home. A smarter slow cooker (or toaster or blender or whatever) can tie into a wireless smart controller to know when you leave home in the morn-ing or arrive home at the end of the day, and perform the necessary operations automatically.

Larger smart appliances operate in much the same fashion. A smart oven can be turned on and heated to a given temperature remotely by a smartphone app when you're ready to leave the office, turned on automatically by either a timer or other program, or triggered by other devices in your smart home system. Same thing with a smart dishwasher or washing machine, but in the opposite fashion—you want these appliances to run when you're not at home (or at night when you're asleep) so the noise doesn't bother you when you are home.

Then there's the smart refrigerator. I'll be honest with you; the current batch of so-called "smart" refrigerators are really, really dumb. Yeah, you can spend some big bucks on refrigerators with LED displays on the door, but that doesn't make the appliance any smarter. Here we're waiting for refrigerators with cameras or other sensors inside that can sense when you're running low on certain types of food or beverages so the fridge can alert you to that fact or automatically place an order for said comestibles from your local grocery store. Like I said, we're still waiting for that kind of intelligence to arrive.

Learn More

Learn more about smart appliances in Chapter 6, "Automating Your Kitchen and Laundry."

Smart Home Entertainment

Home entertainment can also be integrated into a smart home environment. We're talking everything from today's so-called smart TVs (which really aren't that smart, but do make it easy to find and watch programming from a variety of sources) to whole-house entertainment systems. You can use smart hubs to call up movies or TV shows or music on your television or entertainment system, pipe those shows and music to other rooms, and even schedule recordings for when you're away.

Even better, much of this can be controlled with voice commands. Smart hubs such as the Amazon Echo and Google Home let you speak your commands and then they intelligently do the rest. Tell your smart hub that you'd like some mellow music, and it will find what you like on a streaming music service or in your home music library. Tell it that you want to watch the latest episode of your favorite TV show, and it will turn on your television set and recall that program. It's really kind of neat, and makes it a lot easier to watch and listen to the things you like.

Learn More

Learn more about smart entertainment devices and systems in Chapter 7, "Automating Home Entertainment."

Smart Home Control

I just mentioned the Amazon Echo and Google Home smart hubs. These are cool devices that sit in your living room or bedroom and listen for your voice commands. The hubs are connected (wirelessly) to various smart home devices and gateways and let you control those devices with plain English commands. That requires a bit of onboard artificial intelligence, of course, which these hubs have a lot of. They're really smart digital assistants, much like the Siri function on your iPhone. You can ask the Amazon or Google hub not only to control various devices, but also to tell you the current temperature, read the latest news headlines, or suggest a good restaurant. They are literally smart devices.

There are other smart hubs that don't offer all the personal assistant features of the Echo and Google Home devices. Both Insteon and Wink offer smart hubs that control smart devices from their own and other companies. And Apple's Home app lets you control a variety of smart devices from multiple companies from wherever your iPhone or iPad happens to be.

Learn More

Learn more about smart hubs and systems in Chapter 2, "Understanding Smart Home Hubs and Controllers."

And More...

The previous sections cover just the most popular types of devices and activities you can control with smart home technology. There are lots of other devices that don't fit into these general categories that might be of interest to you. I'm talking about things like smart garage door openers, smart irrigation systems, smart car sensors, and more. (And there will be a lot more coming once people and companies get smarter about what smart technology can do!)

Why You Need to Turn Your Home into a Smart Home

Automatic lighting, remote control security, devices that "talk" to one another—all of these things that might have qualified as fiction a decade or so ago are real and available today, with even more coming in the near future. What value might these smart devices offer you in your house or apartment?

You can benefit in many ways by installing various smart devices in your home. Some of the benefits are immediate, some more long-term, but they're all very real. It's not fiction any more.

Saving Time and Effort

First, smart devices can save you time and effort. Admittedly, it doesn't take a lot of effort to get up and flip a light switch, but it still takes a few seconds and a little bit of expended energy. It's kind of like adding a remote control for things that previously weren't remote controlled.

Like most of you, I can remember a time when you had to get up off the couch to change the channel or adjust the volume on the television set. Today, you just reach for the remote and change the channel or volume with the push of a button; you don't have to get up or off the couch. Well, imagine if you can do the same with other devices in your house—your lights, your thermostat, your washing machine. Instead of getting up to flip a switch or turn a dial, you reach for your smartphone and do it all from the comfort of your couch or easy chair, the same as you change channels on your TV.

It may seem like a little thing, but little things add up. All the individual seconds you save by not having to get up to dim the lights or turn up the heat become minutes and then hours as time goes by. The time you save becomes time you can put to better use than flipping switches and turning dials. Your time is more valuable than that.

Saving Money and Conserving Energy

In addition, smart devices can save you money—and, in the process, conserve energy, as well.

- Smart lighting saves money by dimming the lights when it makes sense and turning them off when you're not in the room.

- Smart power plugs, connected to motion sensors, save money by turning on devices only when you're nearby.

- Smart thermostats save money by running more efficiently based on your usage and schedule.

- Smart irrigation systems save money (on your water bill) by running only when your grass needs it, not on some prearranged schedule.

It's all about more efficient operation, and running appliances and lighting and other devices only when necessary. You won't find the lights in a smart home on all day.

Energy Usage

What tasks use the most energy in your home? In a typical residence, heating/cooling is the number-one culprit, contributing to 45% of your home's energy costs. Lighting and appliances come next, comprising 34% of total costs. Next is your water heater, with 13% of costs; everything else fills in the rest. So if you can cut even a little from your heating and lighting costs, it can result in big savings.

Doing More

Finally, smart devices can let you do more with your current appliances and devices than you can do with traditional "dumb" devices. For example, smart lighting kits do more than turn individual light bulbs on or off; they also can control lighting over an entire room or zone. You also can use smart lighting kits to transform traditional on/off lights into dimmable lights. And some smart lighting systems let you adjust a bulb's color temperature, making the light warmer or cooler. That adds a lot of functionality that simply isn't there with traditional light bulbs.

It gets even better when you get multiple smart devices talking to each other. For example, when you connect your smart thermostat to a smart garage door opener, you can turn down the heat the minute your car leaves the garage. Or connect that garage door opener to your smart lighting system, and watch your lights turn on as you walk in the back door. Smart appliances can also tap into the system, starting the washer or dishwasher when you leave the house, or switching the dryer to a low-heat mode when you're gone and don't need dry clothes right away.

There's a lot more potential for synergy and savings as today's smart devices get even smarter in the future. The point is that when you turn dumb devices into a network of connected smart devices, good things happen. And that's why you want to add smart technology to your house or apartment.

>>>Go Further

INDEPENDENT LIVING

Smart devices can also make it easier for you to perform certain tasks that may be becoming more difficult as you age. Smart pill dispensers remind you when it's time to take medication. Smart trackers let family and caregivers know if you wander off, or if there's an emergency. And smart home monitoring systems let others know what you're doing and when, and if you need any help.

And it's not just big stuff. When your knees start to ache or you have trouble breathing, getting up off the couch to turn up the lights or turn down the thermostat requires a lot of effort. It's these little things that add up and cause some to consider moving into assisted living facilities.

If you can use smart technology to perform many of these otherwise mundane tasks, you may be able to stay in your current house or apartment without needing physical assistance. It's even better when you can control these things with voice commands—especially if arthritis or other conditions make it difficult to use your hands and fingers. Let the technology do the work for you and your home can stay your home that much longer.

(By the way, the whole idea of letting smart technology handle traditional assisted living tasks is called *ambient assisted living*. We talk more about it in Chapter 13, "Using Smart Technology for Independent Living.")

Understanding Smart Home Hubs and Controllers

All smart home devices are not created equal. In fact, they may not be (and probably aren't) compatible with each other. There are several competing smart home technologies out there, and you need to know a little bit about them before committing to adding smart devices to your house or apartment. If nothing else, you want to make sure that all the devices you buy and install work with each other!

Understanding Smart Home Technologies

Smart devices have to connect to some sort of controller to work. That is, if you have a smart light bulb, it needs to somehow connect to an app on your smartphone so you can control it. (Most smart devices are controlled via smartphone apps.)

Now, some smart devices connect directly to their own apps, using your home's Wi-Fi system. For example, LIFX smart light bulbs work this way: Screw the smart bulb into the socket, download the LIFX app to your smartphone, and use that app to control the smart bulb, via Wi-Fi.

Smartphone app

Wi-Fi router

Smart light bulb

Controlling a smart bulb with a dedicated smartphone app, via Wi-Fi

More common are those smart devices that connect to some sort of central hub, using their own proprietary protocols. These hubs connect with multiple compatible smart devices and also connect to your home Wi-Fi network. You then connect your smartphone or tablet to the hub via your home's Wi-Fi network and use a mobile app to control the connected smart devices. And, because the hub is connected to your Wi-Fi network, it can interface with devices from other systems that don't necessarily use the hub's proprietary wireless technology.

As an example, consider the Wink Hub. You connect the Wink Hub to your home Wi-Fi network (via Ethernet, actually), then connect Wink-compatible devices to the hub via Wink's proprietary wireless technology. Your smartphone connects to the hub via Wi-Fi and then controls the smart devices via Wink's wireless system.

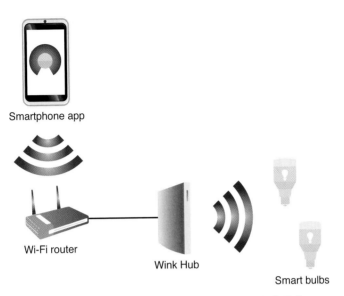

Smartphone app

Wi-Fi router

Wink Hub

Smart bulbs

Controlling a smart bulb via Wi-Fi and the Wink Hub

Fortunately, this isn't near as complicated as it sounds. Read on to learn more.

Protocols

A *protocol* is a set of rules that defines how a given technology works. Wi-Fi is actually a protocol for a wireless technology that all compatible devices must follow to work together. Same thing with ZigBee and Z-Wave. Protocols from one company are not (necessarily) compatible with other protocols—which means a device that uses the ZigBee protocol won't communicate with one that uses the Z-Wave protocol.

X10

I briefly mention X10 in the previous chapter, and when it comes to home automation technologies, X10 is the granddaddy of them all. X10 has been around since the mid-1970s and long has been a favorite among a small but dedicated core of do-it-yourselfers.

X10 is an old-school technology that hasn't really aged well. Compared to the wireless technologies that rule the smart home market today, the original X10 system was all hardwired, using your home's existing electrical connections. In the beginning, every X10 device had to plug into a nearby electrical outlet so it could use your home's power lines to connect to other X10 devices.

Later X10 devices adopted wireless protocols and thus could communicate via either power line or wireless. But that's kind of a moot point, because if you're shopping for smart home devices today, X10 just isn't a viable option. I mention it here only because some more experienced experimenters in home automation may still have some X10-compatible devices—and thus might want to connect them to today's more sophisticated wireless devices.

Insteon

The next generation of home automation/smart home system, from Insteon, mixes wired power line and wireless technologies. The Insteon system, and its two-layer network, enables control signals to jump from one layer to another if problems are encountered, thus enhancing both speed and reliability over older technology. Insteon is also compatible with the X10 protocol, so if you have older X10 devices, they're still usable.

Insteon's wireless networking uses a proprietary standard that operates in a mesh configuration. That is, it doesn't rely on a central hub or controller to distribute signals to all devices, as does Wi-Fi. Instead, each Insteon device wirelessly connects to every other device, creating an ever-expanding mesh network. Connect a new compatible device to the network and it's automatically connected to all the other existing devices in your home.

It gets a little more confusing when you consider that Insteon is a wireless technology and a company that sells smart home devices. Obviously, all Insteon devices are compatible with all other Insteon devices, and Insteon's hubs also let these devices connect to other non-Insteon devices, via Wi-Fi.

All that said, Insteon is more of a closed network than its newer competitors, so if you decide to go with Insteon you're really committing to using Insteon products. Also, because Insteon is an older technology (but still newer than X10), it's not quite as smooth around the edges as its newer competitors.

Wi-Fi

Wi-Fi, short for *wireless fidelity*, is the protocol used by almost all home wireless networks today. Chances are you already have a Wi-Fi network in your home, probably connected to your cable or DSL Internet modem. The Internet signal comes into the modem, which is connected to your Wi-Fi router. The Wi-Fi router centralizes and distributes all the wireless signals in your house (and a few wired ones, too, via the Ethernet connections on the back of the device).

Wi-Fi is a centralized networking technology, in that all the signals come into and go out of the router; individual devices do not directly talk to one another. That's different from the mesh networks created by most smart home hubs, which I discuss shortly.

Interestingly, most smart network hubs do not directly include Wi-Fi technology. Instead, they must be connected (typically via Ethernet cable) to your home's Wi-Fi router, and thus access your Wi-Fi network in this fashion.

Bluetooth

Bluetooth is a little like Wi-Fi, in that it enables wireless communication between devices. However, Bluetooth doesn't require a central hub; instead, it's designed for short-range wireless communication between devices. This is why you see Bluetooth used to connect keyboards and mice to computers, headsets to phones and tablets, and phones to automobiles. These are all very short-range operations, which is what Bluetooth is designed for.

You'll find Bluetooth used to connect devices to nearby hubs in some smart home scenarios. Both Insteon and Wink hubs have Bluetooth support, although it's not yet activated on the SmartThings hub.

Z-Wave

Z-Wave is a newer and more sophisticated wireless technology that creates a *mesh network* between each connected device. In a mesh network, each device communicates with each and every other device directly (or through the nearest device or series of devices), without going through a central hub. This type of mesh network is embraced by the smart home industry, as it quickly sets up its own network and expands in size to wherever the furthest device is located.

Z-Wave networks use a proprietary wireless technology that operates in the 900MHz band (908.42MHz, if you want to be precise), so there's no interference with Wi-Fi networks, which operate at the higher 2.4GHz frequency. That also means Z-Wave is not compatible with Wi-Fi devices, unless they're linked through some sort of central hub. (Most smart home hubs perform this kind of bridge function.) Z-Wave devices create what is called a mesh network that directly connects all the devices in the network to one another. This type of network offers a 30- to 60-foot range between each device.

The Z-Wave Alliance claims that more than 50 million Z-Wave-compatible devices have been sold to date, which makes it one of the, if not the, most popular technologies for connecting together smart devices in the home.

ZigBee

Finally we come to ZigBee, another wireless technology popular with smart home companies. ZigBee is a mesh networking technology that works very similarly to Z-Wave and is supported by a similar number of companies. ZigBee networks operate in the 915MHz band (in the United States, anyway; other bands are utilized in other countries), so there's no competition with either Z-Wave or Wi-Fi networks. Like Z-Wave, ZigBee creates a mesh network with a 30 to 60 foot connection range between devices.

Comparing Smart Home Systems

Now you know a little about the various smart networking protocols that can be used by smart home devices. Fortunately, you don't have to bother much with the technical details. Instead, focus on smart home systems that use these technologies—but make sure the system you choose is compatible with all the devices you want to use.

The three most popular smart home systems today come from Insteon, Samsung (SmartThings), and Wink. Insteon, as you might suspect, uses the Insteon protocol. SmartThings and Wink support both the Z-Wave and ZigBee protocols.

So if you have a Z-Wave or ZigBee device, don't go with Insteon, and if you have an Insteon device, don't go with SmartThings or Wink. Equally important, know that both SmartThings and Wink handle both the Z-protocols and act as bridges to enable devices from one protocol to work with devices from the other protocol.

Insteon

I've already addressed Insteon as a protocol, but now I want to talk about Insteon as a smart home system.

As previously discussed, Insteon is kind of a closed system. You install an Insteon hub, connect it to your Wi-Fi router and then add other Insteon-branded devices to the hub, using Insteon's proprietary wireless technology.

In theory, this should all work fairly seamlessly. In my experience, however, I've found Insteon to be a little rougher around the edges than the newer smart home systems discussed here. Remember, Insteon has been around for a while, that that's both good and bad.

On the plus side, there are a ton of Insteon devices out there for just about any need you might have. Whether you're talking a particular type of light switch or a door or motion detector, it's probably available. Given its time on the market, Insteon has developed a robust infrastructure. (Insteon is a particularly good choice when you're looking at replacing existing wall switches and outlets, with lots of choices there.)

On the minus side, by being a somewhat older technology, Insteon lacks some of the more modern refinements you might find with the newer systems from Samsung and Wink. Because of this, some people might find Insteon more difficult to work with, or not quite as "pretty" to the eye. To be honest with you, I've personally found Insteon to be a little trickier to work with; I've had problems getting some Insteon devices to work with other devices, or in some cases to work at all.

Now, if you're experienced with this type of technology and you don't mind getting your hands dirty, figuratively speaking, then Insteon might be fine for you. On the other hand, if you aren't that technologically adept and don't have any older devices that you need to bother with, you might be better off going with one of the newer smart home systems that are simply easier to use.

Apple Only

One more caveat about Insteon. The latest Insteon Hub Pro can be controlled only via an iOS-compatible smartphone app. That's fine if you have an Apple iPhone, but it means you can't control your Insteon system with any Android phone. That's a deal breaker for many. (SmartThings and Wink are compatible with both iOS and Android.)

SmartThings by Samsung

The SmartThings company was founded in 2012 and was acquired by Samsung in 2014. The SmartThings system is compatible with both Z-Wave and ZigBee wireless protocols, and it works with a variety of both Samsung-branded and third-party devices.

As the newest system on the market, SmartThings is both easy to use yet not quite fully fleshed out, at least in terms of compatible devices. The SmartThings app has a great-looking and easy-to-use interface, but there aren't as many third-party devices compatible with the system as there are for the competing Wink system.

On the plus side, SmartThings is easy to use for consumers of all ages; it's not as confusing or arcane as the older Insteon system. On the minus side, you won't find as many compatible smart devices as you might find for Wink. Make sure you can find the device you want before investing in SmartThings.

Wink

Then we come to Wink, which kind of offers the best of both worlds for the average consumer. It's a newer system that's refined and easy to use, like SmartThings, but it's been around longer so it has better third-party compatibility.

Like SmartThings, the Wink hub utilizes both Z-Wave and ZigBee wireless technologies. It connects to your home network via Ethernet, thus enabling Wi-Fi communication. Oh, and Bluetooth is there too, just in case.

You control the Wink hub with the Wink smartphone app, which is easy on the eyes and is easy to use. Wink itself doesn't sell any smart devices (aside from the hubs), but it's compatible with just about any Z-Wave or Zigbee-compatible device out there. It's easy to connect new devices and control them from the smartphone app, and there's no shortage of devices to choose from.

More Wink

Because of Wink's ease of use and large number of available smart devices, this book includes an entire chapter on how to use the Wink system. Learn more in Chapter 9, "Controlling Your Smart Home with Wink." Note that Wink works in a similar manner to both SmartThings and Insteon, so many of the same operations apply.

And More...

Insteon, SmartThings, and Wink are the three most popular smart home systems today, but they're not the only ones from which to choose. There are a number of other smart home systems you might want to consider, depending on your needs. These include the following:

- **Harmony Hub by Logitech.** The Harmony Hub is a smart home hub designed for use with home entertainment systems as well as traditional smart home devices. Using either the accompanying smartphone app or any compatible Logitech Harmony remote control, you can control not only your home's lights and switches and such but also your television, A/V receiver, home theater system, and more. You can even create multi-device "activities;" for example, press Watch Movie to have your TV and Roku box turn on and switch to Netflix, your lights dim, and more.

More Harmony

Learn more about Logitech's Harmony Hub in Chapter 7, "Automating Home Entertainment."

- **Nest.** What was once a single product (the Nest Learning Thermostat) is now a whole ecosystem built on the Nest thermostat and other products. Nest products communicate via a proprietary wireless standard dubbed Nest Weave;

third-party products can integrate with Nest products via Wi-Fi. Although the Nest system isn't a smart home system per se, you probably need to consider Nest compatibility when choosing other smart home devices.

More Nest

Learn more about the Nest thermostat in Chapter 4, "Automating Heating and Cooling;" learn more about other Nest devices in Chapter 5, "Automating Home Security."

- **WeMo by Belkin.** WeMo is a limited line of smart home devices, consisting primarily of smart plugs, switches, light bulbs, and cameras. WeMo devices work via Wi-Fi, so no central hub is needed.

What Works with What?

When you're considering purchasing smart devices, you need to know which devices work with which systems. As you've learned, some devices work on multiple systems, but that's not something you can depend on; the competing systems are not 100 percent compatible.

With that in mind, the following chart details which devices work on which smart home system, as clearly as can be determined at this point in time.

Things Change

Things do change, so always look at the product description or package for current compatibility.

Devices	Insteon	Samsung SmartThings	Wink
Appliances		Samsung POWERbot vacuum cleaners Samsung ranges Samsung refrigerators Samsung washers and dryers	EcoNet Home Comfort Gardinier ceiling fans Rheem water heaters

Devices	Insteon	Samsung SmartThings	Wink
Controllers	Amazon Echo/ Echo Dot Apple HomeKit	Amazon Echo/Echo Dot Google Home	Amazon Echo/Echo Dot Google Home
Detectors and sensors	Elk FirstAlert Insteon Nest	FortrezZ Leak OSO PlantLink Samsung SmartThings	Kidde smoke and carbon monoxide alarm LeakSmart Nest Protect Pella Insynctive
Dimmers, switches, and outlets	Insteon X-10	Leviton Samsung SmartThings	iHome Smart Plug Leviton Lutron Caseta Switchmate
Garage door controls	Insteon	Linear GoControl	Chamberlain MyQ Linear GoControl
Home entertainment	Sonos	Bose SoundTouch Samsung Wireless Audio Sonos	
Home security	Elk Insteon MiLocks Nest Cam	Arlo D-Link Cloud Camera Ring Samsung SmartThings Schlage Yale	Andersen Arlo August Smart Lock Canary home security Dropcam Pro video camera GoControl KwikSet SmartCode Nest Cam Ring Schlage

Devices	Insteon	Samsung SmartThings	Wink
Hubs	Insteon Hub Insteon Hub Pro Logitech Harmony Hub	Logitech Harmony Hub Samsung SmartThings Hub	GE Link Hub Logitech Harmony Hub Wink Hub Wink Hub 2 Wink Relay Touchscreen Controller
Lawn and patio	Insteon	Spruce irrigation controller	Rachio smart irrigation and sprinkler systems
Lighting	Insteon LIFX X10	LIFX Osram Lightify Philips Hue lighting kits and bulbs WeMo by Belkin	Commercial Electric smart LED lights Cree connected LED bulbs GE Link connected LED bulbs Hampton Bay smart LED lights LIFX Philips Hue lighting kits and bulbs Sylvania smart bulbs
Thermostats	Ecobee Insteon Nest Venstar	Ecobee Honeywell	Carrier Ecobee Honeywell Nest Sensi
Wi-Fi compatible	Via Ethernet connection to wireless router	Via Ethernet connection to wireless router	Via Ethernet connection to wireless router
Window coverings	Insteon Somfy		Bali Lutron Serena Pella Insynctive

Devices	Insteon	Samsung SmartThings	Wink
Wireless protocol(s) used	Bluetooth Insteon (wireless and powerline)	Z-Wave ZigBee	Bluetooth Z-Wave ZigBee

The Normal Caveats

This list is assembled from the best available information at the time of writing, is not intended to be all inclusive, and might not reflect the current status for all devices and systems. As always, check with the device's manufacturer or the system's supporting company to determine the current state of compatibility.

From this list, there are a few generalizations we can make about the compatibility of the three major smart home systems.

First, although Insteon is arguably the oldest system out there, it's mainly a system unto itself. That is, while there are a few third-party devices that work with Insteon, the majority of smart devices available for the Insteon system are made by Insteon itself. You want a light switch or a motion sensor or a whatever to work with your Insteon hub? Then you buy an Insteon light switch or Insteon motion sensor or Insteon whatever. That isn't necessarily a bad thing, and there is a huge selection of Insteon smart devices, but it's as close to a closed system as you can get these days.

Second, Samsung's SmartThings, being one of the newer competitors in this smart space, is compatible with fewer devices than the more established Insteon and Wink systems. That's to be expected; it's also expected to change as Samsung makes its system compatible with more third-party devices.

Speaking of SmartThings, note the apparent focus of this system on home security. Most of the Samsung-branded compatible devices (home appliances and TVs excepted) are security related. We're talking motion detectors, door and window detectors, alarms, and the like. If home security is your thing, SmartThings is worth a look. But for other tasks, you'll find more available devices from either Insteon or Wink.

All things considered, Wink offers the most compatibility with the most number of third-party devices. There are no Wink-manufactured devices (save for its hubs), so this system relies on cooperation and integration with other companies in the smart home space. Even though it's a newer system than Insteon, Wink has been around long enough to form a lot of partnerships, which means you have a lot of devices from a lot of different companies to choose from. That's a good thing.

Controller Compatibility

If you want to use a universal smart home controller, make sure it works with the system you choose. As of this writing, Insteon is the only system that works with Apple's HomeKit. Both SmartThings and Wink work with Google Home, however. And all three systems work with Amazon's Echo/Alexa. (Read on to learn more about all of these smart controllers.)

Comparing Smart Home Controllers

You use a smart hub to connect all your smart home devices. You can control the hub via it's smartphone app, or you can use a third-party controller to do the job.

What exactly is a smart home controller and why would you use it instead of the hub's own app? It's a matter of offering increased functionality.

The simplest type of smart home controller is a smartphone app that does more than the hub's own smartphone app. That's what you have with Apple's Home app, part of its HomeKit system. The Home app integrates with the Insteon hub, Insteon smart devices, and selected smart devices from other companies to offer a one-stop shop for controlling everything in your smart home. Just add all your compatible smart devices to the Home app, and do your controlling from there.

A more sophisticated and functional approach can be found with physical smart home controllers, chief of which are the Amazon Echo and Google Home. These devices, both small enough to sit inconspicuously on your living room end table, are voice activated. Once you (wirelessly) connect your favorite smart hub and smart devices to the controller, all you have to do is say a word or phrase to get your smart home going. Tell Echo or Google Home to "dim the living room lights," and it happens. Say "go to bed" and lights and devices throughout your house will adjust for your sleep time. It's a lot more convenient that punching all those things up in an app.

In addition, these smart controllers function as virtual personal assistants, much like Siri on an iPhone or Cortana in Windows 10. Ask Echo or Google Home a question, and you'll hear an answer. Ask "what's the weather," and you'll get the current temperature and headlines. It's really cool and really useful, and it takes the concept of a "smart" home one step further.

Apple HomeKit

Apple's HomeKit is an app-based system for controlling smart home devices. Naturally, it's only available on Apple phones and tablets, so if you're an Android user, you're out of luck. But if you have an iPhone or iPad, you can use Apple's Home app to control a fairly large number of smart devices in your own home.

Apple's Home app

You can even use the Home app to create "scenes" that operate multiple smart devices at once. Your "good morning" scene might turn up certain lights, turn up the heat (in winter, anyway), and turn on the smart coffee maker. You get the idea.

Because you're using the Home app on your iPhone or iPad, you can control all of this not only via touchscreen but also via voice, using Siri. Just tell Siri to "turn up the lights" or "lock the front door," and it gets done.

Learn More

Learn more about Apple HomeKit in Chapter 10, "Controlling Your Smart Home with Apple Home."

Amazon Echo and Alexa

Amazon was first into the smart controller market with Amazon Echo. The Echo, initially sold as a kind of voice-controlled speaker, quickly evolved into the controller hub for a number of smart home devices.

The Amazon Echo

The Echo looks like a headless table lamp, is voice controlled, and connects to the Internet. It includes a faux intelligent personal assistant dubbed Alexa, so you can ask it any number of questions using plain English sentences. Just say "Alexa, what's on TV tonight?" or something similar, and Alexa tells you.

Amazon has broadened the Echo line beyond the original Echo (which includes a big built-in speaker for listening to music) to include the smaller, coaster-like Echo Dot (much smaller speaker) and the Echo Tap, which is a portable, battery-powered version of the Echo. All offer the same functionality, albeit at different price points.

The Echo and its siblings are compatible with more smart systems and devices than either Apple's HomeKit or Google Home. That's probably because Amazon's controllers have been around longer than the two competitors. That might change in the future, but that's the way it shakes out today.

Learn More

Learn more about Amazon Echo and Alexa in Chapter 11, "Controlling Your Smart Home with Amazon Alexa."

Google Home

Google has also embraced the concept of smart home controllers with its Google Home product. It looks and works much like Amazon's Echo, although it's a little shorter and a little more stylish.

Google Home

Google Home connects to an increasing number of smart hubs and devices, and lets you control them via voice commands. You also get the virtual personal assistant benefits, via the Google Assistant, which ties into the wealth of data at Google's cloud-based fingertips. You can ask it all sorts of questions, or even start movie or music playback via the Google Play streaming service.

Although Google is still playing catchup in terms of third-party compatibility, the Google-based intelligence may be a few steps ahead of what Amazon offers. It's definitely a controller to consider and makes life in a smart home that much easier.

Learn More

Learn more about Google Home in Chapter 12, "Controlling Your Smart Home with Google Home."

Microsoft Invoke

Not wanting to be left out of the game, Microsoft plans to introduce its own smart speaker/controller in the fall of 2017. The Invoke is a tabletop wireless speaker, much like the Amazon Echo and Google Home, that uses Microsoft's Cortana virtual assistant (found in Windows 10) to control smart devices, media playback, and the like. The Invoke will be manufactured and sold by speaker company Harman Kardon, and it will be capable of making voice calls with Skype.

>>>*Go Further*

SMART TECHNOLOGY FOR NEW CONSTRUCTION

Most of the smart devices I discuss in this book are designed to work in existing homes. They use wireless technology to connect to smart hubs and your home network so that you can easily install and control them, no wiring necessary.

If you're building a new house, however, you can build in some of the infrastructure you need for home automation. In particular, talk with your builder about the following:

- Make sure the builder uses deep junction boxes (easier to fit smart switches and connectors) and includes a neutral wire (necessary for some smart controls).

- Install electrical outlets on every wall of every room, and sometimes two; you'll probably be plugging in a lot of smart devices, and you'll need the outlets.

- If you're thinking of whole-house entertainment, run the appropriate speaker wires to all appropriate rooms and consider installing in-wall or in-ceiling speakers.

- Install smart wall switches and keypad controllers instead of normal switches throughout the house.

- Have the builder use smart light bulbs instead of normal bulbs in all fixtures.

- Install smart door locks, doorbells, smoke detectors, and garage door openers from the start.

- Pre-wire your home for a smart home security system, including motion detectors and security cameras.

- Run cat 5 or cat 5e Ethernet cable throughout the house—not necessarily for smart devices, but for computer and home entertainment needs.

- Install a whole-house surge suppressor to protect all your valuable electronics.

When considering smart switches and controllers, Insteon appears to be the system of choice for home builders. You also might want to consider more sophisticated (and more expensive) home automation systems from Lutron and similar suppliers. Ask your builder for recommendations.

In this chapter, you learn how to add smart lighting to your home.

→ Considering Smart Lighting Systems
→ Using the Philips Hue Personal Wireless Lighting System

Automating Your Home Lighting

Most people getting started with smart home technology today start with smart lighting. That's because we all have lights in our homes, and there are some demonstrable benefits for automating the way these lights work.

Considering Smart Lighting Systems

There are several ways to add smart lighting to your house or apartment. You can go with a dedicated smart lighting system, like the Philips Hue, or with a more general smart home system that incorporates smart lighting as part of its operation.

Let's look at some of the more popular options available.

Insteon

Insteon (www.insteon.com) is a smart home system that uses its own smart hub and smartphone app to control a variety of branded and third-party smart devices. You can use the Insteon hub and app to directly control a variety of smart light bulbs, as well as smart plugs and outlets into which you can plug traditional light bulbs. (Going the smart plug/outlet route lets you use lower-priced non-smart LED bulbs, which can save a lot of money in the short term.)

Insteon

The Insteon system—including smart lighting—is covered in Chapter 2, "Understanding Smart Home Hubs and Controllers."

LIFX

LIFX (www.lifx.com) manufactures smart light bulbs that can be controlled directly by the LIFX smartphone app via your home's Wi-Fi network. Unlike the other systems discussed here, there is no central hub necessary; the smart bulbs connect to the app directly via Wi-Fi.

In addition, LIFX bulbs can be controlled by other systems' controllers. You can control LIFX bulbs with Amazon Echo, Apple HomeKit, Google Home, the Insteon Hub, the Logitech Harmony Hub, Samsung's SmartThings Hub, and the Wink Hub. LIFX is not yet compatible with Google Home, although it's likely to be so in the near future.

Philips Hue

Philips is known worldwide as a major supplier of residential and commercial lighting. Walk down the lighting aisle in any big-box store and you'll find a variety of Philips light bulbs—both traditional and smart.

It's not surprising that Philips developed its own smart lighting system, dubbed Hue (www.meethue.com). Philips sells individual Hue light bulbs and controllers in a variety of types and sizes, along with Hue starter kits that include bulbs, switches, and the Hue bridge, which you use to connect all the Hue products together.

The Hue smart lighting system is covered in depth later in this chapter.

Wink

Wink (www.wink.com) is another whole-house smart home system, like Insteon. You can connect a variety of smart light bulbs, smart plugs, and smart outlets to the Wink smart hub; you control those devices from Wink's smarthome app.

Wink

Chapter 9, "Controlling Your Smart Home with Wink," covers the Wink system— including smart lighting—in depth.

Other Systems

Insteon, Philips, and Wink aren't the only companies providing smart lighting solutions. You can also find smart lighting and plugs/outlets from the following companies:

- Belkin WeMo (www.wemo.com)
- Cree (www.creebulb.com)
- GE Link (www.gelinkbulbs.com)
- Lutron (www.lutron.com)
- MiPow (www.mipow.com)
- OSRAM LIGHTIFY (www.osram.com)
- Samsung SmartThings (www.smartthings.com)
- Stack (www.stacklighting.com)
- TP-Link (www.tp-link.com)

Many of these smart lights and controllers work with the Insteon and Wink systems, as well.

Using the Philips Hue Personal Wireless Lighting System

The most popular smart home lighting system available today is arguably the Philips Hue Personal Wireless Lighting System. The Hue system connects and controls all manner of smart bulbs and lights from a single Hue bridge—a small, hockey puck-like device that connects to your home's wireless router and then wirelessly to all your Hue lights. You can control each individual light or all the lights in a given room from remote control switches or the Hue app on your smartphone.

It's the Hue smartphone app that adds extensive functionality. Not only does the light let you turn on, turn off, or dim individual lights or groups of lights, it also lets you control the color temperature (warmer or cooler) of individual lights, create *scenes* with specific types of lighting for specific activities, and program *routines* that turn on or off your lights at a given time or when something specific happens, such as you leave home in the morning or arrive home at night.

The Hue system is incredibly versatile, and will let you do things with your lights that you didn't know you could do. To get started with Hue, you need to invest in a starter kit that includes a Hue bridge and one or more Hue light bulbs. You can add extra bulbs and accessories as you need them.

Connect the Hue Bridge

Everything you do with Hue is done through the Hue bridge. While individual Hue lights connect to the bridge wirelessly, via your Wi-Fi network, the bridge itself has to be connected directly to your router via Ethernet cable.

(1) Insert all the Hue light bulbs you want to use into your lamps or light sockets.

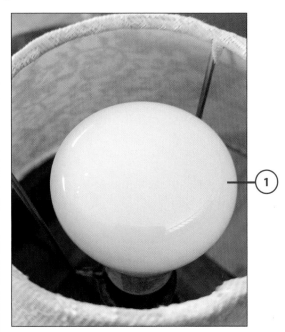

(2) Make sure all the lamps and lights are turned on.

(3) Plug the Hue bridge into a power source.

(4) Connect one end of the Ethernet cable (supplied) to the LAN jack on the back of the Hue bridge.

(5) Connect the other end of the
Ethernet cable to an open port
on your Wi-Fi router.

(6) When all three blue lights along
the top of the Hue bridge are lit,
the bridge is connected to your
home Wi-Fi network.

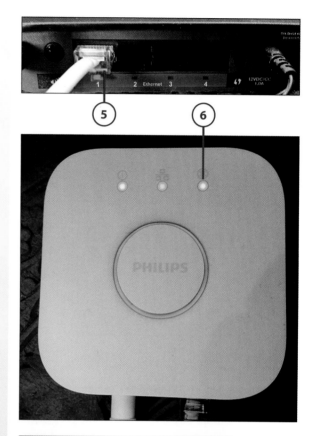

Hue Range

The Hue Hub has an effective range of
about 100 feet, which means any bulb
or controller within this radius should
work fine. In addition, each Hue bulb
works as a range extender, extending
how far the signal reaches. So you have
100 feet from the Hub to the first bulb
then another 100 feet from that bulb to
the next, and so on.

Connect to the Hue Dimmer Switch

Some Hue kits come with a wireless
dimmer switch, which is actually a
handheld remote control that can be
attached to a wall-mounted plate. You
don't need to connect any wires, and
you can place the switch anywhere
in your house. This switch controls all
nearby Hue lights.

(1) Use the two-sided tape on the
back of the mounting plate to
attach the plate to your wall.

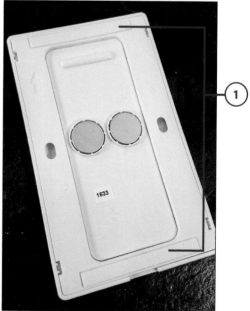

2 Remove the pull strip from the bottom of the dimmer switch.

3 Place the dimmer switch on the mounting plate. They're both magnetic, so they should hold in place automatically.

4 The dimmer switch is automatically connected to the Hue bridge and can immediately control the connected lights.

Handheld Operation
You can also use the dimmer switch apart from the mounting plate as a handheld remote control.

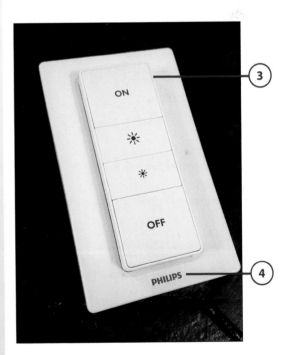

Control Your Lights with the Dimmer Switch

Using the wireless dimmer switch is just like using a traditional dimmer switch. There are only four buttons to be concerned with.

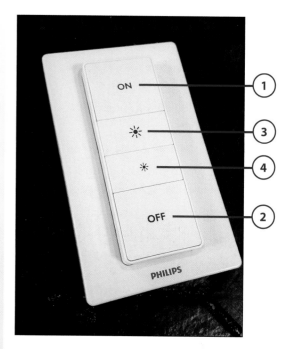

(1) Press the **On** button to turn on the connected Hue lights.

(2) Press the **Off** button to turn off the connected Hue lights.

(3) Press the **Bright** button to increase the lights' brightness.

(4) Press the **Dim** button to decrease the lights' brightness.

Scenes

Keep pressing the **On** button to cycle through the default scenes—Relax, Read, Concentrate, and Energize.

Connect to the Hue App

The Hue system is even more versatile when you control it via the Hue smartphone app. The app is available for both Apple iOS (iPhone) and Android smartphones.

Download the App

If you have an iPhone or iPad, you can download the Hue app (for free) from Apple's App store. If you have an Android phone or tablet, you can download the Hue app (also for free) from the Google Play Store.

For the app to work with your Hue bridge, they both must be connected to the same Wi-Fi router and network. So connect your smartphone to your home network and follow these steps.

1. Launch the Hue app on your smartphone.

2. The app automatically searches for nearby Hue bridges. When your bridge is found, tap **Set Up**.

3. Press the large round push-link button on the Hue bridge.

4. On your phone, you're notified if an update is available for the Hue bridge. (There probably is.) Tap to agree to the terms and conditions and then tap the **Update** button. Make sure you keep the Hue bridge and lights powered on during this process.

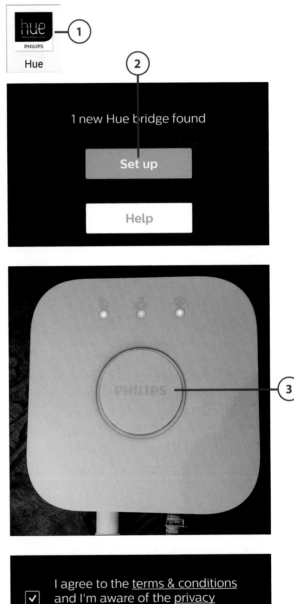

(5) The app notifies you when the update is completed. Tap the **Done** button.

(6) Press the large round push-link button on the Hue bridge again. The Hue bridge is now connected to the Hue app.

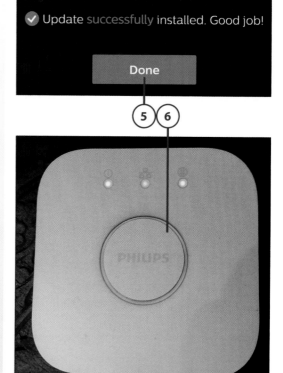

Create a Room

Once you've connected the Hue app to your Hue bridge, the setup process continues by asking you to create a *room*. With the Hue system, a room is just what you'd think it is—a room in your house in which you've installed one or more Hue lights. You can create as many rooms in the Hue app as you have lights installed in your house. For example, you may need to create a living room, one or more bedrooms, den, and so forth.

(1) In the Hue app, tap the + button to view the New screen.

(2) Enter the name for your room in the text box at the top of the screen.

(3) Tap **Room Type** to view the available types of rooms.

(**4**) Tap the type of room you're in. You return to the New screen.

(**5**) Tap to select which lights are in this room. You can (and probably do) have multiple lights in this room.

(**6**) Tap **Save**.

(**7**) When the room is saved, you return to the Room Setup screen. Tap the **+** button to create additional rooms.

(**8**) When you're done setting up your rooms, tap the right arrow.

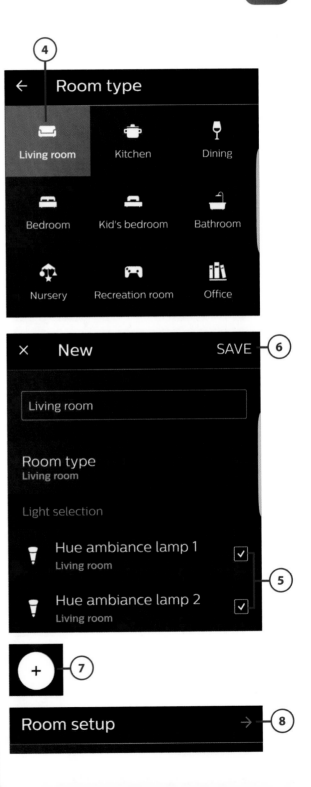

(9) Tap **Let's Go** to begin using the Hue app.

New Rooms Anytime

You can create a new room at any time after the initial setup. From within the Hue app, tap the Home icon to view the Home screen and then tap the + at the bottom of the screen. You need to create a room on the app for each room in your home where you want to use a Hue bulb.

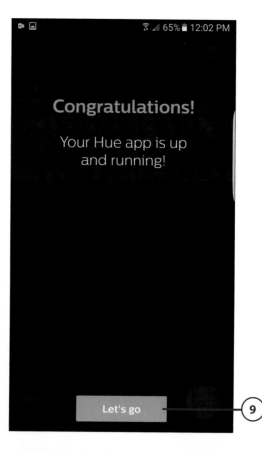

Add More Lights or Accessories

You're not limited to using the lights included with your Hue starter kit. You can add other lights, switches, and accessories at any time to outfit your entire house or apartment with Hue smart lighting.

(1) From within the Hue app, tap to view the **Settings** tab.

(2) Tap the type of item you want to add to your system—Hue bridges, new rooms, new lights, or new accessories.

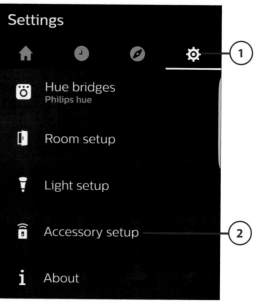

(**3**) From the next screen, tap the **+** at the bottom of the screen.

(**4**) If you're adding a new light, make sure it's powered on and then tap **Search**. Follow the onscreen instructions to add and name the new light when it's found by the Hue app.

(**5**) If you're adding a new accessory, tap the type of item you want to add. Follow the onscreen instructions to activate the accessory and have it found by the Hue app.

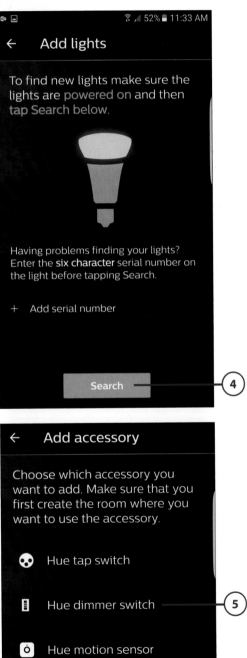

Turn Lights On or Off with the Hue Smartphone App

At its most basic, the Hue smartphone app lets you perform the same basic operations available with a traditional wall switch.

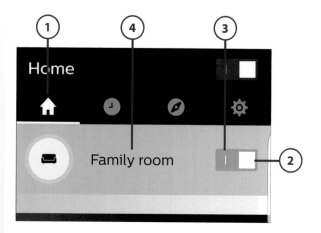

(1) Within the Hue app, tap the **Home** icon to view the Home tab.

(2) Tap "on" the switch for a given room to turn on the lights in that room. (The switch in the app turns white.)

(3) Tap "off" the switch for a given room to turn off the lights in that room. (The switch in the app turns black.)

(4) Turn on or off an individual light by tapping the name of the room you're in.

(5) Tap the "on" switch for a given light to turn it on.

(6) Tap the "off" switch for a given light to turn it off.

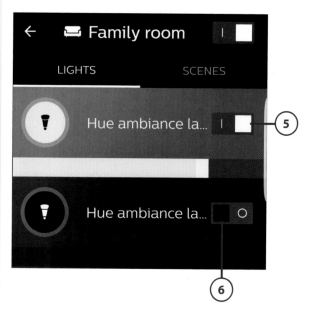

Control Over the Internet

Once you've completed your initial setup, you can control your Hue lights from anywhere via your smartphone. Just make sure your smartphone has an Internet connection and your Hue app is signed in to your Hue account, then you can use the app to control your home lights even if you're away from home.

Dim Your Lights

You can also use the Hue app to dim all the lights in a room or to adjust each light individually.

1. From within the Hue app, tap to select the **Home** screen.

2. Make sure the lights in this room are turned on; then tap and drag the slider underneath a given room to raise or lower the brightness for all the lights in that room.

3. Dim an individual light by tapping that room to display the lights in that room.

4. Make sure the given light is turned on; then tap and drag that light's slider to raise or lower the brightness.

Adjust a Light's Color Temperature

One of the unique features about smart lighting, and Philips' Hue system in particular, is the ability to change the type of light emitted by a given bulb. That is, you can change a bulb's color temperature so that the light is either warmer (more reddish) or cooler (more bluish).

1. From within the Hue app, tap to view the **Home** screen.

2. Tap a room to view the lights in that room.

Room Temperature

To adjust the color temperature for all the lights in a room, tap the round icon for that room on the Home screen.

(3) Make sure the light you want to adjust is turned on, and then tap the round icon for that light.

(4) Tap **Whites** at the top of the screen.

(5) Tap and drag the circle to the color temperature you'd like.

(6) Tap the check mark when done.

Recipes

When you go to adjust the color temperature for a given light, you also see a Recipes icon at the top of the screen. Recipes are another name for the Applets created by something called If This Then That (IFTTT), a web-based service that lets you create chains of conditional commands for multiple smart devices. Learn more about IFTTT in Chapter 14, "Adding More Functionality with IFTTT."

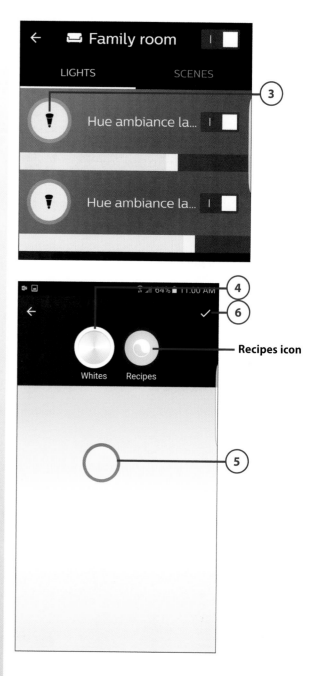

Recipes icon

>>>*Go Further*

COLOR TEMPERATURE

The temperature of white light is measured in degrees Kelvin, or K. Warmer white light (between 2700K and 3000K) is good for general use; it's what most of us are used to in residential lighting. Cooler white light (between 3500K and 4100K), which looks a bit more artificial, is typically used in offices, retail shopping spaces, and household work areas such as garages and laundries. And so-called natural white light (between 4600K and 6500K) is a blue-white light that mimics bright daylight.

For comparison, traditional incandescent light is typically on the warm side, between 2700K and 3300K. The type of fluorescent lighting you find in offices is typically cooler, around 5000K.

So if you want a soothing type of lighting for your living room or bedroom, go with warmer lighting. If you want something a little more modern that looks a little brighter then go with cooler lighting. Cool white is also good for areas where you need to concentrate, such as your kitchen, bathroom, or home office.

Select a Scene

Rather than adjust color temperature and brightness level separately, the Hue app lets you create *scenes* for specific tasks that incorporate both temperature and brightness settings. If you want to sit down and read a book, you might select the Read scene; when you just need to relax a little, select the Relax scene. You can use any of Hue's built-in scenes or create your own scenes.

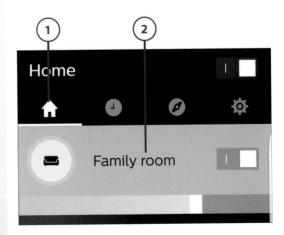

① From within the Hue app, tap to view the **Home** screen.

② Tap to select the room you want to adjust.

3 Tap the **Scenes** tab.

4 Tap to apply the desired scene.

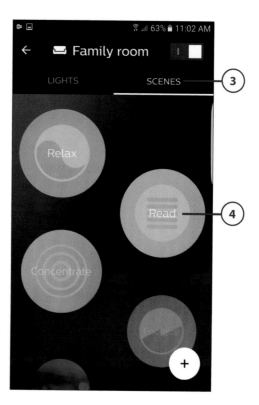

Create a New Scene

You're not limited to the default themes included with the Hue app. You can create your own scenes with the color temperature based on a picture you select. These are called *picture scenes*, and the Hue app includes several built-in photos you can use to create them.

1 From within the Hue app, tap to view the **Home** screen.

2 Tap to select a given room.

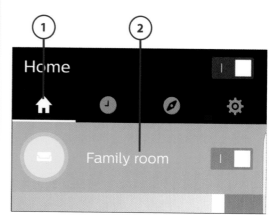

3. Make sure at least one light in this room is turned on then tap to select the **Scenes** tab.

4. Tap the + at the bottom of the screen.

5. Save the current settings as a new scene by tapping **Store Current Light Settings**.

6. Create a new scene by tapping **Picture Scene** to display the New Scene screen.

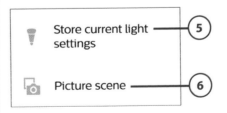

Store current light settings — 5

Picture scene — 6

(7) Select a picture supplied with the Hue app by tapping **Philips**.

(8) Select one of your pictures stored on your phone by tapping **Camera Roll**.

(9) Tap the picture that best represents the lighting scheme you'd like to create.

(10) The color temperature for this scene is set to reflect that of the selected picture.

(11) Tap and drag the slider at the bottom of the screen to select the desired brightness level.

(12) Tap **Save** to display the New Scene dialog box.

(13) Enter a name for this scene.

(14) Tap **Save**. The scene is now saved and available for future use.

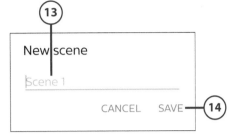

Create a New Home & Away Routine

In addition to lighting scenes, the Hue app lets you create automated *routines* that turn your lights on or off based on various conditions. Some routines are time-based (that is, they turn lights on or off at a given time); others are proximity based.

The most popular proximity-based routines are the Home & Away routines, which turn your lights off when you leave home and turn them back on when you come home. These routines work by using the location services on your phone. When you're near, the lights go on, and when you're further away, they turn off.

(1) From within the Hue app, tap to view the **Routines** tab.

(2) Tap **Home & Away**.

(3) Tap "on" the **Location Aware** switch. The app displays a map of your current location.

(4) Tap **Coming Home** to control which lights turn on when you arrive home.

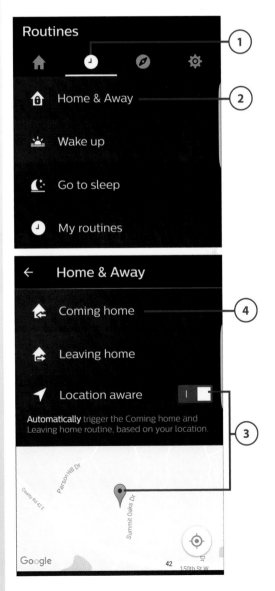

(5) Tap "on" the **Only After Sunset** switch if you only want your lights turned on after dark.

(6) Tap **Turn On** to display the Where? Screen.

(7) Tap to select **Home** to turn on all the connected lights in your home. *Or...*

(8) Tap a specific room or rooms to turn on the lights in only the selected rooms.

(9) Tap the back arrow to return to the Coming Home screen.

(10) Tap the name of the room you just selected.

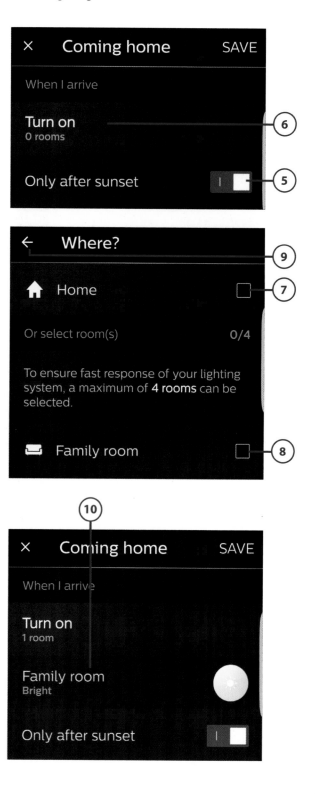

11 Tap the type of lighting you want to see when you get home, from either the Defaults (Bright, Dimmed, or Nightlight) or your Scenes.

12 Tap the back arrow to return to the Coming Home screen.

13 Review your commands, then tap **Save**. You're now returned to the Home & Away screen.

14 Tap **Leaving Home** to adjust which lights turn off when you leave your house or apartment.

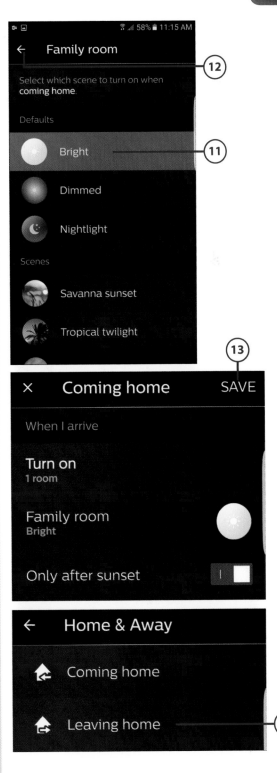

(15) Tap **Where?** to display the Where? screen.

(16) Tap to select **Home** to turn off all the connected lights in your home. *Or...*

(17) Tap a specific room or rooms to turn off the lights in only the selected rooms.

(18) Tap the back arrow to return to the Leaving Home screen.

(19) Tap **Save** to return to the Home & Away screen.

(20) Tap the back arrow to return to the Routines screen.

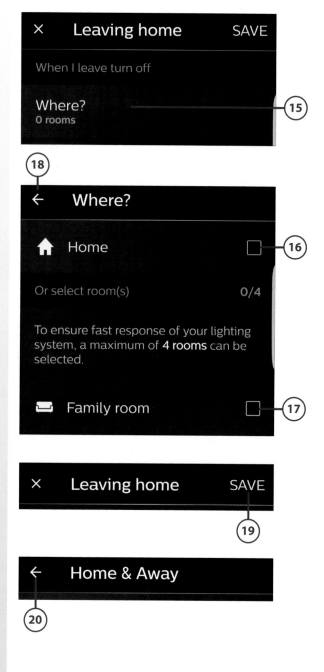

Create a Wake Up Routine

If you have Hue lights in your bedroom, you might want to create a wake up routine. This type of routine turns on your lights at a given time in the morning, but at a low brightness level. It then gradually increases the level until full brightness is reached and you are presumably awake.

1. From within the Hue app, tap to view the **Routines** tab.

2. Tap **Wake Up**.

3. Tap the + to create a new routine.

4. Enter a name for the new routine in the top text box.

5. Enter the time you want woken up.

6. Tap to select the days of the week you want for this routine.

7. Tap the **Fade In** box to select how long you want the fade-in routine to take—10, 20, or 30 minutes.

8. Tap **Where?** to select which room you want this routine to apply.

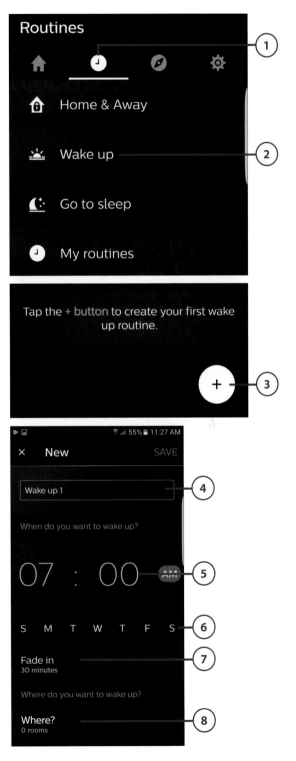

(9) Tap to select which room you want for this routine, or tap **Home** to have it affect all the lights in your home.

(10) Tap the back arrow to return to the New screen.

(11) Tap **Save** to save and activate this routine.

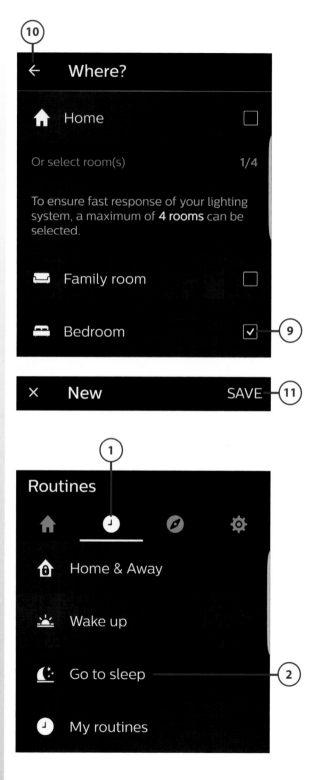

Create a Go to Sleep Routine

Just as you can create a lighting routine to wake you up in the morning, you can also create a routine to apply when you go to sleep at night.

(1) From within the Hue app, tap to view the **Routines** tab.

(2) Tap **Go to Sleep**.

(3) Tap the + to create a new routine.

(4) Enter a name for the new routine into the top text box.

(5) Enter the time you want to go to sleep.

(6) Tap to select the days of the week you want for this routine.

(7) Tap the **Fade Out** box to select how long you want the lights to fade to darkness.

(8) Tap **Where?** to select which room you want this routine to apply.

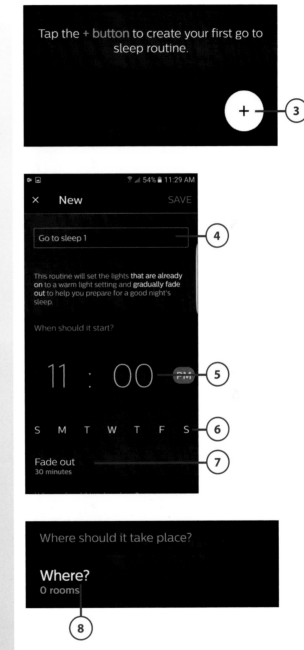

9 Tap to select which room you want for this routine, or tap **Home** to have it affect all the lights in your home.

10 Tap the back arrow to return to the New screen.

11 Tap **Save** to save and activate this routine.

Different Rooms

You can create different Wake Up and Go to Sleep routines for different rooms. For example, you might create one Go to Sleep routine for your living room with a short fade out time, and a different Go to Sleep routine for your bedroom, with a later activation time and longer fade out.

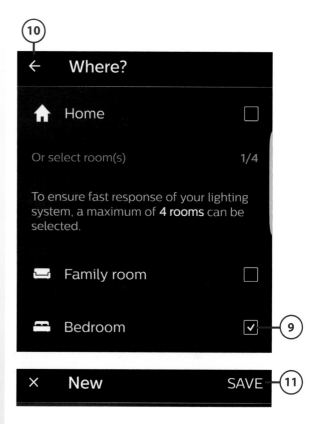

>>>Go Further

SMART LIGHTING PRICING

Let's address the elephant in the room—pricing. Yes, smart lighting costs more than traditional lighting. A lot more. Is it worth it?

First, the costs. If you head down to your local hardware store, you can buy the LED equivalent of a 60-watt traditional incandescent bulb (no longer available, of course) for anywhere from $2 to $8. Halogen bulbs are even less expensive, often available for $1 or less.

In contrast, 60-watt equivalent smart LED light bulbs run from $15 to $30. And to get started with many bulbs, you need to buy a starter pack that includes a few bulbs and a smart bridge, which is even more expensive; Philips' basic Hue Starter Kit (with no switches included) costs around $70.

Given the choice of buying a $2 dumb bulb versus a $20 smart one, which would you choose? I know if I'm on a budget, the $2 bulb is a lot more appealing. Now, I know the smart bulb can do a lot more, but when I'm replacing half a dozen bulbs at a time (common in my house), that's a $100+ expenditure versus a $10 to $15 one. That's tough to swallow.

That said, if you're committing to using smart lighting in your home, or in the process of converting to a larger smart home system, you need to swallow the higher immediate cost for all the long-term benefits you get from smart lighting and control. With smart lighting, after all, you should use your lights less, and thus save on electricity costs over time. Plus you get all the convenience of smart lighting, which can't be easily measured in dollars and cents.

So if you're on a budget, by all means stick with traditional lighting. But if you want the benefits that smart lighting offers—including longer-term energy savings—then find a way to put smart lighting in your budget. (And always, always, look out for short-term deals and longer-term price reductions!)

In this chapter, you learn how to automatically control your home's heating and cooling with a smart thermostat.

→ Understanding Smart Thermostats
→ Evaluating Smart Thermostats
→ Using the Nest Learning Thermostat

Automating Heating and Cooling

When it comes to smart home technology, the one thing that gets the interest of a lot of folks is the so-called smart thermostat. This is a device that learns your temperature preferences and automatically adjusts your furnace and air conditioner accordingly—while interfacing with other smart devices in your home as well.

This chapter introduces you to the various smart thermostats on the market today, with a special focus on the first—and still most popular—model: the Nest Learning Thermostat.

Understanding Smart Thermostats

When I was a kid, my grandfather worked for Bryant Heating and Cooling in Indianapolis. I have a memory of being about five or six and going with him to the opening of their new factory on the west side of town, where I got a hot dog and a Coke and bright blue balloon. I also remember losing my grip on the balloon, watching it sail away into the equally blue sky, and feeling sad about it.

Naturally, my grandparents had a Bryant furnace and air conditioner in their small two-bedroom house. The Bryant thermostat back then was a small round affair with a switch to select either heating or air conditioning, and a dial you turned to set the temperature. That was as fancy as it got in the 1960s, but it got the job done.

Over the years, thermostats got a little smarter. I got a new furnace and air conditioner a few years ago, and the accompanying thermostat was all digital and programmable. I could create a schedule that told the equipment what temperature I wanted and when, and I got to see the results on a fancy LED display—although I still had to manually switch between heating and cooling.

Today, however, even smarter thermostats exist. These truly smart thermostats not only let you create your own schedules but they also learn from how and when you change temperatures to automatically create heating and cooling schedules—and automatically switch between heating and cooling as necessary, too.

So while the most popular of these thermostats—the Nest Learning Thermostat—has the same general dimensions and round shape as that primitive Bryant thermostat from half a century ago, it does much, much more. (And saves energy, too!)

How Smart Thermostats Work

A traditional thermostat has one job, to adjust the temperature in your house or apartment. That is also job one for a smart thermostat, although a smart thermostat handles the task in a much different way.

Before we get too far into this, know that you can use a smart thermostat just as you do a traditional one. That is, you can set the temperature you'd like in your home, and the thermostat communicates with your furnace or air conditioner to run until that temperature is reached. Easy stuff.

A smart thermostat goes further, however, in a lot of different ways.

First, smart thermostats, like many newer non-smart thermostats, let you set up a schedule for heating and cooling. You tell the thermostat you'd like to wake up to a 72-degree house, but can live with lower temperatures (in the winter; higher in the summer) after 11:00 pm when you're asleep, and the thermostat manages the heating and cooling to this schedule.

With a smart thermostat, however, this type of schedule setting is made easier by the use of the thermostat's smartphone app. It's simply a lot easier to set a schedule on your phone's touchscreen than it is by pushing all the little buttons and such on a standard thermostat.

Even better, a smart thermostat can create a heating/cooling schedule for you by learning from when you manually adjust the temperature. If it detects that you always turn up the heat in the morning or turn down the air in the afternoon, it learns from your habits and automatically creates a schedule based on your past behavior and preferences. (That's why some of these smart thermostats are called "learning thermostats.")

Even better, most smart thermostats will set up "home" and "away" modes. When the thermostat knows you're home, it adjusts the temperature one way; when it knows you're away, it adjusts the temperature another.

The smart thermostat's smartphone app also adds a lot of functionality. We're talking graphing and displaying your temperature settings over time, and even calculating energy costs. Plus, of course, you can use the app to change the temperature with your smartphone, even if you're not at home.

Finally, many smart thermostats connect to other smart devices in your home, typically via Wi-Fi. If you link your smart thermostat to your Amazon Echo or Google Home device, for example, you can change the temperature by using simple voice commands. ("Alexa, turn up the heat.") Or if you link your smart thermostat to your smart lighting system, you can have your lights turn off automatically when your thermostat goes into away mode.

All this is accomplished via the microprocessor built into the smart thermostat, and the accompanying software programming. The thing is smart because it's programmed to be smart. (And, on some models, that built-in intelligence is augmented by remote sensors that monitor temperature and humidity in other rooms.)

The smart thermostat itself connects to your heating/cooling system the same way your old thermostat does. In fact, installation is typically a matter of disconnecting a few wires from your old thermostat and reconnecting them in a similar fashion to your new thermostat. It's that easy.

After you have your smart thermostat in place, you synchronize it to the accompanying smartphone app. You can then wirelessly connect the thermostat to other smart hubs and devices in your home.

Should You Upgrade to a Smart Thermostat?

Smart thermostats aren't cheap; you'll pay anywhere from $150 to $300, more if you need professional installation. Is a smart thermostat worth that kind of money?

The smart answer, as it seems to be with most smart home technologies, is "maybe."

What benefits can you gain by installing a smart thermostat in your house or apartment? Let's look at the major advantages:

- **You'll save money—over time.** For most people, heating and cooling account for more than 40 percent of the home's energy use. Even if a smart thermostat saves you just a little each month, those little bits can add up to big bucks over time. The savings come, of course, from the smart thermostat's ability to more accurately turn the temperature down (or up, depending on the season) when you're gone or sleeping. You don't need to heat or cool your house when you're not there, and sensing that is something most smart thermostats excel at.

How Much Savings?

Estimates of savings vary from manufacturer to manufacturer but promise to be significant. For example, Nest estimates that using its learning thermostat saves 10 to 12 percent in heating costs and 15 percent on cooling. Ecobee claims an average savings of 23 percent using its device. If these claims are accurate, the average household will save $130 or more over the course of a year. At that rate, you'll pay for your smart thermostat in two years or so.

- **It's more convenient.** This is important for users of any age, but especially for us older folks who really don't want to keep getting up and down all day to adjust the thermostat. Smart thermostats are easier to program (especially when they program themselves), and it's a lot easier to adjust the temperature via smartphone app or using your Echo or Google Home voice-controlled device than it is by walking across the room and doing it by hand. As with most smart devices, convenience matters.

- **You can control it from anywhere.** When you use your smart thermostat's smartphone app, you can adjust the temperature from any room in the house or when you're away from home. For that matter, you can adjust the temperature from any room in any house; your smartphone connects to your smart thermostat over the Internet, which lets you control the temperature even when you're out on the town or on vacation.

- **You get more information**. Traditional thermostats display the current temperature and the desired temperature, and not much else. Many smart thermostats display (either on the unit itself or in the smartphone app) a lot more information, including current weather conditions, future weather forecasts, energy usage, and more.

- **It's easier to make changes.** Whether you're making changes to your heating/cooling schedule or adjusting the clock for Daylight Saving Time, it's a lot easier to do with a smart thermostat or its accompanying smartphone app. (By the way, most smart thermostats are more than smart enough to automatically adjust for Daylight Saving Time, so there.)

- **It works with other smart devices in your home**. Most smart thermostats either directly or indirectly connect to other smart devices in your home. That means that your smart lighting (or other devices) can be programmed to turn off or on when you leave or arrive home, based on the home/away settings on your smart thermostat. The possibilities here are myriad.

Bottom line, a smart thermostat makes sense for you if you're interested in saving energy and like the convenience of automated learning and remote control over your home's temperature. The fact that you can use your smart thermostat to help control other smart devices in your home is just icing on the cake.

Evaluating Smart Thermostats

Thermostats first got smart in 2011, when Nest Labs introduced the first-generation Nest Learning Thermostat. Although the Nest set the mold for what we now consider a smart thermostat, other companies soon jumped into the market with their own variations on the theme. Today you can find smart thermostats from a half-dozen or so companies, most of which perform similarly.

Enter Google

The original Nest thermostat was so impressive that Google bought the parent company in 2014. So today, Nest is part of Google and works very well with the Google Home and the company's other smart devices and services.

Most smart thermostats offer some combination of automatic learning, Internet connectivity, and smartphone control. The most versatile also easily connect to and interface with other popular smart devices.

Carrier Cor Wi-Fi Thermostat

Carrier is one of the larger manufacturers of heating/cooling equipment in the United States (They also own the Bryant brand, among others.) As such, Carrier's entry into the smart thermostat market is not totally unexpected.

The Carrier Cor Wi-Fi Thermostat

The Cor is a nice-looking unit with a big full-color touchscreen display. The touch-screen display in essence replaces traditional up and down buttons, along with other physical controls; just touch or tap the corresponding onscreen control.

In terms of operation, it's a fully programmable model that uses remote temperature and humidity sensors to maintain a comfortable temperature while conserving energy. Unfortunately, it's not a learning thermostat, so you have to program in your heating/cooling schedule manually, or via the accompanying smartphone app.

The Carrier Cor is compatible with the Amazon Echo/Echo Dot, Apple HomeKit, and Wink hubs and devices.

Unlike many of the other smart thermostats described here, Carrier requires professional installation for the Cor. It sells for about $250, not including installation. Learn more at www.carrier.com.

Bryant Housewise

The Carrier Cor is also sold under the Bryant Housewise brand.

Ecobee

While the Nest Learning Thermostat got out to an earlier and large lead in the smart thermostat marketplace, Ecobee has become a strong number-two player in the market. They currently offer three different models.

The low-priced ($170) Ecobee 3 Lite offers full programmability and remote smartphone control. It doesn't have learning capabilities, but it's a good, solid, app-controlled thermostat. It's compatible with the Amazon Echo/Echo Dot, Apple HomeKit, Logitech Harmony, Samsung SmartThings, and Wink hubs and devices. It also works with IFTTT commands.

The mid-priced ($200) Ecobee3 includes everything the Lite has and adds support for up to 32 wireless remote temperature sensors. Put a sensor in each room of your house and the Ecobee3 uses them to match the target temperature you set for each room. When a room's occupancy changes, the sensor sends that information to the thermostat to adjust the heating or cooling accordingly.

Ecobee's new top-end model is the Ecobee4. Like the Ecobee3, it offers remote sensor capability and compatibility with a wide range of smart hubs and controllers. It adds built-in Amazon Alexa Voice Service, with integrated microphone and speaker, which is a pretty big deal. This means you can control the thermostat with voice commands and also use it to control other smart devices in your home. (In essence, if you have the Ecobee4, you don't need a separate Amazon Echo or Echo Dot device in the room.) The Ecobee4 is kind of an all-in-one smart thermostat/controller solution, and sells for around $250.

Learn more about all of Ecobee's smart thermostats at www.ecobee.com.

The Ecobee4 smart thermostat

Emerson Sensi Wi-Fi Thermostat

The Emerson Sensi costs a little less than some of the other smart thermostats available today but offers similar features. You get full programmability and remote smart phone control, but no learning capabilities. The design is a little more old school than some of its competitors and uses physical control buttons instead of a touchscreen display—but you may be comfortable with that.

The Emerson Sensi Wi-Fi Thermostat

The Sensi is compatible with Amazon Echo/Echo Dot and Wink hubs and devices. It sells for around $160. Learn more at www.sensicomfort.com.

Honeywell Lyric Round Wi-Fi Thermostat

Like Carrier, Honeywell is a big player in the heating/cooling space, and the Lyric Round Wi-Fi Thermostat is its answer to the Nest Learning Thermostat. Like the Nest, the Lyric is a big round controller with a fancy display in the middle; you turn the controller to select an option, then press in to select.

Honeywell's Lyric Wi-Fi Thermostat

Also like the Nest, the Lyric is fully programmable and can be remote controlled via the accompanying smartphone app. It doesn't have learning capabilities, but it does offer *geofencing*, which sets home and away modes based on how far away you are from your house or apartment. (It gets this information from the location sensing on your smartphone.)

The Lyric thermostat is compatible with Amazon Echo/Echo Dot, Apple HomeKit, Google Home, Logitech Harmony, Samsung SmartThings, and Wink hubs and devices. It also works with IFTTT.

Honeywell sells the Lyric thermostat for around $200. Learn more at yourhome. honeywell.com.

Honeywell Wi-Fi Smart Thermostat

Honeywell's Wi-Fi Smart Thermostat is an older model that might appeal to some smart home users. It has a full-featured color touchscreen display that offers more information than you find on the Nest/Ecobee-type thermostats. It's fully programmable, of course, and you can also control it with the accompanying smartphone app.

The Honeywell Wi-Fi Smart Thermostat

The Wi-Fi Smart Thermostat is compatible with Amazon Echo/Echo Dot and Google Home controllers, as well as SmartThings and Wink hubs and devices. It's priced around $200. Learn more at yourhome.honeywell.com.

Nest Learning Thermostat

The most popular smart thermostat on the market today, and the one that pretty much defined the entire category, is the Nest Learning Thermostat. The Nest looks like a round dial with a colorful LED display; you turn the outside of the dial (the *ring*) to rotate through the available options and then press the ring to select.

The Nest Learning Thermostat

Like most other smart thermostats, the Nest is fully programmable and can also be controlled by the accompanying smartphone app. What's unique about the Nest is its ability to learn from your behavior; as you turn the temperature up or down throughout the day and across several days and weeks, it learns your routine and automatically creates a heating/cooling schedule that fits. So although you can program it manually, you don't have to.

The Nest is compatible with most major smart home systems and devices out there. You can connect the Nest to Amazon Echo/Echo Dot and Google Home devices for voice-controller operation; it's also compatible with dozens of other smart devices, from August smart locks to Zuli smart plugs, and just about everything in between.

Works with Nest

To view a current list of devices that work with the Nest Learning Thermostat, go to www.nest.com/works-with-nest/.

Naturally, the Nest thermostat is also compatible with other Nest devices, including the Nest Protect smoke alarm and Nest Cam Indoor and Outdoor security cameras.

What you can't use with the Nest is a shorter list. You can't use it with Apple HomeKit or with SmartThings by Samsung. That's about it.

Because of this broad compatibility across multiple smart platforms, it's easy to use the Nest thermostat with the smart devices in your home. Connect the Nest thermostat to a given device and either use that device to trigger a temperature change or use the Nest to turn on or off a given device.

The Nest Learning Thermostat is available in most home improvement stores and online. Nest sells it in four colors (the original stainless steel, white, copper, or black); it's priced at about $250. Learn more at www.nest.com.

>>>Go Further

INSTALLING A SMART THERMOSTAT

Most smart thermostats are surprisingly easy to install. You need a very small flathead screwdriver, and maybe a larger Philips screwdriver (for removing the mounting screws).

The installation consists of six basic steps:

1. Turn off the power to your heating/cooling system. You might find a master switch by your furnace, or you might need to disengage the system's circuit breaker.

2. Remove your current thermostat from the wall. You might need to detach a few latches, or remove a few screws.

3. Use the small screwdriver to disconnect the wires from the current thermostat. These wires should be color-coded or labeled; if not, use small pieces of tape to label them now.

4. Connect these wires to the new smart thermostat. Match the wire colors to the colors or labels on the thermostat.

Connecting wires to a Nest Learning Thermostat

5. Mount the new thermostat to the wall. You might need to use the mounting plate that came with the thermostat, or you can mount it to the wall directly.

6. Turn on the master switch or circuit breaker for your heating/cooling system.

That's it. Once your system is turned back on, the new smart thermostat boots up and walks you through a setup procedure. Follow the onscreen instructions to get everything set up properly.

If you're comfortable doing this little bit of wiring, you can probably install the smart thermostat yourself. If not, call your local handyman or heating/cooling firm to do it for you. The hardest part for me was getting the old thermostat off the wall; everything else was a breeze.

Using the Nest Learning Thermostat

Because the Nest is the big dog in smart thermostats, the rest of this chapter focuses on how to set up and use a Nest Learning Thermostat in your home. I'll assume you've installed your Nest and are ready to start the configuration process.

Set Up and Configure Your Nest Thermostat

Once you've installed your Nest thermostat and restored power to your heating/cooling system, the Nest walks you through a fairly simple configuration process. To make a selection, rotate the Nest's outer ring left or right. To confirm the selection, press in on the ring.

(1) When prompted, select the language you want to use.

(2) Select **Internet Connection** to connect your thermostat to your home network.

(3) Select your network from the list.

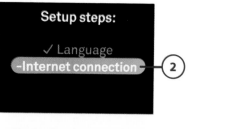

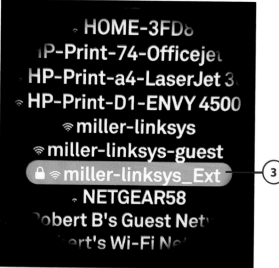

4. Enter the password for your home network. Rotate the ring to choose a letter and then press the ring to select it.

5. Select **Your Location** to enter your home's location.

6. Nest attempts to guess your location based on your Internet connection. If this is the correct location, select **Yes**. (If not, select **No** and enter your ZIP Code manually.)

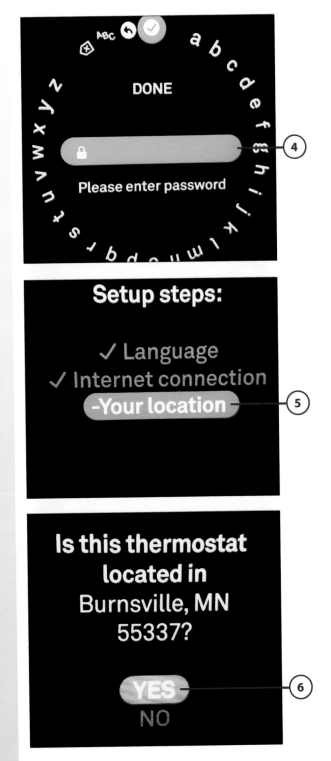

7. Select the most appropriate description for your home—**Single-family, Multi-family, Apt./Condo,** or **Business**.

8. Select which room the thermostat is in.

9. Select **Heating and Cooling**.

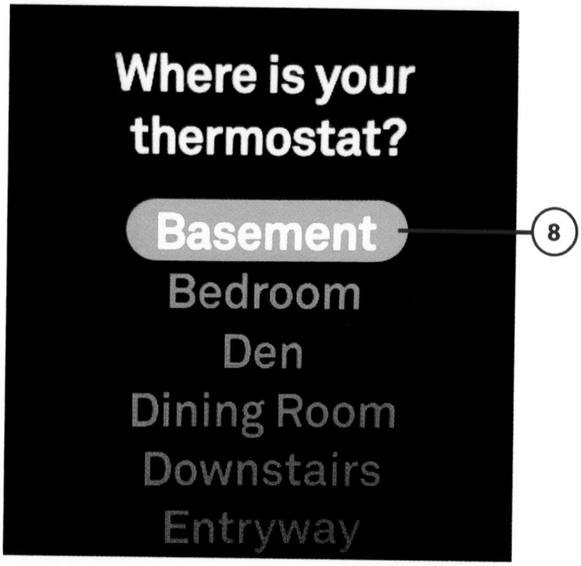

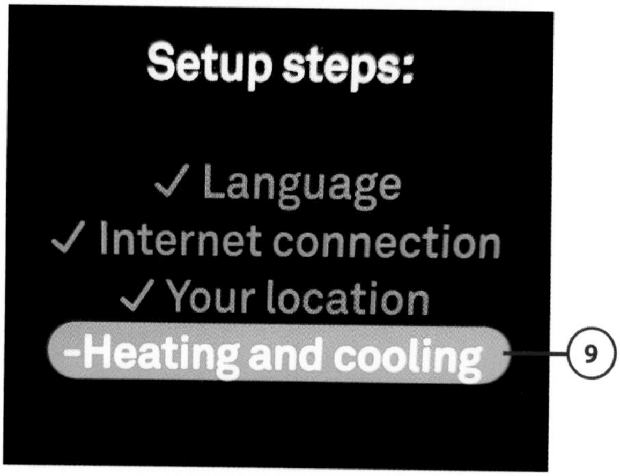

Please describe this location:

SINGLE-FAMILY ⟵ 7
MULTI-FAMILY
APT. / CONDO
BUSINESS

Where is your thermostat?

Basement ⟵ 8
Bedroom
Den
Dining Room
Downstairs
Entryway

Setup steps:

✓ Language
✓ Internet connection
✓ Your location
-Heating and cooling ⟵ 9

10 If you're installing the thermostat yourself, select **Homeowner**.

11 Review your connections and then select **Continue**.

12 Nest displays the components of your system—typically Heating, Cooling, and Fan. Select **Continue**.

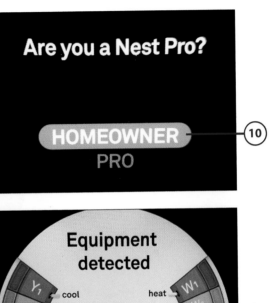

(13) Identify the fuel source for your heating—Gas, Electric, Oil, etc.

(14) Select what type of heating you have—Forced air, radiant, and so forth.

(15) Select **Temperature**.

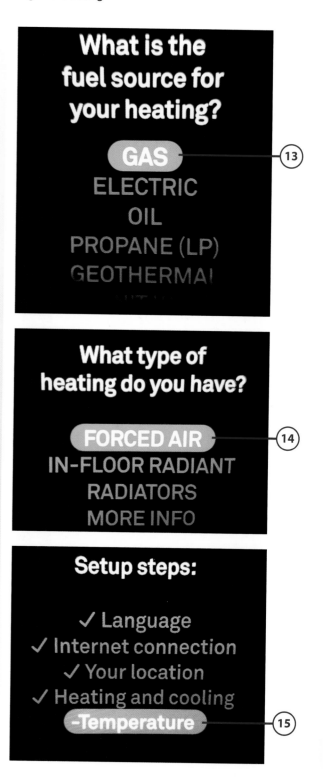

(16) Select whether you want to begin by **Heating** or **Cooling** your home.

(17) Enter the lowest and highest temperatures you want while you're away.

(18) If you want, select **System Test** to see if everything works, or select **Finish** to complete the set up.

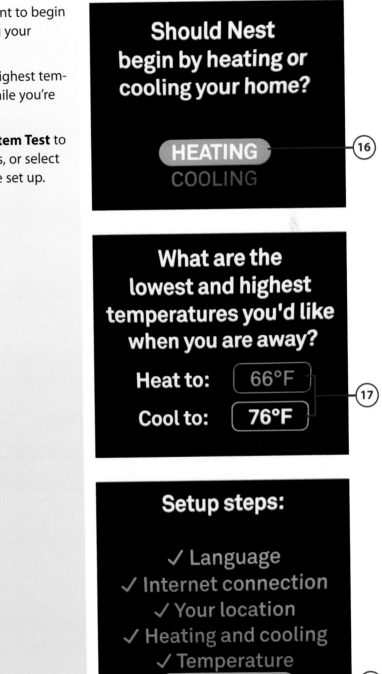

Control Your Thermostat

You can control various operations from the Nest menu on the device's display. You access the menu screen by pressing the outside ring.

The center of the menu screen displays the current temperature, day and time, outside temperature, and weather forecast. Rotate the ring to highlight the available options.

(1) Select **Heat/Cool** to switch between heating (furnace) and cooling (air conditioner).

(2) Select **Fan** to turn your fan on or off.

(3) Select **Energy** to view how much energy you've used over the past ten days.

(4) Select **Schedule** to create, edit, or view your heating/cooling schedule.

(5) Select **Settings** to configure the device's various settings.

(6) Select **Home/Away** to enter Away mode when you're leaving the house and want to save energy while you're gone. (Select this again when you get home to switch to Home mode.)

(7) Select **Done** to see the current time, temperature, and weather conditions in the center of the screen.

Set the Temperature

Manually setting the temperature on the Nest thermostat is as easy as turning a dial.

(1) By default, the Nest thermostat displays the current room temperature. Rotate the ring to select the temperature you want.

(2) Press the dial. The display lights up blue if you're cooling to the selected temperature or orange if you're heating to that temperature. It also displays how many minutes will pass until you reach the selected temperature.

(3) You can also control the temperature from the Nest mobile app. From the main screen of the app, tap the room where the thermostat is installed.

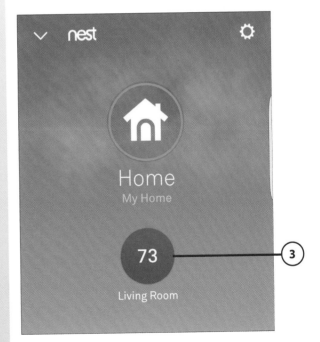

(4) You now see the current inside (big) and outside (small) temperatures. Tap and drag the temperature indicator to the temperature you want. (Alternatively, you can tap the up and down arrows to raise or lower the temperature.)

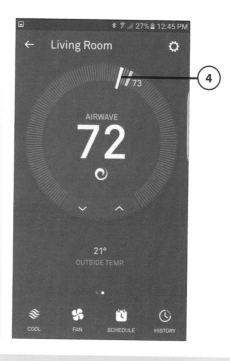

>>>Go Further
INSTALLING AND CONFIGURING THE NEST APP

You use the Nest app to control all Nest products—the Nest Learning Thermostat, Nest Protect smoke detector, and Nest Cam security camera. The app itself is free; you can download it from your phone's app store. You'll need to create a Nest account (also free) to use the app with your Nest devices.

When you first launch the Nest app, you're prompted to sign in to your Nest account. If you've previously created an account, enter your email address and password, and then tap **Sign In**. If you've not yet created a Nest account, tap **Sign Up** and follow the onscreen instructions.

You need to configure the app the first time you use it. When prompted, tap **Continue** and follow the on-screen instructions to create a name for your home, enter your home's address, and select whether you want to use your phone's location for Nest's Home/Away assist function. (You probably do.)

You then need to add your Nest thermostat to the Nest app. From the app's main screen, tap **Add**, select **Nest Thermostat** from the list of products, and enter the seven-digit key from the Settings screen of the thermostat. You can then start using the app to control your Nest thermostat.

Program Your Nest

As with most smart thermostats, you can program your desired heating/cooling schedule into the Nest thermostat. You can do this from the Nest thermostat itself (select **Schedule** from the menu screen) or from the Nest mobile app. This is a lot easier to do on your smartphone or tablet, so the following steps describe that method.

1. From the main screen of the app, tap the room where the thermostat is installed.

2. Tap **Schedule**.

3. Turn your phone or tablet sideways to view the Schedule screen. Tap the day where you want to add a temperature change.

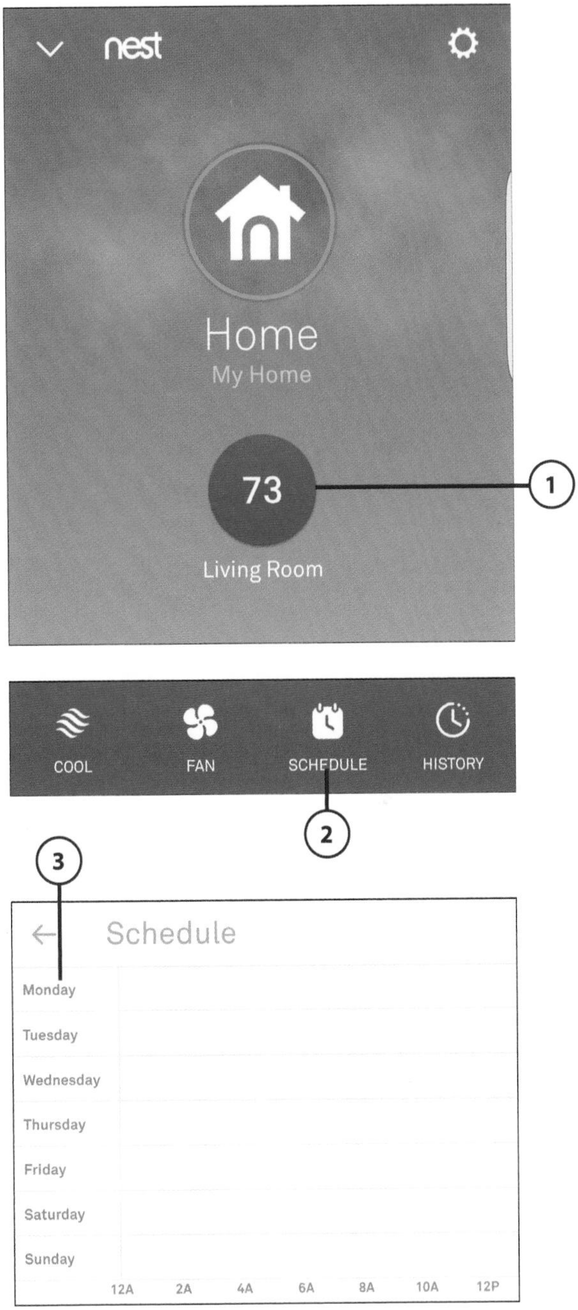

nest

Home
My Home

73

Living Room

COOL   FAN   SCHEDULE   HISTORY

Schedule

Monday
Tuesday
Wednesday
Thursday
Friday
Saturday
Sunday

12A   2A   4A   6A   8A   10A   12P

(4) You now see a schedule for that day. Tap **Add**.

(5) Tap the time you want the temperature change (left to right) and the temperature you want (top to bottom). Repeat steps 4 and 5 to add more temperature points.

(6) To change the temperature for one of the points you've added, tap and drag it up or down.

(7) To remove a temperature point, tap **Remove** and then tap that point.

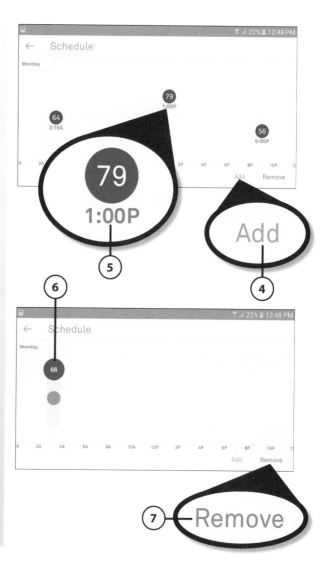

Learning Your Routine

Creating your own heating/cooling schedule is useful. Having your Nest thermostat do it for you, automatically, is even better.

The Nest Learning Thermostat gets its name from its ability to learn your heating and cooling preferences. This takes a little time—several days to a few weeks, depending—but it's a lot easier than manually punching in all your desired temperatures into a preprogrammed schedule.

How do you get your learning thermostat to learn your preferences? It's simple; all you have to do is tell it what you want. You do this by manually changing the temperature when you want it changed. So if you like to turn up the heat when you wake up, turn up the heat when you wake up. If you want to turn down the heat when you go to bed, turn down the heat when you go to bed. Turn down the air when you leave the house, or turn it up when you get home in the late afternoon. Make whatever changes you want, manually, to the Nest thermostat.

Over time, Nest learns from the changes you make and starts making them for you. After you have turned up the heat each morning for a few days, Nest turns up the heat automatically. It truly learns your preferences and creates its own schedule based on them. There's nothing more you need to do than rotate the ring from time to time. (And if your preferences change, Nest learns that, too!)

Connecting Your Nest to Other Smart Devices

As we discussed previously in this chapter, the Nest Learning Thermostat is compatible with all manner of smart systems and devices. But how do you get your Nest talking to all those smart things?

For most devices, it's a matter of adding the Nest to your connections in that device's smartphone app. For example, if you have a Wink system, open the Wink app, tap **Add a Product**, select **Heating and Cooling**, then select **Nest Learning Thermostat**. You're prompted to sign in to your Nest account to be connected. You can then control your Nest thermostat from the Wink app, as well as add the thermostat to any shortcuts or robots you create.

Here's another example. If you want to control your Nest thermostat from your Amazon Echo device, you have to add a skill for the Nest thermostat to the Alexa mobile app. Tap **Smart Home** and then tap **Get More Smart Home Skills**. Search for Nest and tap **Nest** in the search results. Tap **Enable** and follow the onscreen instructions to connect your thermostat to Alexa. Once connected, you can change temperature by saying "Alexa, raise the temperature" or "Alexa, set the temperature to 72 degrees."

>>>Go Further

SMART VENTS AND CEILING FANS

If you want to make your home heating/cooling system even more efficient, consider install-ing smart vents. These vents, like the Keen Home Smart Vents (www.keenhome.io/smart-vent), can be programmed to open and close automatically based on the desired temperature for that particular room. They're not cheap ($80 or so per vent, which adds up fast), but they do address the challenge of achieving different temperatures in different rooms.

Of course, you don't have to turn on the air conditioner to cool a given room. For many of us, ceiling fans are great for moving the air around and cooling things off without running the air conditioner. There are several brands of fans that can be controlled via smartphone app; some even connect to the Nest thermostat for more integrated control. Check out smart fans from Bond (www.fan-bond.com), Haiku (www.haikuhome.com/senseme), and Hunter (www.hunterfan.com/SimpleConnect) if you're interested.

In this chapter, you learn how to make your home safer with smart home technology.

→ Adding a Smart Doorbell
→ Installing a Smart Door Lock
→ Using Smart Security Cameras
→ Working with Smart Smoke and CO Detectors
→ Assembling a Smart Home Security System

Automating Home Security

How safe is your house or apartment? When the doorbell rings, do you know who's at the door? Did you remember to lock your door when you left home? Do you know what's happening on the other floors or rooms of the house? What happens if there's smoke, or a fire? And how safe are you from break-ins, anyway?

We're all concerned about our personal safety. Fortunately, smart home technology can actually make your home safer. There's a variety of smart devices you can employ, from smart doorbells and door locks to whole-house security systems. You can choose the level of security that's best for you.

Adding a Smart Doorbell

You're sitting on your couch or lying in bed when the doorbell rings. You're not expecting any visitors, and you don't know whether you should get up to answer the door. Is it someone you know? Is it a delivery person with a package? Is it someone asking for donations? Or is it a bad guy who's thinking of breaking in?

Wouldn't it be great to know who's at the door before you open it—or even got up out of bed? Well, you can do just that when you install a smart doorbell outside your front door. When someone presses the button on a smart doorbell, you can see who's there without getting up and walking across the room. That's a safer and more convenient solution.

How Smart Doorbells Work

Most smart doorbells operate in a similar fashion. The doorbell installs outside your front door, replacing your current doorbell. Some connect to your existing doorbell's wiring for power and chime inside your house; some have their own built-in batteries for power without involving any wiring. (These latter types are ideal if you live in an apartment and can't replace the existing doorbell.)

All smart doorbells have built-in video cameras. So when someone presses the doorbell button, not only do you hear a chime letting you know someone's at the door, you also get a notification on the doorbell's mobile app. Just tap the button on your smartphone or tablet and you see, in real time, who's at your front door. You can then decide whether you want to get up and let them in.

Some smart doorbells have a built-in speaker and microphone, so you can talk to and hear whoever's at your door. And, thanks to the Internet, you can see who's at the door (and talk with them) when you're not at home; that way it can look like you're at home even if you're hundreds of miles away.

There are several popular models of smart doorbells available today. This chapter examines the three most popular, as detailed in Table 5.1.

Table 5.1   Popular Smart Doorbells

	August Doorbell Cam	**Ring Video Doorbell**	**SkyBell HD**
Built-in video camera	Yes	Yes	Yes
Build-in microphone	Yes	Yes	Yes
Built-in speaker	Yes	Yes	Yes
Connects to existing wiring	Yes	Yes (optional)	Yes
Optional battery power	No	Yes	No
Motion sensing	Yes	Yes	Yes
Smartphone app	Yes	Yes	Yes
Two-way communication	Yes	Yes	Yes
Live video feed	Yes	Yes	Yes
Video quality	1080p HD	720p HD	1080p HD
Night vision video	No	Yes	Yes
Cloud recording	Yes, $4.99/month	Yes, $3/month	Yes, free
Price	$200	$200	$200

As you can see, all three of these popular models sell for around $200 and offer similar features. Because of its built-in battery, however, the Ring Video Doorbell is the easiest of the three to install, and really the only choice if you live in an apartment where you can't tamper with the existing doorbell wiring.

August Doorbell Cam

The August Doorbell Cam is a small round device that replaces your existing doorbell. Like the other smart doorbells discussed here, it includes a built-in HD video camera, microphone, and speaker, so you can see, hear, and talk to anyone at your front door. It also includes a motion sensor so you're alerted if someone's knocking instead of ringing (why do people do that?), or if someone suspicious is hanging around your front door.

The August Doorbell Cam

Like the other smart doorbells here, you get alerted in two ways when someone pushes the doorbell button. First, your existing doorbell chime makes its sound, just as your current doorbell does. Second, you get an alert on the August smartphone app. This way you're alerted to activity even when you're not at home.

At this point you can choose to ignore the doorbell, get up and answer the door, or open the smartphone app to see who's at the door. This last option is the safest and most useful; if it's someone you don't want to see, you can then ignore them.

When you're using the smartphone app, you also have the option of talking to the person at the door. You see and hear the person, via the doorbell's camera and microphone; they hear you but don't see you, which is an added layer of protection. And, since you're doing all this over the Internet, you can talk to someone at your door even when you're at work, out for dinner, or on vacation. (This is especially useful for making people think you're at home when you're really not!)

The feature that makes the August doorbell unique is that it interfaces with August's smart door lock, which is covered later in this chapter. By connecting the two August products together, you can opt to unlock the door if it's someone you trust—again, even if you're not at home. Let's say, for example, that you have a housecleaning service. The cleaning lady rings the August doorbell, you see who it is on the August smartphone app, and then tell the person you're unlocking the door. You do just that by tapping the button in the August app that unlocks the August door lock. Pretty nifty!

The August doorbell keeps a record of all operations, so you know when your doorbell is being rung (or when there's been motion at the front door). All interactions are recorded by the doorbell's camera, and you can call up past recordings at will—if you subscribe to August's cloud recording service, that is. That costs $4.99 per month.

As to price, expect to pay around $200 for the August Doorbell Cam. Learn more at www.august.com.

Ring Video Doorbell

The Ring Video Doorbell is different from the other models discussed here in two ways. First, it isn't round; it's rectangular. Second, it doesn't have to use your existing doorbell's wiring for power. (Although it can, if you want.) It includes a built-in rechargeable battery, which makes it a better choice if you live in an apartment or condo where you can't remove the existing doorbell.

The Ring Video Doorbell

Battery Operation

A single battery charge should last between 6 and 12 months. You recharge the unit by removing the Ring doorbell from its mounting plate (loosen two screws and it lifts off) and connecting it to a power outlet via the supplied USB cable.

Aside from those two features, you get pretty much the same functionality as with the August and SkyBell models. There's an HD video camera, microphone, and speaker, as well as night vision and motion-sensing technologies. You receive alerts on your smartphone (via Ring's mobile app) when someone rings the bell or there's motion at the front door; you can then view what's happening via the doorbell's built-in camera and microphone, and talk with the person at the door if you want.

Viewing a visitor on Ring's smartphone app

The Ring app records and stores (in the cloud) all the interactions at your front door, so if you miss an alert you can go back and see who or what was there. (My Ring doorbell's motion sensor caught me shoveling snow from my doorstep a few weeks ago!) Ring charges $3/month (or $30/year) for its cloud recording service.

If you connect the Ring doorbell to your existing doorbell's wiring, you hear the doorbell through your existing system's chime. If you use the Ring doorbell with its built-in battery, you probably want to purchase the optional Chime or Chime Pro. These devices connect to a power outlet and your Wi-Fi network, and ring when someone presses the button on your Ring doorbell. (They can also be configured to sound a different alert when the motion detector is activated.) The basic Chime unit sells for $30; the Chime Pro also functions as a Wi-Fi extender (nice if your front door is a far distance from your wireless router) and sells for $50.

Ring's Chime Pro

Like the smart doorbells discussed here, the Ring Video Doorbell sells for around $200. Learn more at www.ring.com.

Ring Video Doorbell Pro

Ring also offers the Video Doorbell Pro. This model sells for about $50 more than the standard model and offers slightly better video recording, at full 1080p HD. (The regular Video Doorbell only offers 720p HD—which is more than adequate for viewing on your smartphone.) In addition, the Video Doorbell Pro does *not* have a built-in battery, so it only installs as a replacement for an existing doorbell.

SkyBell HD Wi-Fi Video Doorbell

Like the August Doorbell Cam, the SkyBell HD Wi-Fi Video Doorbell is a round device with a round button. It contains an HD video camera, microphone, and speaker. It connects to your existing doorbell wiring and has its own smartphone app.

The SkyBell HD Video Doorbell

When someone rings the SkyBell HD, you get a sound from your existing doorbell chimes as well as an alert on the SkyBell app. You can get up to answer the door (or not) or view who's at the door on your phone. You can also talk to the person at the door via the mobile app, if you want.

Unlike the August doorbell (but like the Ring), the SkyBell HD has night vision technology to make it easier to view visitors after dark. You can also opt to just turn on the SkyBell camera to monitor what's happening outside your front door. All video interactions are recorded and stored in the cloud for future viewing; unlike the other systems discussed here, SkyBell's cloud recording service is free of charge.

The SkyBell HD sells for around $200. Learn more at www.skybell.com.

Installing a Smart Door Lock

Knowing who's at your door is one thing. Being able to lock or unlock your door remotely is another.

Welcome to the world of smart locks. A smart lock replaces some or all of your existing deadbolt lock and offers a number of useful features. Some smart locks let you unlock the front door with a touch, or just by being near. Others let you lock or unlock your door with a smartphone app, even when you're not at home. And some even interface with your other smart devices—such as a smart doorbell—to automatically lock or unlock your door when certain conditions are met.

How Smart Door Locks Work

When we talk about smart locks, there's a lot of variety. The term "smart lock" is a fairly broad definition for number of different smart features that you might find on these products.

What they all have in common is that they replace some or all of your existing deadbolt lock. That means a bit of work to do the installation, which you may or may not be comfortable with. If you've never installed a lock before, you might want to hire a locksmith or handyman to do the job.

Almost all smart locks let you lock or unlock your door without using a traditional key. Some offer a touchscreen or touchpad you use to tap in a keycode for entry. Others connect to a special key fob or your smartphone via Bluetooth, and they lock or unlock with a touch of your finger or just when you're physically close enough. (Most also let you use a physical key for backup, if you want.)

Then there's remote operation. Some smart locks connect directly to your home Wi-Fi network so that you can operate them via smartphone app wherever you have an Internet connection. Others offer this type of Wi-Fi connectivity only when you purchase an additional bridge unit; the lock connects to the bridge via Bluetooth then the bridge talks to your smartphone via Wi-Fi.

A smaller number of smart locks use either Bluetooth or Wi-Fi to connect to other smart systems or devices. Some smart locks connect to Apple's HomeKit, some to Nest products, and others to Wink hubs and devices. In addition, some smart locks connect to other devices sold by the same company. (The August Smart Lock works seamlessly with the August Video Doorbell, for example.)

Prices range anywhere from $200 to $350 for the smart lock itself, and an additional $100 or so for the optional Wi-Fi bridge, if necessary.

There are several different smart door locks available today. This chapter covers some of the most popular, as detailed in Table 5.2.

Table 5.2   Popular Smart Door Locks

	August Smart Lock	Kwikset Kevo	Kwikset Premis	Schlage Connect	Schlage Sense	Yale Assure
Bluetooth entry	Yes	Yes	Yes	No	Yes	Yes
Touchpad entry	No	No	Yes	Yes	Yes	Yes
Smartphone operation	Yes	Yes	Yes	Yes	Yes	Yes
Virtual electronic keys for guests	Yes	Yes	No	No	Yes	Yes
Network bridge required for remote operation	Yes, $80	Yes, $100	Yes, Apple TV or iPad	Yes, SmartThings or Wink hub	Yes, Apple TV or iPad	Yes, $75
Smart home compatibility	Amazon Alexa, Apple HomeKit, Google Home, Nest	Honeywell, Nest, Ring, SkyBell	Apple HomeKit	Amazon Alexa, SmartThings, Wink	Apple HomeKit	Apple HomeKit, SmartThings, Wink
Price	$230	$230	$230	$230	$230	$200

August Smart Lock

Let's start with the August Smart Lock. This is a good choice if you're using the August Video Doorbell, discussed previously in this chapter. These two devices work together to let you remotely unlock the door if whomever rings the bell is someone you want to see.

The August Smart Lock

The August Smart Lock uses Bluetooth technology to connect to your smartphone when you approach the front door. When configured to do so, it senses when you're near and automatically unlocks the door; you don't have to physically touch or tap or turn anything. It also senses when you leave via the front door and automatically locks itself after you.

You can also create virtual keys for family and guests. You create a limited-time electronic key and send it to a person's smartphone via email. They then use their phone to unlock the door. (You can track their comings and goings via the August smartphone app, too.)

Rental Guests

August's virtual keys are perfect for when you have guests visiting, or need to let in a repair person if you're away from home. It's also great if you offer your home as an Airbnb vacation rental—just send each guest their own limited-time keys to use.

The one truly unique feature of the August Smart Lock is that it doesn't require you to replace your entire existing lock. You leave the outside part of your lock and the deadbolt in place and install the August lock in place of the inside portion of your lock. It's the easiest installation of all these smart locks, and perhaps the only one suited for installation in apartments.

Installing the August Smart Lock

To take advantage of remote locking features, you need to purchase the optional August Connect device. This diminutive unit connects to your August lock via Bluetooth, and then to your home network (and the greater Internet) via Wi-Fi. It sells for about $80.

In addition, the August Smart Lock is compatible with Apple's HomeKit. This means you can operate it via the Home app on your iPhone or iPad, or via Siri voice commands. It's also compatible with the Google Home voice-controlled device.

The August Smart Lock sells for around $230. Learn more at www.august.com.

August Smart Keypad

August also makes a Smart Keypad that lets visitors unlock the smart lock by punching in a preprogrammed numeric code. This is good if you have repair people or house cleaners who need access to your home while you're away; just give them a one-time code so they can enter.

Kwikset Kevo

Kwikset offers two different types of smart locks. First is the Kevo, which is currently in its second generation.

Kwikset's Kevo smart lock

The Kevo totally replaces your existing deadbolt lock. When you approach your front door from the outside, all you have to do is touch the Kevo to unlock it. (That's assuming you have either your smartphone or a Kevo key fob in your pocket; they have to connect to the Kevo lock via Bluetooth for this whole thing to work.) You can also unlock the door via Kevo's smartphone app or a standard key.

You can also send virtual electronic keys to others to use with their smartphones. This lets anyone you approve unlock the front door just by touching the Kevo lock.

Kevo works with a variety of smart devices, including Honeywell thermostats, the Nest Learning Thermostat, the Ring Video Doorbell, and the SkyBell HD smart doorbell. It also functions with IFTTT commands.

IFTTT

IFTTT (If This Then That) is a cloud-based service for automating multiple smart devices. Learn more in Chapter 14, "Adding More Functionality with IFTTT."

To work with these other devices, or to enable remote locking/unlocking, you need to purchase the Kevo Plus hub. This hub connects your Kevo to the Internet and lets you do all sorts of remote access and monitoring. It runs around $100.

The Kevo smart lock itself sells for around $230. Learn more at www.kwikset.com/kevo.

Kwikset Premis

Kwikset offers another smart lock, called the Premis Touchscreen Smart Lock. This lock's claim to fame is that it's compatible with Apple's HomeKit system and Siri voice-controlled assistant.

Kwikset's Premis Touchscreen Smart Lock

Unlike its Kevo cousin, the Premis includes a touchscreen you can use to manually key in a code for entry. Otherwise, you use your phone to do the locking and unlocking. You can use the Premis mobile app, Apple's Home app, or just talk to Siri and tell her to lock or unlock the door.

To work with Apple HomeKit, you need some sort of Apple hub—either an Apple TV set top box or an iPad that you keep inside your home. Unfortunately, the Premis is an Apple-only smart lock; there's no Premis app for Android devices.

The Premis smart lock sells for around $230—the same price as the Kevo. Learn more at www.kwikset.com/premis.

Schlage Connect

Schlage is one of the leading lock makers in the world, and the Connect is its lead smart lock.

The Schlage Connect

The Connect isn't as smart as some other smart locks, however. You can't open it at your door with your smartphone or a key fob; you have to manually key in an entry code via its touchscreen control. You can, however, connect it to your Amazon Echo device and control it via voice commands to the Alexa personal assistant. It does connect to Z-Wave-compatible smart systems, such as the SmartThings and Wink hubs, so you can use those systems (and their smartphone apps) to control it remotely.

The Schlage Connect sells for $230 or less at most retailers. Learn more at www. schlage.com.

Schlage Sense

The Schlage Sense is similar to the Schlage Connect in that it offers a touchscreen for keying in manual entry. Unlike the Connect, the Sense is compatible with Apple's HomeKit, so you can use your iPhone to open the door, either via the Home app or Siri voice commands. You can also assign virtual keys to guests' iPhones.

The Schlage Sense

If you have an Apple TV or iPad in your home, you can use Apple's HomeKit to control your lock remotely via your iPhone. Unfortunately, this is an Apple-only device, so it doesn't work with Android devices.

The Schlage Sense sells for around $230. Learn more at www.schlage.com.

Yale Assure Lock with Bluetooth

Our final smart lock is the Yale Assure Lock with Bluetooth. It's a keyless lock that you operate solely via your smartphone or its built-in touchpad.

Yale's Assure Lock

To lock or unlock the Assure, hold your phone up to the lock and make a key-like twisting gesture. The connection is via Bluetooth, of course. You can hand out virtual keys for friends or guests to use with their smartphones. Friends and guests (and you, too) can also unlock the Assure by keying in a code on the built-in touchpad.

Yale's Assure integrates with any ZigBee or Z-Wave-compatible system, which includes SmartThings and Wink hubs and devices. It's also slated to be compatible with Apple's HomeKit in the near future.

To work with these smart systems, you need to invest in a Yale Network Module. This device serves as a bridge between the Bluetooth-enabled Assure lock and your smart system's Wi-Fi hub. It sells for $75.

The Yale Assure Lock sells for around $200. Learn more at www.yalehome.com.

Using Smart Security Cameras

You can add another level of security to your home by installing indoor and/or outdoor security cameras. Smart security cams broadcast what they're seeing to an accompanying smartphone app; some even connect to your existing smart home network to trigger other devices and events.

How Smart Cameras Work

A smart camera is more or less a standard video camera that connects to the Internet and offers remote viewing capability via the accompanying smartphone app. Some smart cameras also connect to your smart home hub to interface with other smart devices.

Smart cameras are a lot smaller than the traditional video cameras or security cameras you might be used to. Some of them resemble the smallish webcams you can add on to your desktop computer system. Others, designed for outside use, are in slightly larger housings for protection from the elements.

What most smart cameras have in common is the ability to operate in always-on mode or to be triggered by motion in the room or area. This type of motion detection can also alert you that there's someone nearby and show you what's happening.

In terms of connecting a smart camera, you don't have to worry too much about cables and wiring. Most operate off of built-in rechargeable batteries, and they connect to your home network (and other devices) via Wi-Fi, so everything's wireless.

These smart cameras also record everything they see, and upload the videos to the manufacturer's cloud storage system. You'll probably pay a small monthly fee for this service, but it lets you review what was recorded in the past.

This section covers a few of the most popular smart cameras on the market today. Table 5.3 presents details for these products.

Table 5.3 Popular Smart Security Cameras

	Arlo Q	Arlo Pro	Canary Flex	Nest Cam Indoor	Nest Cam Outdoor
Indoor use	Yes	Yes	Yes	Yes	No
Outdoor use	No	Yes	Yes	No	Yes
Battery power	No	Optional	Optional	No	No
Wi-Fi wireless operation	No	Yes	Yes	Yes	Yes
Video quality	1080p HD	720p HD	1080p HD	1080p HD	1080p HD
Motion detection	Yes	Yes	Yes	No	No
Night vision	Yes	Yes	Yes	Yes	Yes
Two-way audio	Yes	Yes	Yes	Yes	Yes
Smartphone app	Yes	Yes	Yes	Yes	Yes
Compatibility	SmartThings, Wink	SmartThings	None	Amazon Alexa, Nest, Wink	Amazon Alexa, Nest, Wink

	Arlo Q	Arlo Pro	Canary Flex	Nest Cam Indoor	Nest Cam Outdoor
Cloud storage	Yes, free (7-day storage), $9.99/month (30-day storage)	Yes, free (7-day storage), $9.99/month (30-day storage)	Yes, $9.99/month (30-day storage)	Yes, $10/month (30-day storage)	Yes, $10/month (30-day storage)
Network hub required	No	Yes, included	No	No	No
Price	$200	$250	$200	$200	$200

Arlo Q

Netgear is the company behind the Arlo family of security cameras. The Arlo Q is designed for indoor-only use, and it looks a little like a computer-type webcam. It comes with a short stand and sits on a desk or table in your home. It includes a 130-degree wide-angle lens to take in as much of your room as possible.

Netgear's Arlo Q indoor smart cam

As to features, it's up there with most of the other cams we're looking at. You're talking 1080p HD video, two-way communication so you can talk to anyone in the monitored room, night vision technology for better video in the dark, and a built-in motion sensor to activate the camera when someone walks into the room.

You can view what the Arlo Q sees via its smartphone app from anywhere you have an Internet connection. Unlike most of these other cams, you get free cloud storage for seven days' worth of recordings; upgrade to the Premier plan ($9.99/month) to store 30 days' worth of recordings online.

The Arlo Q connects to your home network via Wi-Fi. It's compatible with SmartThings and Wink hubs and devices.

Netgear sells a whole range of Arlo security cams at various price points; the Arlo Q sells for around $200. Learn more at www.arlo.com.

Arlo Pro

If you need a more rugged security camera, especially for outdoor use, consider the Arlo Pro. This model is designed for outdoor use but can also be used indoors; power comes from either a wall outlet or from the unit's built-in rechargeable battery. It connects to your home network via Wi-Fi, of course, and you can view what's happening from its smartphone app.

Netgear's Arlo Pro indoor/outdoor smart cam

As to specs, it's similar to the Arlo Q. You get a 130-degree wide-angle lens, two-way audio, built-in motion detection, and night vision viewing. Video isn't quite as sharp as with the Q, maxing out at 720p HD, which should be good enough for most users.

The Arlo Pro is a great choice for an outdoor camera, as its case is totally waterproof. Just hang it up on the outside of your house, switch to battery power, and you're good to go. It also includes a siren you can trigger remotely or program to sound when there's motion in the area.

You can take advantage of the same Basic (free) and Premier ($9.99/month) cloud storage plans you get with the Arlo Q. It's compatible with SmartThings hubs and devices.

To use the Arlo Pro, you need a Wi-Fi base station. Netgear sells a package of one Arlo Pro camera and base station for about $250, and offers other packages with more cameras as well. Learn more at www.arlo.com.

Canary Flex

Canary sells a complete home security system, including cameras, that are covered later in this chapter. For now we're looking at its standalone security camera: the Canary Flex.

The Canary Flex indoor/outdoor smart cam

The Flex is a weatherproof indoor/outdoor camera that's powered by a rechargeable battery. It connects to your home network via Wi-Fi and is operable by its accompanying smartphone app.

In terms of features, the Canary Flex includes a 116-degree wide-angle lens, 1080p HD video, motion detection, and night vision technology. At present it's not compatible with other smart systems and devices—it works only with the Canary home security system.

The Canary Flex sells for around $200 and is available in both white and black casings. Learn more at www.canary.is/flex.

Nest Cam Indoor and Outdoor

You learned about the Nest Learning Thermostat in Chapter 4, "Automating Heating and Cooling." Well, the Nest thermostat was just the first of several smart products from the folks at Nest. They also offer two smart security cams, the Nest Cam Indoor and the Nest Cam Outdoor.

The Nest Cam Indoor

The Nest Cam Indoor looks like a small computer webcam on a stand, and it operates via normal wall power. The Nest Cam Outdoor is weatherproof and can mount on the side of your house; it still needs to be plugged in for power, however, as it doesn't have an internal battery.

The Nest Cam Outdoor

Both cameras share similar specs; it's just that one is designed for indoor use and the other for outdoor use. The Nest Cams offer 130-degree wide-angle lenses, 1080p HD video, night vision technology, and two-way audio communications. Both are operable via the Nest smartphone app, and both connect to your home network via Wi-Fi.

Unlike other smart cams discussed here, the Nest Cams don't have motion detectors. They record everything they see, constantly, 24/7. Nest says this is a good thing, as you'll never miss anything that happens. It's certainly a different approach than the motion-activated cams. The camera's software can tell the difference between a person and a thing in the picture, and only notifies you if there's a human being in the frame.

Naturally, both Nest Cams connect to and interface with the Nest Learning Thermostat and the Nest Protect smoke detector. For example, when your Nest thermostat goes into Away mode, it can turn on your Nest Cams—or turn them off in Home mode. Another example is what happens if the Nest Protect detects smoke or high carbon monoxide (CO) levels; it turns on the Nest Cam's streaming video in the smartphone app and records an emergency video clip.

The Nest Cams are also compatible with Wink hubs and devices. You can also interface your Nest Cam with Amazon Echo/Echo Dot and Google Home voice-controlled devices.

The Nest Cam Indoor and Nest Cam Outdoor both sell for around $200. Learn more at www.nest.com.

Working with Smart Smoke and CO Detectors

When it comes to protecting your home, it isn't all about making your home safe from intruders. You also need to worry about protection from other types of emergencies, such as fires and unhealthy air quality. To that end, let's examine some of the smart smoke and air quality detectors available, which are also compared in Table 5.4.

Table 5.4   Popular Smart Smoke and CO Detectors

	Birdi	Halo+	Nest Protect
Smoke detection	Yes	Yes	Yes
Carbon monoxide (CO) detection	Yes	Yes	Yes
Air quality monitoring	Yes	No	No
Temperature sensor	Yes	Yes	Yes
Humidity sensor	Yes	Yes	Yes
Photoelectric smoke sensor	Yes	Yes	Yes
Ambient light sensor	Yes	No	Yes
CO sensor	Yes	Yes	Yes
CO_2 sensor	Yes	No	No
Particulate sensor	Yes	No	No
Barometric pressure sensor	No	Yes	No
Motion sensor	No	No	Yes
Weather alerts	Yes	Yes	No
Connect via Wi-Fi	Yes	Yes	Yes
Smartphone app	Yes	Yes	Yes
Compatibility	N/A	Amazon Alexa, SmartThings	Google Home, Nest, Wink
Price	$120	$130	$100

Birdi

Birdi is a "smart detector," a combination smoke detector, carbon monoxide (CO) detector, and air quality monitor. It can alert you in case of fire, high CO levels, and even earthquakes and tornados. In terms of air quality, Birdi monitors temperature, humidity, dust, volatile organic compounds (VOCs), and more.

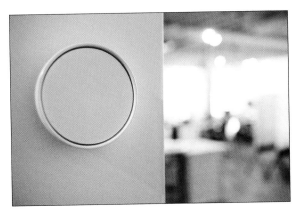

The Birdi smart smoke/CO detector and air quality monitor

The number of different alerts offered by Birdi is impressive. You can be alerted either in person (via the physical alarm) or via smartphone app of smoke and fires, high CO levels, high or low temperatures (especially freezing temperatures), weather emergencies, and more. If a home emergency is detected, not only do you get alerted, but Birdi calls the appropriate authorities.

The Birdi app not only alerts you to dangerous conditions, it also presents weather forecasts and air quality information. You can track pollen levels, allergy outbreaks, high UV levels, and more.

Birdi sells for about $120. Learn more at www.getbirdi.com.

Availability

As this book is written in spring of 2017, Birdi is not yet shipping in large quantities. Look for wider availability by the time you read this book.

Halo+

The Halo+ is a combination smoke and CO alarm with bonus weather alerts. Not only do you get notified in the instance of smoke, fire, or high carbon monoxide levels, the Halo+ also lets you know when there's bad weather on the way.

The Halo+ smoke/CO detector with weather alerts

The alerts come your way via either in-person alarms from the device or alerts on Halo's smartphone app. The unit also lights up red or blue, depending on the type of alert. It connects to your home network via Wi-Fi.

The Halo+ is able to handle all its tasks because it includes a variety of sensors. Packed inside this little round device are photoelectric, ionization, CO, temperature, humidity, and barometric sensors. The weather alerts come courtesy of the National Weather Service.

The Halo+ is compatible with Amazon Echo/Echo Dot voice-controlled devices, as well as SmartThings hubs and devices. It sells for around $130; there's also a simpler Halo (non-plus) model that lacks weather alerts and sells for around $100. Learn more at www.halosmartlabs.com.

Nest Protect

Nest Protect is yet another product from the folks who brought you the Nest Learning Thermostat and Nest Cams. This one's a smart smoke and CO detector that does a lot more than the typical $20 smoke detector you find at your local big box store.

The Nest Protect smoke + CO alarm

First off, the Nest Protect senses both smoke and CO. It also tests itself automatically, which is nice, and it's supposed to last a lot longer than a cheap smoke detector. And here's something unique: It contains a motion sensor and automatically lights up when you walk underneath. (That's great for when you're up foraging for food in the middle of the night.)

When it senses something's wrong, the Nest Protect talks to you during an emergency and tells you what's going on. Instead of issuing only an annoying beep, it plays a chime tone and says something like "Heads up; there's smoke in the kitchen."

Even better, the Nest Protect sends emergency alerts to your smartphone, so you know if there's a problem even when you're away from home. You can configure it to send alerts not only to you but also to other family members, friends, and emergency response services.

The Nest Protect connects to and interfaces with Nest's other products, of course. It connects to your home network via Wi-Fi. It's compatible with the Google Home voice-controlled device, as well as Wink hubs and devices.

The Nest Protect is available in both battery-operated and wired versions. It's also more expensive than traditional smoke detectors; it sells for around $100. Learn more at www.nest.com.

>>>Go Further
SMART WATER SENSORS

If you've ever been the victim of a big water leak—from a faulty water heater, an overflowing tub or toilet, or a leaky washing machine or dishwasher—then you know the damage that can result. (Our household recently had a gusher in our 150-gallon saltwater aquarium, which is about as big a leak as you're likely to encounter; unfortunately, it happened in the dead of night and I didn't have a leak detector nearby.) Fortunately, smart home technology can alert you when there's water where it shouldn't be.

There are a variety of smart leak detectors or water sensors on the market. These devices connect via Wi-Fi to alert you, via smartphone app, when there's a leak. It's pretty simple, really.

Some of the more popular models come from D-Link (www.dlink.com), Fibaro (www.fibaro.com), and LeakSMART (www.leaksmart.com). If you've ever had to deal with massive water damage, you know the value these sensors can bring.

Assembling a Smart Home Security System

When it comes to protecting your home from break-ins, burglaries, home invasions, and the like, it's a matter of you versus the bad guys. In the past, if you wanted more security than you were offered from a simple deadbolt, you had to contract with a home security service to monitor your home. That is a good solution that can certainly make you feel safe. The downside, though, is that you're stuck with that firm and its service and equipment, and you're stuck paying a pricey monthly fee.

If you want more control over your home security—and you want to reduce that monthly subscription fee—you can now turn to smart home technology. By combining the right smart devices, you can assemble your own home security system at a fraction of the cost.

There are various ways you can put together a smart home security system. You can piecemeal together individual devices and sensors that work with a given smart hub; you can use an all-in-one device that includes a motion detector, security camera, and alarm; or you can buy a full-featured system that includes multiple sensors, cameras, and such that work together as a whole. The following sections examine a few of each kind of system.

No Fees, No Contracts

The advantage of putting together your own smart security system is that you don't have to subscribe to a monitoring service, which means you don't have to sign any contracts or pay any monthly fees. The downside is that you're doing the monitoring yourself; you'll receive alerts if there's a break-in or intruder, and you'll need to contact the authorities yourself.

Samsung SmartThings

Samsung offers a SmartThings Home Monitoring Kit—for about $250—that gives you everything you need to put together a basic home security system. If you're already using SmartThings devices (or thinking of doing so), this is a good way to go.

Samsung's SmartThings Home Monitoring Kit

Here's what you get in the bundle:

- SmartThings Hub
- SmartThings Motion Sensor
- SmartThings Multipurpose Sensors (2)
- SmartThings Outlet

You can use the motion sensor to alert you to unexpected motion in a given room or area. The multipurpose sensors can monitor whether doors or windows are open or closed. And they all connect to the SmartThings Hub, which can also control other SmartThings devices. Buy this bundle and then purchase additional sensors as needed to protect your entire home. You can even add SmartThings-compatible sirens to complement the alerts you'll receive on your phone via the SmartThings app.

Learn more at www.smartthings.com.

Wink

Unlike Samsung, Wink doesn't sell its own sensors and devices (other than the Wink Hub, that is). To use a smart home security system that works with Wink, you need to assemble compatible sensors and devices offered by third parties.

You start with the Wink Hub, of course, and then add a variety of motion sensors and door/window sensors. You can top the whole thing off with an alarm, as well. You can then program the Wink app to sound the alarm and send you an alert when one of the sensors is triggered. (You might want to configure the alert so that it triggers only after a certain time, or when you're away from home—otherwise, you won't be able to open a door or window without sounding the alert!)

If you don't want to assemble your own system from scratch, and don't yet have a Wink Hub installed, Wink does offer a Security and Monitoring Kit, which sells for around $170. This kit includes the following components:

- Wink Hub
- GoControl Motion Detector
- GoControl Door-Window Sensors (2)
- Levitron DZC Plug-In Appliance Module

These are essentially the same components in Samsung's competing SmartThings bundle, but they're from different companies and at a slightly lower cost. If you're in the Wink ecosystem, this is a good way to get started.

Learn more at www.wink.com.

Canary

If you want simplicity, take a look at Canary. This is an all-in-one indoor security solution—a small table-top device that combines a built-in security camera, various air-quality sensors, and a siren to monitor a given room. If something is amiss, you get an alert on your smartphone. (And the alarm sounds, of course.)

The Canary smart security device

Inside this nifty little device you'll find

- Security camera with 147-degree wide-angle lens, 1080p HD video, and night vision technology
- Microphone and speaker for two-way communication
- Motion sensor
- Temperature sensor
- Humidity sensor
- Ambient light sensor
- Accelerometer
- 90dB siren

The Canary system connects to your home network via either Wi-Fi or Ethernet. It's a good solution for a small apartment, and can be supplemented by additional Canary Flex cameras to cover additional rooms in your home.

The basic Canary unit sells for around $200, although Canary sells various packages with additional Canary devices and Canary Flex cameras as well. Learn more at https://canary.is.

Piper

Piper is an all-in-one security device, similar to Canary. This little table-top wonder combines a security camera with a motion sensor and siren, and it sends alerts to the accompanying smartphone app.

The Piper smart security device, along with the Piper smartphone app and optional door/window sensor

Here's what's inside each unit:

- Security camera with 180-degree wide-angle lens, night vision (Piper nv only), and pan-and-tilt capability
- Microphone and speaker for two-way communication
- Motion sensor
- Sound sensor
- Temperature sensor
- Humidity sensor
- Light sensor
- 105dB siren

You monitor and control Piper with the Piper smartphone app. It connects to your home network via Wi-Fi and is Z-Wave compatible.

The Piper Classic sells for around $200. The Piper nv, which adds night vision capabilities, sells for around $280. You can augment the basic Piper unit with door/window sensors, smart switches, and the like, if you want.

Learn more at www.getpiper.com.

iSmartAlarm

If you have a larger house and want complete coverage, you need to move beyond the all-in-one devices and invest in a more sophisticated home security package, such as iSmartAlarm, which is an expandable, self-monitored, DIY security system.

The company sells several different kits and some standalone devices. The system is built around the CubeOne hub, which has a built-in 110 dB siren. The CubeOne is the brains of the system, and it alerts you via smartphone or email when there's been an intrusion.

You can get started with the iSmartAlarm Starter Package. This package includes one CubeOne hub, one motion sensor, one contact sensor, and one remote tag. It sells for around $150.

The iSmartAlarm Preferred Package, with accompanying smartphone app

If you need to cover more doors/windows/rooms, consider the Preferred Package. This one gives you one CubeOne hub, one motion sensor, two contact sensors, and two remote tags. It sells for around $200.

iSmartHome also sells additional contact and motion sensors, sirens, and security cameras that link together via the CubeOne hub. Learn more at www.ismartalarm.com.

SimpliSafe

SimpliSafe offers one of my favorite smart home security packages. Unlike iSmartHome, SimpliSafe is a 24/7 monitored solution which provides an added layer of security (at a small monthly cost, of course). Like iSmartHome, there are a variety of packages and devices to choose from.

When a sensor senses that something's wrong, it wirelessly contacts the SimpliSafe base station. (This unit is the brains of the system and also includes an 85 dB siren.) The base station then sends you an alert and notifies the SimpliSafe support desk, which will contact the appropriate authorities, if necessary.

SimpliSafe's Starter Home Security System

You can build your own system from available components, or go with one of SimpliSafe's existing packages. A good place to start is the Starter System, which is good for condos and apartments. It includes one base station, one motion sensor, one entry sensor, one wireless keypad, and one keychain remote. It sells for about $230.

For bigger homes, consider the Classic System. This one includes one base station, one motion sensor, three entry sensors, one wireless keyboard, one smoke detector, one extra siren, and one keychain remote. It sells for around $350. (Other systems are available.)

SimpliSafe's monitoring is done over a cellular connection, so if a bad guy cuts your phone lines it still works. You'll pay $14.95/month for the monitoring service.

Learn more at www.simplisafe.com.

Automating Your Kitchen and Laundry

Smart appliances represent a lot of potential for the smart home. Note that I said "potential." That's because there are a number of smart appliances available today, but what's coming in the future is more interesting.

Wait a few years and you'll see smart refrigerators that monitor food usage and text or email you detailed shopping lists when necessary; smart ovens that know what you're cooking and when you eat, and turn themselves on automatically; and smart laundry machines that run when you're away from home so you won't hear the noise.

Some of this functionality is available now, but most of it is still a few years away. Read on to learn what's here and what's coming.

Understanding Today's Smart Appliances

All the appliances you have in your kitchen and laundry room today are rather dumb. Let's face it—your refrigerator is just a big insulated box designed to keep food cool. Your dishwasher has only enough brains to start the designated cycle at the time you set. Your oven has a timer, but you have to manually set the desired temperature. Your microwave oven is a little smarter, in that it probably has a few preprogrammed power levels for specific types of food, but the clock doesn't know enough to reset itself for Daylight Saving Time. And although your washer and dryer include some preprogrammed cycles for different types of fabrics, and the dryer maybe even has a moisture sensor to tell you when everything's properly dry, both are still simple machines, waiting for you to tell them what to do.

All of that doesn't mean that smart technology isn't coming to your kitchen and laundry. In fact, there's a little bit of smarts in some of the higher-end appliances currently available in your local big box store. Let's take a look at what's currently available, and what you can look forward to in the future.

Smart Operation

When we think of smart appliances, the first thing we'd all like to see is smart operation. That starts with the ability to manage your appliances remotely. This is not what we're used to, by the way; with most appliances today you need to set a timer or a given start time to fire up a cycle. It's semi-automatic operation, but not really the smart technology we're looking for.

With a true smart appliance, operation gets more flexible. Instead of manually setting a timer on the front panel of a device, you can use an app on your smartphone to remotely press the start button on an appliance. Some apps will even let you program operations in advance—like setting a manual timer, but more sophisticated.

Even better, smart interactive technology connects your smart appliances to other smart devices and hubs in your home. Connect your smart dishwasher to your smart thermostat or garage door, and it will know when you've left home so it can start a noisy cycle without bothering you. Connect a smart oven to your smart lighting system so it knows when you're coming home to start cooking dinner.

Smart Monitoring

For a smart appliance to be truly smart, it must monitor its environment and operation to let you know about things you need to know. That means sending out some sort of alert or notification when an operation is done or when something unexpected happens.

In the past, appliances typically alerted you with a loud buzzer or rinky-dink snippet of music. (I absolutely hate the notification music from our laundry equipment!) Smarter appliances send out smarter notifications.

For example, a smart washer might send a notification to its corresponding smartphone app when the washing cycle is complete. Or maybe you'll get a text message notifying you that your dinner is finished cooking in your smart oven. Or how about a smartphone alert if somebody leaves the refrigerator door open?

The key is to use connected technology to notify you of important stuff happening in the kitchen or laundry room. We have the technology; we *can* do this.

Smart Energy Savings

Some of today's smart appliances use their smarts to cut down on energy usage. If an appliance knows when power consumption is lower or rates are cheaper, it can program itself to operate during those times. In addition, smart appliances typically include other energy-efficient functionality, such as a dishwasher using less water per cycle or a refrigerator incorporating more insulation to keep things frosty.

Smart Maintenance

Then there's the process of keeping your smart appliance up to date and in tip-top operating condition. This involves having the right sensors within each appliance to determine when some maintenance needs to be done or when some function isn't properly working. Then, instead of just flashing a light on the appliance's front panel, you get notified (via app, text message, or email) about the issue at hand. Ideally, the message includes advice or instructions for what you should do next.

For example, you're probably used to seeing an alert light above your refrigerator's water dispenser when the water filter needs to be changed. With a smarter refrigerator, instead you'd get an alert in a smartphone app or a text message to that effect. Same thing when you need to add more fabric softener to your smart dryer, or if the hot water in your dishwasher isn't getting hot enough.

It's all about smart diagnostics and alerts making you more aware of things you need to be aware of—and aiding in the diagnosis when things go wrong.

Smarter Food Storage with Smart Refrigerators

Let's focus our attention on individual kitchen and laundry appliances, and look at the smartest of today's crop of smart appliances.

GE Connected Refrigerators

GE (www.geappliances.com/ge/connected-appliances) offers a variety of what it calls "connected appliances." These appliances can be controlled by the GE Kitchen smartphone app, as well as the Amazon Echo smart hub.

Here's just some of what GE's connected refrigerators and the GE Kitchen app let you do:

- Alert you if the refrigerator door is open, when the water filter needs to be replaced, or if the refrigerator's temperature is too high

- Provide status updates that let you view the current temperatures of the fresh food and freezer compartments, as well as the status of the icemaker (full or empty)

- Control various operations, including turning the icemaker on or off, adjusting the temperature, scheduling hot water for your morning coffee (on models with the hot water feature), and controlling various special modes

GE currently offers a half-dozen or so connected refrigerators, all in the popular French door configuration from 22.2 to 27.8 cubic feet capacity. Prices are all more than $3,000.

LG SmartThinQ Refrigerators

LG (www.lg.com/us/discover/smartthinq offers several different kitchen appliances that can be controlled and monitored via their SmartThinQ smartphone app, including two smart refrigerators. Here's some of what the app lets you do:

- Activate Ice Plus mode to increase the amount of ice when you need it

- View the status of various functions, including refrigerator and freezer temperatures

- Receive alerts when the water filter and fresh air filter need to be replaced

- Conserve energy by having the refrigerator run in a power-saving mode when you're away from home

- Troubleshoot common problems directly from the app—even if you're not at home

Monitoring an LG smart refrigerator with the SmartThinQ app

At present LG offers two SmartThinQ refrigerators, both with 30 cubic foot capacity in the French door configuration. Both are priced around $4,000.

Samsung Family Hub Refrigerators

Samsung's (www.samsung.com/us/home-appliances) smart refrigerator offering is called the Family Hub, and it has a really big LCD touchscreen in the door. The touchscreen connects to your home Wi-Fi network and provides a lot of non-refrigeration functionality, including family calendars, notes and reminders, photo display, and streaming music. (Okay, so it's kind of like having a big tablet taped to your refrigerator door.) You can also use the touchscreen to compile family grocery lists, and send those lists to your smartphone. Oh, and if you have a Samsung Smart TV, you can mirror whatever you're watching in the living room on the refrigerator screen.

Samsung Family Hub refrigerator

Inside the refrigerator are three cameras that take photos every time the doors close. You can view what's inside the fridge from your smartphone, as well as control refrigerator and freezer temperatures, check the status of the water filter, and control the ice maker.

Currently, Samsung offers four Family Hub models, all in the French door configuration, with capacities from 22 to 27.9 cubic feet. Prices hover between $5,600 and $6,000, although many retailers offer these models at discounted prices.

>>>Go Further
SMART REFRIGERATORS IN THE FUTURE

Today's smart refrigerators are just nudging into the "smart" category—and smart refrigerator technology is typically only available in high-end, high-priced models. What can we expect to see in the smart refrigerators of the future?

First, expect smart features to filter down into lower-priced models. Yes, the fancy stuff will start out in the high-end models, but over time prices come down and you will be able to get a bevy of smart features—especially smartphone connectivity—in mid-range and even lower-end models.

Beyond that, look for new smart features behind the refrigerator doors. How about a refrigerator that lets you know when foods expire? Or one that knows what foods you like and monitors its own inventory? Even better, the smart fridge of the future should know when you're low on your favorite foods and beverages, and use that information to assemble a grocery list. Take that one step further, and the fridge should then send (via text or email or whatever) the grocery list to your local grocery store, which then will then fill the order and deliver those groceries right to your front door—and send you an electronic invoice for the goods purchased. (You'll still have to manually stock the groceries in the fridge, however, unless someone invents a handy-dandy robot to do that chore.)

Once you start thinking outside the box, there's a lot more a truly smart refrigerator could do, especially when connected to other smart devices. Envision your smart refrigerator connected to your smart TV, and that you're watching your favorite cooking show on the Food Network. You see a recipe you like and tell your smart TV to save the recipe and send it to your smart refrigerator. The fridge stores the recipe and determines whether you have all the ingredients necessary. If you don't, it either tells you what you need or automatically adds those items to the next grocery list. And all this happens before the show you're watching goes to commercial.

Even better, why not let your smart fridge figure out what to cook, based on what ingredients you have on hand? Using a combination of sensors and internal cameras, your refrigerator will know what's inside and use its own built-in intelligence (matched to a database of recipes, of course) to figure what you can cook, based on how well stocked it is. That will take all the guesswork out of meal planning.

Within the kitchen, you'll be able to connect your smart refrigerator to your smart oven to make cooking easier. Send a recipe from your smart refrigerator to your smart oven to automatically set the precise cooking time and temperature, and then get alerted when it's time to start cooking.

And what about using a smart fridge to help you diet? Connect your smart refrigerator to your smart scale or fitness band and it'll know what foods you should be avoiding. Imagine your smart refrigerator nagging you not to eat that bowl of ice cream or slice of pie as you start to take it out of the fridge. Annoying, perhaps, but also nudging you toward a healthier lifestyle. (Or maybe the fridge is so Draconian it refuses to stock unhealthy items? It's possible!)

All that's a bit in the future, but it's something to look forward to. I know I am!

Smarter Cooking with Smart Ranges and Ovens

There's a world of possibilities when you add just a little intelligence to your oven and cooktop. It's all a matter of trying to make cooking easier—and more accurate.

Let's see what's currently available.

GE Wi-Fi Connected Ovens and Ranges

GE's Wi-Fi connected ovens and ranges connect to the same GE Kitchen smartphone app as do GE's connected refrigerators. The app lets you do the following:

- Preheat your oven in advance from the app
- Set timer alerts when you're baking or roasting
- Change the oven's temperature from wherever you happen to be

Controlling a GE double oven with the GE Kitchen app

And when you connect your connected oven to the Amazon Echo hub, you can use the Alexa personal assistant to turn your oven on or off via voice commands.

GE offers a variety of connected freestanding ranges and single and double wall ovens. Prices range from $1,500 to $4,000, depending on the configuration.

LG SmartThinQ Ranges

LG's SmartThinQ gas and electric ranges let you monitor and control their operation via smartphone. You can set and monitor cooking time and temperature, as well as use the My Recipe app to send cooking information about your favorite recipes directly to your oven or range.

LG currently sells three different models of SmartThinQ Ranges—two electric and one gas. They range in price from $1,300 to $2,000.

Samsung Wi-Fi Ranges

Samsung offers two smart ranges—one gas, one electric—with Wi-Fi connectivity. Use Samsung's Smart Home smartphone app to do the following:

- Turn the oven on and off

- Monitor cooktop and oven functions

- Preheat the oven and adjust cooking temperatures

- Set a timer

- Receive alerts on oven temperatures and if you accidentally left the burners on

The ovens run around $3,000.

Samsung slide-in gas range with Wi-Fi connectivity

Smarter Dishwashing with Smart Dishwashers

Today's smart dishwashers are a lot like the current batch of smart ranges. You get remote control via smartphone app, but not a lot more.

Bosch Dishwasher with Home Connect

Bosch's Wi-Fi-enabled dishwasher (www.bosch-home.com/us/smart-dishwashers. html) lets you control basic functions with the company's Home Connect smartphone app. The app lets you do the following:

- Start the dishwasher from anywhere you are
- Receive an alert when the cycle is done
- Receive a notification when you're low on detergent tabs
- Receive an alert if there's a leak

There's one dishwasher in Bosch's current lineup that offers the Home Connect feature. It's priced at about $2,000, although discounts are available.

GE Wi-Fi Connected Dishwashers

As with other appliance categories, GE offers several Wi-Fi connected dishwashers. When used with the GE Kitchen smartphone app, you can do the following:

- Monitor dishwasher status and cycle time
- Remotely lock and unlock the controls
- Determine if the rinse agent is low
- Receive alerts if anything is wrong with the cycle, including door leaks
- Receive an alert when the cycle is done

GE built-in dishwasher with Wi-Fi Connect technology

GE currently offers three smart dishwasher models, all priced around $1,500.

Smarter Cleaning with Smart Washers and Dryers

How smart do a washer and dryer need to be? All they do is wash and dry clothes, right? Well, there's a lot you can automate about your laundry operation—and become more efficient to boot.

First off, the smarter the equipment is, the better it can wash and dry your clothes. Moisture sensors in both washers and dryers can help fine tune wash and dry cycles based on the clothing being laundered. Automatic sensing of fabric type can help the washer set the correct wash cycle and the dryer adjust the heat accordingly. These features are found in almost all of today's washers and dryers.

If you want to get smarter, think about remote control operation. Use your smartphone app to start your washer remotely, even when you're not at home. You can also use the smartphone app to monitor your laundry's progress and be notified when the load is done.

Let's see what's available.

GE Wi-Fi Connected Washers and Dryers

GE offers several different washers and dryers with Wi-Fi connected technology. Use the GE Laundry smartphone app to do the following:

- Monitor cycles and time remaining
- Extend the dryer tumble dry cycle for hard-to-dry clothes
- Receive an alert when the cycle is complete
- Monitor levels of laundry detergent and fabric softener

Control GE's smart washers and dryers with the GE Laundry app

You can also add functionality to your appliances by downloading new custom cycles to the GE Laundry app.

GE offers two washers with Wi-Fi Connect, priced around $1,200, and four Wi-Fi connected dryers (two gas, two electric), also priced around $1,200.

LG SmartThinQ Washers and Dryers

LG offers several washers and dryers that incorporate its SmartThinQ technology. Use the SmartThinQ app to do the following:

- Choose wash and dry cycles
- Start the washer and dryer
- Customize existing and download additional cycles

Currently, LG has two smart washers and four smart dryers (two gas, two electric) available. Prices range from around $1,500 to $2,000.

Whirlpool

Whirlpool (www.whirlpool.com/smart-appliances/) has offered smart laundry appliances before and has recently updated its line by smartifying the latest top-loading laundry pair. Using Whirlpool's smartphone app, you can do the following:

- Remotely start and pause wash and dry cycles
- Track cycle progress
- Track energy usage
- Activate a special cycle to keep wrinkles from setting in
- Receive notifications when cycles are complete
- Start a special Load Fresh cycle to keep clothes fresh while you're gone
- Download new cycles specialized for various types of clothing

Whirlpool Smart Cabrio washer and dryer with smart technology

Even better, Whirlpool's smart washers and dryers work with Google's Nest Learning Thermostat for enhanced functionality. When connected to the Nest system, your smart washer and dryer will know when you're home and when you're away, and adjust operation accordingly. The appliances will know to keep your clothes fresh if the cycle ends when you're away, use longer and more efficient drying cycles when you're away, and automatically delay operation when energy usage is at its peak. This is all good stuff, and it's a great demonstration of how different smart devices can work together for you.

Whirlpool offers one smart top-loading washer and two matching smart dryers (one gas, one electric). All models are priced around $1,500 each.

Nest

Learn more about the Nest Learning Thermostat in Chapter 4, "Automating Heating and Cooling."

>>>*Go Further*
DO SMART APPLIANCES MAKE SENSE FOR YOU?

As you've seen, most of today's big appliance manufacturers—including Whirlpool, GE, LG, and Samsung—include smart functionality on many of their high-end models. Despite these companies' best efforts, though, smart appliances have been a tough sell. Appliance manufacturers have been trying to integrate smart technology into their lines for several years now, but consumers just aren't buying. Why is that?

First, and perhaps most important, smart appliances are expensive. Very expensive. If you're in the market for a new refrigerator, you might have a budget of $1,000 or so for a mid-range model. If you want a smart fridge, however, be prepared to shell out $3,500 or more. That's an incredibly large price differential, and more than most consumers are willing to consider.

Second, the appliance replacement cycle is much longer than for typical consumer electronics items. You might replace your smartphone every 2 years, your PC every 4 or 5 years, and your TV every 8 to 10. But your refrigerator or laundry pair? Think 15 years or more in between purchases.

And you typically don't replace your appliances because they're losing their luster. You replace them because they wear out. A 20-year-old refrigerator cools your groceries just as well as a shiny new model. There's little to no technological reason to upgrade your appliances on a more rapid cycle, so you don't.

This brings us to the question—should you invest in new smart appliances? For most people, the answer is probably not; that is, you shouldn't (and probably won't) buy a new fridge or clothes washer unless your old one breaks down. Appliances are major purchases, and they're built to last. You don't buy new ones on a whim.

That said, if you do need a new dishwasher or range, you should probably look at the available smart models. In some instances, a smart appliance might be worth the extra cost—especially if you're already considering a high-end model. But for most of us, the current smart features just aren't smart enough to warrant the additional expense.

This probably will change in the future as costs drop and functionality increases. Today's smart appliances really aren't that smart; what you get for all that extra dough is, in most instances, nothing more than remote control operation via your smartphone. But the smart appliances of tomorrow promise more intelligence and more interconnectivity, and costs are bound to drop.

We just have to get there, but if you can get truly smart operation at a nominal price increase, then the question of upgrading might get a different answer.

So unless you're forced into a new appliance purchase in the near future, taking a wait-and-see attitude may be best. Smart appliance technology is progressing rapidly, and the options available five years from now are apt to be much more appealing than what's available today.

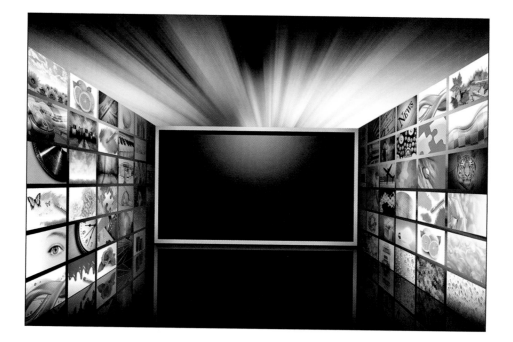

7

Automating Home Entertainment

Smart technology goes well beyond lighting, home security, and heating/cooling. There's a lot of smart technology available for your living room, much of it designed to enhance your viewing and listening pleasure.

Smart home entertainment starts with today's crop of smart TVs and set-top boxes, and it progresses quickly to whole-house audio and smart entertainment/hub integration. Read on to learn more.

Watching Smart TV

If you've purchased a new television set anytime in the last 10 or so years, or just browsed the aisles of your favorite big box retailer, you've heard the term *smart TV*. Given the overall emphasis on smart home technology and devices, you'd be excused for thinking that these smart TVs had something to do with smart homes.

Except they really don't. The term *smart TV*, as it's used today, is nothing more than marketing hype. The appellation refers to television sets or set-top boxes that offer connectivity to the Internet, typically via Wi-Fi, as well as built-in apps that enable viewing of various streaming video services, such as Netflix and Hulu. There's nothing inherently smart about one of today's smart TVs; it's a marketing term used to convey the ability to view Internet-based programming.

You can tell something's up with the term when you realize that it predates today's fascination with smart home technology. These so-called smart TVs have been around since 2007 or so, under many different labels, including connected TV, hybrid TV, IPTV, and Internet TV.

Smart TVs, then, don't necessarily have anything to do with the smart home technology we've been discussing in this book. For that matter, a smart TV doesn't actually have to be a TV. Streaming media boxes and dongles that connect to a TV and offer the requisite streaming video connectivity also fit under the broad category of smart TV devices. So Roku and Apple TV set-top boxes are smart TV devices, as are the Google Chromecast, Roku Streaming Stick, and Amazon Fire Stick. For that matter, Blu-ray players and videogame consoles that offer streaming video connectivity are also classified as smart TV devices.

What's Inside a Smart TV

Still, with millions of smart TVs in homes today, the whole smart TV phenomenon is worth examining. What exactly is a smart TV?

At its most basic, a smart TV is a television set that can connect to and interact with the Internet, primarily for the purpose of streaming videos and music over the web. In practical terms, that means the television must include the following:

- Wi-Fi connectivity, for a wireless connection to your home network.
- Central processing unit (CPU), the computer brain that manages all the device's operations and commands.
- Operating system that serves as the interface between the CPU and software-based applications.
- Graphical user interface (GUI) for displaying menus and other options.
- Software-based apps that enable connection to various web-based streaming video and audio services. For example, a smart TV might have built-in apps for Netflix, Hulu, Pandora, and more. Most smart TVs come with several apps pre-installed; some smart TVs enable additional apps to be installed after purchase.

Some smart TVs also include apps and associated technology that enable the device to play back media stored on your home network. In some cases, this capability is built into the operating system, as with the Apple TV; in other cases, this capability is enabled by DNLA or UPnP compatibility.

DNLA

DNLA stands for Digital Network Living Alliance, an industry trade group that promotes interoperability between different devices. In practical use, the DNLA specification indicates that a device is capable of playing digital media (video, music, and photos) from computers and other devices connected to the same network. UPnP stands for Universal Plug and Play. It's a set of networking protocols that enables connected devices to discover each other's presence on a network.

Some smart TVs include a built-in camera and microphone for connecting with video-sharing and chat services, such as Skype. Some more advanced smart TVs employ the built-in camera/microphone so you can navigate the onscreen menus via a series of hand gestures or voice commands.

Naturally, a smart TV (not a set-top box) also includes a traditional television tuner for viewing broadcast, cable, or satellite programming. You typically switch from the normal viewing screen to a GUI menu for the web-based services and apps.

And remember that a smart TV doesn't have to be a literal TV. A smart TV device, like the aforementioned Roku set-top box, contains the same circuitry and apps as a literal smart TV, but without the TV part. Instead, the set-top box connects to a regular TV (typically via HDMI), enabling the TV to display media played on the external device.

What a Smart TV Does

So a smart TV is a TV or set-top box that connects to the Internet for streaming video. What exactly does that mean?

Most smart TVs can perform the following functions:

- Connect to the Internet via a local network. That means connecting to your home network and sharing your Internet connection. Most smart TVs connect via Wi-Fi, although some can connect via Ethernet, too, for a faster connection.

- Play video content from web-based streaming video services, such as Netflix, Hulu, and Amazon Video.

- Play music from web-based streaming music services, such as Pandora, Spotify, and TuneIn Radio.

- Play digital media stored on other devices connected to your home network. (Some smart TVs can do this, but not all.)

- Access selected websites and web-based services, such as Facebook, Twitter, and AccuWeather. Some smart TVs offer full-fledged web browsers, although it's more common to find discrete apps for specific sites and services.

Using a Typical Smart TV

Most of today's smart TVs offer similar features and functionality. In addition to the normal TV features (screen, tuner, remote control, and so on), you get the Wi-Fi or Ethernet connectivity, onscreen GUI menus, and built-in apps that are part and parcel of the "smart" experience. Naturally, the onscreen menus and included apps differ from manufacturer to manufacturer and model to model, but the same general approach is offered by all.

For example, let's look at a typical higher-end smart TV, as of spring 2017: the Samsung UN55J6200, a 55" diagonal LED-LCD model that sells for around $500. This model has all the bells and whistles that you'd expect from a TV in this price range, including smart TV functionality in the form of what Samsung calls its Smart Hub.

Before you can access the Smart Hub, you first have to connect the TV to your home network. This particular model includes both wireless and wired connectivity, so there is an Ethernet connection on the back if you want to use it.

Wired Versus Wireless

If you have the option (and a convenient Ethernet cable), connecting a smart TV via Ethernet is a better option than using Wi-Fi. A wired connection is not only more reliable than a wireless one (you don't have to deal with weak or flakey Wi-Fi signals), but it's also faster—which is a godsend when you're watching HD streaming video.

To access the Smart Hub, press the Smart Hub button on the TV's remote. This displays pre-installed apps and those apps you've added to the Smart Hub. Click to open an app, sign into the service (if necessary), and then start watching, listening, communicating, or whatever.

Browsing streaming media apps in Samsung's Smart Hub

Roku TV

Samsung, Sony, and other major television manufacturers typically offer their own proprietary interfaces and collections of smart TV apps. Other manufacturers team with Roku (discussed next) to incorporate the popular Roku interface in their smart TVs. These so-called Roku TVs offer the same experience as a freestanding Roku set-top box.

Using a Smart Set-Top Box

If you have an older TV (or even a lower-priced newer one without built-in connectivity), you can add smart TV features by purchasing a streaming media set-top device. There are lots of these devices, with the most popular being the Roku models, Apple TV, and Amazon Fire TV. All these devices are small enough to hold in your hand and sell for $100 or less.

Consider the Roku Premiere. This one's more or less in the middle of the Roku line (between the Roku Express and Roku Ultra) and sells for about $80. It connects to your home network via Wi-Fi and to your TV via HDMI, and it includes its own remote control. Configuration is as easy as navigating through a handful of setup screens.

Roku Premiere streaming media player and accompanying remote control

Like all Roku models, the Roku Premiere comes with a number of popular apps (they call them "channels") preinstalled, including Netflix, Hulu, Amazon Video, HBO GO, Vudu, YouTube, Vevo, Pandora, Spotify, and TuneIn Radio. You can download a plethora of additional channels online for a variety of different streaming services; because of its popularity, Roku has the most available third-party apps of any of the currently available smart TV devices.

Navigating online content from the Roku home screen

If one of these little boxes is too big for you to deal with, consider a smart TV on a stick. These are streaming media devices in the form factor of a USB dongle, such as Google's Chromecast, the Roku Streaming Stick, and Amazon's Fire TV Stick. As you can see in the next figure, these devices plug into any open HDMI connector on your TV and provide similar app functionality for web-based streaming media services. There are fewer cables to worry about, plus the cost is lower, ranging from $35 for the Chromecast to $50 for the Roku Streaming Stick. The Roku and Fire sticks come with their own remotes; you operate the Chromecast with the accompanying smartphone app. It's a nifty way to add smart TV functionality to any TV set that has an HDMI connection.

Streaming Audio Throughout Your Home

If you're an audiophile, you probably know all about sophisticated whole-house audio systems. These are systems where you hardwire speakers throughout your house and drive them with a separate audio amplifier or the multiroom connections on a high-end audio/video receiver. These systems run multiple thousands of dollars and produce high-fidelity sound from a central source.

That's not the kind of system we're talking about here, mainly because most people don't have multiple thousands of dollars to run high-fidelity sound throughout their homes. Most of us just want to play a little music in the bedroom, basement, or kitchen, and don't want to spend a fortune—or run the wires—to do so.

Fortunately, two of the smart devices we discuss in this book are ideally suited for this sort of wireless multiroom audio. So let's look at how you can use your Amazon Echo or Google Home devices as speakers throughout your home.

Using the Amazon Echo as a Speaker

The Amazon Echo is a smart home hub that you control via voice commands. It's also a wireless speaker that can stand by itself or be linked with other Echo devices to play music throughout your house or apartment.

On its own, the Amazon Echo device *is* a wireless speaker. It's a cylindrical device that contains two internal speakers, a 2.5" woofer and a 2" tweeter, along with a reflex port to enhance the bass response. As such, it's small enough to sit on any table yet can still fill a good-size room with quality sound.

You control the Echo with Amazon's Alexa virtual personal assistant. When you want to play music, just tell it what you want to hear. Say "Alexa, play 'Jumping Jack Flash,'" or "Alexa, play some Fleetwood Mac," or "Alexa, play country music." Alexa will find the music you want and start playback. (To stop playback at any time, just say "Alexa, stop.")

By default, Alexa plays music from the Amazon Music service. (It's an Amazon device, after all.) You can, however, configure Alexa (from the Alexa smartphone app) to play music from other sources. Or you can just ask Alexa to do so, as in "Alexa, ask Pandora to play my Easy Listening channel," "Alexa, ask Spotify to play my Party playlist," or "Alexa, ask TuneIn Radio to play the Oldies channel."

While you can install multiple Echo devices in different rooms of your house, you can't sync the audio between them. That is, you can't play the same music at the same time on multiple devices.

You can, however, play different music in different rooms. You can have your living room Echo play music from Amazon Music, while the Echo in your bedroom plays a Pandora channel and the Echo in your kitchen plays a Spotify playlist. Just ask each Echo to play what you want in that room, and that's what you hear.

Amazon Echo

Learn more about the Amazon Echo in Chapter 11, "Controlling Your Smart Home with Amazon Alexa," or visit www.amazon.com online.

Using Google Home as a Speaker

Google's answer to the Amazon Echo is the Google Home smart wireless speaker. Like the Echo, you control Google Home with simple voice commands (via the Google Assistant virtual assistant), and it can be used to not only play music but also control many of your home's smart devices.

The Google Home device is a little shorter than the Amazon Echo. It contains a 2" high-excursion speaker and two 2" passive radiators, for a surprisingly big sound from such a little device. Just put it on a table and let it do its thing.

When you want to play music on Google Home, just tell it what you want to hear. Say "Hey Google, play some Dave Brubeck," or "Hey Google, play 'California Dreamin'," or "Hey Google, play some classical music." By default, the Google Assistant plays music from your Google Play Music account, although it can be configured or instructed to play music from other sources. For example, you can say "Hey Google, ask Pandora to play some classic rock" or "Hey Google, ask Spotify to play my Motown playlist."

Unlike the Amazon Echo, you can sync playback to multiple Google Home devices throughout your house. You do this by creating what Google calls an *audio group*, consisting of multiple Google Home devices.

Create an Audio Group

To create an audio group, open the Google Home smartphone app and tap **Devices** to display all your Google Home devices. Tap **Create Group**, give the group a name, and then tap to select which devices you want to include. Finish by scrolling to the bottom of the screen and moving the **Link This Group to Your Google Account** slider to the right. Now you can control playback on all the group's devices with a single command.

Let's say you created an audio group called "Cocktail Party." To play music, say "Hey Google, play some jazz on Cocktail Party." All the Google Home speakers start playing the same music, exactly in sync.

Google Home

Learn more about Google Home in Chapter 12, "Controlling Your Smart Home with Google Home."

Using the Harmony Hub

One of the promises of smart home technology is being able to control just about everything in your home from a single device, either a smartphone app or voice-controlled device, like the Amazon Echo or Google Home. While we've talked about control of lights and switches, doorbells and door locks, even kitchen appliances, the one piece of equipment we've skipped so far is your living room TV—or, if you're really fancy, your home theater system.

Unfortunately, none of the smart hubs and systems we've discussed—Insteon, SmartThings, and Wink—interface with your home electronics. But there *is* a hub that controls both your smart home devices and your TV and home/theater receiver. It comes from Logitech, the company behind many popular universal remote controls, and it's called the Harmony Hub.

Getting to Know the Harmony Hub

The Harmony Hub is a small black hockey puck-type piece of hardware that is actually two devices in one.

Logitech's Harmony Hub with smartphone app and Harmony Elite remote control

First, the Harmony Hub functions as a universal remote control gateway for all your electronics devices, essentially replacing all your traditional handheld remote controls. You can configure the Harmony Hub like any Logitech Harmony remote control to control your TV set, Blu-ray or DVD player, audio/video receiver, Roku or other smart set-top box, and just about anything else you have connected to your system.

Second, the Harmony Hub functions as a smart hub, much like the Insteon, SmartThings, and Wink hubs. You connect your various smart devices to the Harmony Hub (via your home's Wi-Fi network), and then control them through the Hub.

In terms of control, you have several options. First, you can control the Harmony Hub via your smartphone or tablet using the Harmony app. Second, some models of the Hub come with an accompanying remote control unit, so you can control both your entertainment system and selected smart devices in that fashion, too. And third, if you have the Harmony Hub connected to your Amazon Echo or Google Home device, you can control the Hub via voice commands.

Logitech sells three variations of the Harmony Hub. The basic package comes with just the Harmony Hub, no remote control (you control it via smartphone app), and sells for about $100. The Harmony Companion includes the Harmony Hub and a basic universal remote, and sells for about $150. The Harmony Elite comes with the Harmony Hub and a more sophisticated touchscreen universal remote, and sells for about $350.

Learn more at www.logitech.com.

What's It Work With?

In terms of compatibility, the Harmony Hub works with just about anything you can think of.

As a universal remote control, the Harmony Hub is compatible with all manner of home electronics. It'll work with any brand TV, disc player, set-top box, and just about everything else manufactured in the last dozen or so years.

As a smart hub, it's the most compatible hub I've found. It works with both the Amazon Alexa and Google Home smart controllers, along with Insteon and SmartThings hubs and devices. It can control devices from Aeon Labs, August, Cree, Ecobee, Ecolink, GE Link, Honeywell, Hunter Douglas, Jasco, Kwikset, Leviton, LIFX, Lutron, Osram LIGHTIFY, PEQ, Philips Hue, Schlage, Yale, and more. It also works with IFTTT commands.

Setting Up the Harmony Hub

If you've ever set up a Logitech Harmony universal remote control, you're familiar with how to set up the Harmony Hub. You can configure the Hub via either the Harmony smartphone app or the MyHarmony software on your computer. (I find it's easier to use the MyHarmony software, but either method works.)

You start by telling the app or software which components and devices you have. Based on what you have, the software then automatically creates certain activities, such as Watch TV or Listen to Music. You can then add your own custom activities; just select which devices should be included and in what order. The app or software figures out the rest and creates the activity.

You can create as many activities as you need. Activities can be strictly entertainment based (Watch a Movie, Watch the Food Network, Listen to Pandora, and so on), strictly smart home based (Leave Home, Go to Sleep, Reading Lights, and so forth), or both.

Using the Harmony Hub

Once you have all devices connected to the Hub and the Hub configured for all the activities you need, operating your devices is as simple as pushing (or tapping) the right button on the Harmony app.

Launch the app on your smartphone or tablet, then tap the **Activities** tab. Here you see all the activities you've created—Watch TV, Play Games, Listen to Music, and so forth. Tap the desired activity, and everything else is triggered automatically. The Harmony Hub turns on the necessary devices, switches inputs and channels and such, and even raises or lowers the lights and locks the doors, if that's part of the scene. It's the most automatic operation for smart home devices (and electronics equipment!) you can imagine.

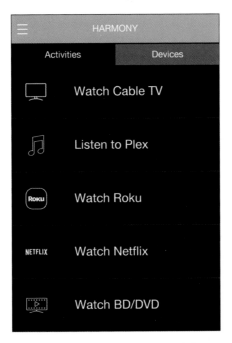

Selecting activities in the Android version of the Harmony app

>>>Go Further

VOICE CONTROL

If you have the Harmony Hub connected to your Echo or Google Home device, it can trigger complicated operations with a single voice command. This is extremely easy if you have an Amazon Echo device. For example, if you say "Alexa, turn on Netflix," it might signal the Harmony Hub to turn on your TV, switch to the HDMI input for your Roku set-top box, and switch to the Netflix channel on your Roku.

If you have a Google Home device, you have to add a few words to ask Harmony to do what you want, as in "Hey Google, ask Harmony to…." So if you say "Hey Google, ask Harmony to watch HGTV," it might signal the Harmony Hub to turn on your TV and cable box, switch to the HDMI input for your cable box, and switch to the HGTV channel.

Examining Other Smart Devices and Applications

Over the past few chapters we've covered the most popular smart devices for the home—smart lighting, smart thermostats, smart smoke and CO_2 detectors, smart security systems, smart door locks, smart doorbells, smart kitchen appliances, smart TVs, and more. But there are a lot of other smart devices out there to serve your specific needs. Let's look at a few of them.

Smart Devices for the Living Room

Let's start with a few more smart devices you can employ to automate those things you do in your living room. It's not just about smart lights and thermostats—there are also smart plugs, switches, outlets, motion detectors, window coverings, and even vacuum cleaners!

Smart Plugs

Obviously, smart bulbs are great for automating your home lighting. But what if you have a lamp that isn't suited for the typical 65-watt (equivalent) smart bulb? Maybe you need something brighter, like a 100-watt bulb? Or maybe you don't have the budget to replace all the light bulbs in your home (or even in a room)? How can you automate your home lighting without replacing every single existing bulb?

The answer is to use a smart plug or smart outlet. With a smart plug, just plug in your current light and plug the smart plug into the existing wall outlet. No bulbs to replace, no re-wiring necessary. Just buy a smart plug, and that's that.

There are lots of smart plugs on the market. You can find smart plugs that work on both the Insteon and Wink systems, and in various configurations. (Some smart plugs are just plugs; others have their own dimmer controls on the side.) And smart plugs can be used for more than just lighting; you can also plug in other appliances—room fans, space heaters, even small kitchen appliances—to add them to your smart home system.

The Smart Plug from iHome, works with most smart home systems

For example, the iHome Smart Plug, from iHome (www.ihomeaudio.com/ experience/smarthome), lets you turn any device into a smart connected device. All three available Smart Plugs (priced from $40 to $50) will handle appliances up to 1800 watts, don't need a central hub, and work with the company's iHome Control app (for either iOS or Android smartphones).

Plug the iHome Smart Plug into the electrical outlet you want to use. (Don't plug anything into the Smart Plug yet.) Launch the iHomeControl app on your smartphone, and allow the app to find the Smart Plug. Once the Smart Plug is paired with the app, you can plug in whatever light or appliance you want. You control the Smart Plug (and what's plugged into it) from the iHomeControl app on your smartphone; you can turn the Smart Plug on or off as well as create "rules" for turning the outlet on or off under specified conditions.

The iHome Smart Plugs are also compatible with Amazon's Echo/Alexa devices, Apple's HomeKit/Home system, Google's Nest devices, Samsung's SmartThings hub and app, and the Wink hub and app. When you plug the Smart Plug into a wall outlet, open your system's smartphone app to discover and pair the Smart Plug with your app. You can then use your smart home app to control the Smart Plug as it does other smart devices.

Smart Outlets

The nice thing about iHome's Smart Plugs is that they're not locked into one place; you can easily move a Smart Plug from one outlet or room to another, and use it to control lots of different devices. If you want a more permanent solution, look at replacing an existing wall outlet with a smart outlet. The smart outlet contains all the wireless technology and smarts necessary to connect to your smart home system.

You can buy smart outlets from a variety of companies. For example, if you have an Insteon-based system, try the Insteon On/Off Outlet. If you have a SmartThings or Wink system, go with the Leviton Decora smart outlet. Both of these units work in similar fashion, just with different systems. (They both work with Amazon Echo/Alexa, too.)

The thing you have to remember is that you need to be a little comfortable with basic electrical work; you need to turn off the appropriate circuit breaker, disconnect the existing outlet and plate, connect the new smart outlet, then flip the circuit breaker back on. If that worries you, don't do it; stick to a much easier-to-install smart plug instead.

Smart Wall Switches

You can also insert smart functionality on the control end of things by replacing an existing wall switch with a smart one. Connect the smart wall switch to the corresponding smart hub, and then you can adjust whatever's connected to that switch from your smartphone. (Or you can add that switch to your room control scheme, if you want.)

The easiest smart wall switches to install are those that connect directly to your home Wi-Fi network, no hubs required, such as the WeMo Light Switch from Belkin. If you have an Insteon hub, look at any number of wall switches from Insteon. If you have a SmartThings or Wink system, go with the Universal In-Wall Switch from Leviton (www.leviton.com). All three of these switches work in much the same fashion.

Smart Motion Detectors

Chapter 5, "Automating Home Security," discusses motion detectors, and they certainly have their place in a smart home security system. But you can also use smart motion detectors to activate other smart home devices. For example, connect a smart motion detector to your smart lighting system and have your lights turn on when you walk into a room.

There are lots of smart motion detectors out there. If you have an Insteon system, go with the Insteon Motion Sensor. If you're a SmartThings or Wink user, go with Ecolink's Z-Wave PIR Motion Detector (www.discoverecolink.com). They'll both do a good job.

>>>*Go Further*

SMART ARRIVAL SENSOR

If you're using Samsung's SmartThings hub and system, check out the SmartThings Arrival Sensor (www.smartthings.com). This little doohickey looks like a normal key fob, but it tracks when people, pets, or cars leave or arrive at your house. Somewhat unique to the SmartThings ecosystem, this sensor is one of the most useful things around for controlling other smart devices in your home.

Here's the practical use. You have an arrival sensor on your keyring. When you leave the house, the arrival sensor notifies other smart devices that you've left. In turn, the smart thermostat gets dialed down, the smart lights go off, the smart door lock locks your front door, and so on.

When you come back home, the arrival sensor notifies those same smart devices to turn up the heat, turn on the lights, and unlock the door for you. You don't do anything; the arrival sensor is the trigger for all these other activities.

Naturally, the SmartThings Arrival Sensor is compatible only with Samsung's SmartThings hub; it runs around $30. If you're using another hub/system, check out the Automatic car monitoring system, discussed later in this chapter.

Smart Window Coverings

The concept of smart lighting begs the question of why you have to get up and manually raise or lower your blinds and shades. Well, you don't. Not surprisingly, there are a number of smart blind systems out there that automatically open and close your window coverings, either on a prearranged schedule or from a command from a smartphone app.

These window coverings are motorized; when you tap a button to open or close them, the motor raises or lowers them accordingly. That makes these systems more expensive than conventional blinds and drapes (we're talking $200 or more per window), but you're paying for convenience.

Serena motorized shades from Lutron

Some of the more popular smart blind systems include the following:

- Bali Blinds (www.baliblinds.com)
- Lutron Serena Shades (www.serenashades.com)

- MySmartBlinds (www.mysmartblinds.com)
- Pella Insynctive (www.pella.com/insynctive/)
- Somfy (www.somfysystems.com)

Most of these systems are self-contained—that is, they use their own smartphone apps and don't integrate with other smart hubs or controllers. (The Wink system is a major exception and is compatible with smart window coverings by Bali, Lutron, and Pella.) Expect this to change, however, as more and more people want to control all their room lighting options with a single command.

Smart Vacuums

Robotic vacuum cleaners, such as the category-defining Roomba, have been around for a while. These are self-propelled cleaning machines that bumble and stumble around from room to room, cleaning the carpet or floor as they move around.

Plain old robot vacuums are old tech, however. Newer self-contained vacuum cleaners add wireless remote operation (via Wi-Fi and accompanying smartphone app) that lets you start, stop, and schedule in advance your vacuuming operations. Some models even show you a map (on the app) of where they've vacuumed.

Samsung's POWERbot smart robot vacuum cleaner

As of yet, there's not a lot of connectivity with smart home hubs and controllers. The big exception here is the Samsung POWERbot, which interfaces just fine with Samsung's SmartThings hub and app.

Here are some of the models available now:

- Dyson 360 Eye (www.dyson.com)
- iRobot Roomba 980 (www.irobot.com)
- Neato Botvac Connected (www.neatorobotics.com)
- Samsung POWERbot (www.samsungpowerbot.com)

These are all very expensive vacuum cleaners, by the way. Prices range from around $400 up to $1,000.

Smart Devices for the Bedroom

Many of the smart devices we've already discussed can also be put to use in your bedroom. Smart lighting, smart switches and plugs, smart entertainment—they all make sense for bedroom use, too.

But there are other bedroom-specific smart devices you might want to consider. Let's look at a few.

Smart Bedding and Accessories

The biggest and most important thing in your bedroom is your bed. Component-wise, we're talking a mattress, box spring, pillows, and bed frame. Nothing necessarily "smart" about any of them, at least not traditionally. But there are new smart sleep systems that can adjust to the way you (and your spouse) sleep, and provide a better sleep experience.

When it comes to so-called smart betting, here are a few products to consider:

- Kingsdown Sleep Smart (www.kingsdown.com/collection/sleep-smart). This "intelligent mattress" adjusts to your sleeping position and habits and tracks your sleep via a corresponding app on your smartphone.

- ReST Smart Bed (www.restperformance.com). The ReST Smart Bed is constructed with pressure-sensing fabric beneath the outer layer of the mattress that measures pressure from each part of your body. This data is sent to the brains of the smart bed, which then adjusts the firmness and such throughout the night as necessary. It sends your sleep data to its smartphone app and connects via Wi-Fi to other smart devices in your house, including smart thermostats, smart lighting, and more.

- Sleep Number 360 Smart Bed (www.sleepnumber.com/360). This version of the best-selling Sleep Number bed adjusts firmness, comfort, and such, much like other Sleep Number beds, but also warms your feet, senses snoring and raises that half of the bed automatically, and captures all your sleep data in the accompanying smartphone app. The app also integrates with Nest thermostats to help control room temperature, too.

- Eight Sleep Tracker (www.eightsleep.com). You don't have to invest in a completely new bed to go smart; instead, use the Sleep Tracker smart mattress cover with your existing bed to add smart features. This mattress cover warms or cools your bed as necessary and then tracks your sleep via its own smartphone app. There's even a built-in smart alarm that identifies the right moment in your sleep cycle to wake you up at the maximum energy level. In terms of smartness, it interfaces with other smart devices in your home to lock your smart door locks, turn off your smart lightbulbs, adjust your smart thermostat, and more.

Smart Control

The bedroom is a prime room for you to use a voice-controlled smart hub, such as the Amazon Echo or Google Home. These units can also replace your existing clock radio, as both let you program daily alarms. They also function as pretty good wireless speakers when you want to listen to music.

Smart Devices for the Kitchen

We've already discussed the big appliances in your smart kitchen—smart ranges, refrigerators, and dishwashers. There are also a number of smaller appliances that function as smart devices. Let's take a look at them.

Smart Coffee Makers

If you're like a lot of folks, you want to wake up to a hot cup of coffee. Yes, a lot of coffee makers today come with timers that let you schedule when you get that first cup. But there are also smarter coffeemakers that let you integrate your morning coffee with other smart home activities. Here are a few:

Control the Mr. Coffee Smart Optimal Brew coffeemaker with the WeMo smartphone app

- Bosch Home Connect Coffee Machine (www.bosch-home.com/us/smart-coffee-makers.html). Bosch's smart coffee maker uses the company's Home Connect app to let you start up your next cup from the comfort of your smartphone—even if you're not home yet. You can use the app to select from a variety of hot drinks, and register everyone's favorite coffee in advance.

- EzPro BrewGenie Wi-Fi Smart Coffee Maker (www.fanstel.com/brewgenie/). Use the accompanying EZPro smartphone app to set up a brewing schedule, start brewing, and receive alerts when you need fresh filters, grounds, or water.

- Mr. Coffee Smart Optimal Brew Programmable Coffee Maker (www.mrcoffee.com). Use the accompanying smartphone app to schedule or adjust brew times. Works with Belkin's WeMo smart home system and app.

- Nespresso Prodigio (www.nespresso.com/prodigio). This is a Bluetooth-enabled deluxe coffee machine that lets you schedule brew times, remotely start brewing, and manage your capsule stock directly from your smartphone.

Smart Cooking Appliances

Slow cookers and pressure cookers are must-have kitchen appliances for many household chefs. And there are smart versions of both available.

- Crock-Pot Smart Slow Cooker with WeMo (www.crock-pot.com). Slow cookers are great for cooking meals when you're away from home for the day; just gather together all the ingredients for your favorite chili or Salisbury steak or whatever, turn the slow cooker on low, and let things simmer until dinnertime. Unfortunately, most slow cookers are kind of dumb. Not so Crock-Pot's Smart Slow Cooker, which connects to Belkin's WeMo system and app and lets you control key operations with your smartphone. You can start cooking, adjust the heat mid-way through cooking, and receive a notification when your meal is done. It's pretty neat.

- Instant Pot IP-Smart Pressure Cooker (www.instantpot.com). Pressure cookers are kind of the opposite of slow cookers; they let you cook foods quicker than normal. The Instant Pot Smart Pressure Cooker is a high-end model with 14 built-in programs, dual pressure, and more. You can control it from its front panel display or via remote control through its smartphone app. The app not only controls the pressure cooker, it also helps you find new recipes and adapt them for the cooker.

Smart Devices for the Garage

Your garage can be part of your smart house, too. In particular, check out these smart garage door openers and a smart adapter/monitoring device for your car.

Smart Garage Door Openers

Adding a smart garage door opener to your smart home makes a lot of sense. You can have other smart devices trigger your garage door when you're leaving or arriving home, of course, based on the "home" or "away" modes in your smart hub or smart thermostat. You can also have the opening or closing of your garage door trigger other in-home operations, such as locking/unlocking your back door, turning your thermostat up or down, turning on or off your lights, and so forth.

There are only a few smart garage door openers on the market today. Some are complete units, others are smart add-ons you attach to your existing garage door opener mechanism. Here's what's available:

- Chamberlain MyQ Garage Door Openers and Controllers (www.chamberlain. com/smartphone-control-products). Garage opener company Chamberlain offers perhaps the largest and most versatile line of smart garage door products, all enabled with its MyQ smart technology. You can choose from a variety of dedicated garage door openers, as well as several MyQ smart controllers you can add to any existing garage door opener to add the desired smart operations. With MyQ you can open and close your garage door with the MyQ smartphone app, get notified if your garage door opens when you're away or if you accidentally left it open, and more. MyQ-enabled openers and controllers are also compatible with Wink hubs and the Nest learning thermostat. (Future compatibility with Apple HomeKit and Samsung SmartThings is promised, but not yet there.)

- Garageio (www.garageio.com). Garageio is a smart controller you connect to your existing garage door opener. You then control Garageio (and your garage door opener) with the company's smartphone app. Garageio is currently compatible with the Amazon Echo; future support for Samsung SmartThings is promised.

- Genie Aladdin Connect Garage Door Controller (www.geniecompany.com/ aladdinconnect). This add-on box connects to any existing Genie garage door opener and lets you control and monitor operations from the accompanying smartphone app. You can receive notifications when the garage door is opened or closed, open or close the door remotely, and track usage history.

- GoControl Garage Door Opener Remote Controller (www.gocontrol.com). Connect the GoControl box to any existing garage door opener to add remote open/close operations. GoControl is a Z-Wave device and is compatible with Insteon, SmartThings, and Wink.

- Gogogate2 (www.gogogate.com). This add-on device lets you remotely open, close, and monitor any garage door opener or gate from the accompanying smartphone app. It even includes video monitoring in real time, with optional video cameras.

- Insteon Garage Door Controller (www.insteon.com). If you have an Insteon system, check out the Insteon Garage Door Control & Status Kit. You can remotely open and close your garage door, as well as find out if you accidentally left the door open, all via the Insteon app.

Smart Car Adapter

The Automatic Pro car adapter (www.automatic.com) is a nifty little device that connects to your car's data port and provides a variety of operations and services. You can use the Automatic Pro to find your car in a crowded parking lot, notify authorities if you're in an accident or other emergency, troubleshoot engine problems, track your driving habits, and more.

Even better, the Automatic Pro connects to your Amazon Echo and Nest learning thermostat to provide information to your other smart home devices. When connected in this fashion, the Automatic Pro can let your smart home know when you're on your way home and activate all the necessary devices to greet you when you arrive. It costs around $130.

The Automatic Pro car adapter and smartphone app

Smart Devices for Outdoors

The smart home isn't just an indoor thing. There are even smart devices available to control various outdoor devices.

Smart Irrigation Systems

Let's start with the simple home irrigation system, a necessity if you have a house on a lot of significant size. Today's irrigation systems let you schedule start/stop times by zone and day; smart irrigation systems integrate additional data to provide more effective and efficient watering.

Here's a smattering of what's available:

- Melnor Wi-Fi Aquatimer (www.melnor.com). This relatively low-priced (around $100) device lets you control watering in four zones via smartphone app.

- Orbit B-Hyve Smart Wi-Fi Sprinkler Timer (www.orbitonline.com). Connect this control unit to your existing irrigation system to control everything via Wi-Fi, using the company's smartphone app or website. In addition to normal zone scheduling (up to 12 zones included), this device provides smart monitoring based on your yard's condition—slope, soil type, sun or shade, and live weather feeds.

- Rachio (www.rachio.com). Rachio is a smart sprinkler controller you can operate with a smartphone app. You program details about each zone and then let Rachio calculate the most appropriate watering cycles.

- RainRobot (www.rainrobot.com). Like the other controllers presented here, RainRobot is smart and Wi-Fi connected. Use the smartphone app to set up and control watering cycles by zone.

- Spruce (www.spruceirrigation.com). This is another remote smartphone-controlled irrigation controller. Unique to this system is the compatibility with Samsung's SmartThings hub and app.

Smart Lawn Mowers

You have a robotic vacuum cleaner to clean the inside of your house. Why not a robotic lawn mower to cut the grass outside your house?

Take it easy while the Robomow smart lawn mower cuts the grass.

Robomow (usa.robomow.com) is a robotic lawn mower that can cut your grass with minimal input on your part, based on the schedule you set up. Or, if you prefer, you can control the thing in real time via its accompanying smartphone app. In either case, you get to take it easy while Robomow does all the hard work for you.

There are a half-dozen Robomow models available, each suited for a specific lawn size. Prices run from $500 to $2,500.

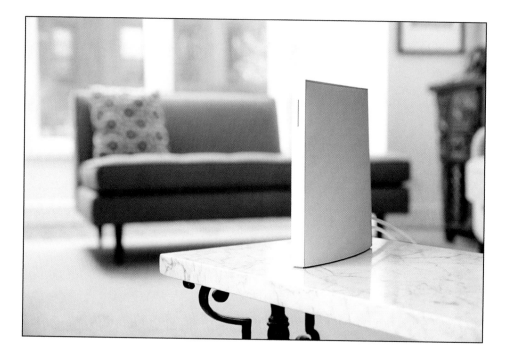

In this chapter, you learn how to set up the Wink hub and compatible devices, and automate their usage with the Wink smartphone app.

→ Getting to Know Wink
→ Setting Things Up
→ Using the Wink App
→ Automating Activities with Robots and Events

Controlling Your Smart Home with Wink

Chapter 2, "Understanding Smart Home Hubs and Controllers," covers all the different smart home technologies and systems on the market today. For various reasons, many nontechnical users have gravitated to the Wink system, which links smart devices from a number of different companies into the Wink Hub, where they can be controlled by the Wink app. It's an elegant and full-featured solution when you want to convert your traditional home into a smart home.

Getting to Know Wink

Wink is a system that ties multiple smart devices into a single system. You can use the Wink system to control smart lighting from GE, Philips, and Sylvania; smart switches and plugs from iHome, Leviton, and Lutron; smart doorbells and cams from Arlo, Nest, and Ring; smart detectors from Kidde, Leaksmart, and Nest; smart locks from August, Kwikset, and Schlage; smart thermostats from Ecobee, Honeywell, and

Nest; smart window treatments from Bali, Lutron, and Pella; smart garage door openers from Chamberlain; smart home security systems from GoControl; and smart control from Amazon's Echo devices.

All Things Wink

For a full list of Wink-compatible devices, go to www.wink.com/products/.

These devices all connect to a single Wink Hub, which also connects to your home Wi-Fi system. Once a device is paired with the Hub, it can interact with other Wink-compatible devices and be controlled by the Wink smartphone app—either in your home or while you're away, as long as your phone is connected to the Internet. It's a smart interactive system that is easy to set up and just as easy to use, with minimal hassles, which is why it's so popular.

Wink works with all these different devices because the system utilizes a number of popular smart home technologies. The Wink Hub is compatible with Wi-Fi wireless networks, Bluetooth devices, and Z-Wave and ZigBee mesh networks. Setting up new devices is quick and easy, thanks to the system's auto-discovery capabilities.

All you need to set up a Wink system in your house or apartment is a Wink Hub, the Wink app installed on your Apple or Android smartphone, and one or more Wink-compatible smart devices. Given the relatively low cost of the Wink Hub (less than $100), it's a minimal investment with a lot of future potential.

>>>Go Further
WHY WINK?

Chapter 2 discusses a number of different smart home systems, including Insteon, Samsung's SmartThings, and Wink. Although all these systems have their pros and cons, this chapter focuses on Wink. Why is that?

First, there's the matter of compatibility. Insteon is the oldest system of this bunch, but it's still pretty much a closed system; although Insteon is compatible with some third-party devices, the vast majority of compatible devices are manufactured and sold by the Insteon company itself. SmartThings has a little bit more compatibility with third-party devices, but frankly it's so new that there are far fewer devices available than with the other systems. That leaves Wink, which far and away is compatible with more different devices than the other two systems.

Next is the ease of use. All three systems are relatively easy to set up and use, but in my opinion Wink is just easier. The system's been around long enough to work out the kinks and provide a very user-friendly setup and user experience. Not that the others are hard to use; Wink's just a little easier.

Finally, there's the issue of issues—how likely are you to have problems setting things up? Here both SmartThings and Wink shine and Insteon falls down a bit. Frankly, I had issues setting up an Insteon Hub in my home, and if I had trouble with it the average consumer is going to be really flummoxed. Now, this may be an issue just in my particular house, but searching online reveals that others have found Insteon a sometimes-tricky system to get up and running, too. I didn't have a lick of trouble setting up multiple Wink devices, and that's a good thing.

Those are the reasons I decided to focus on Wink in this chapter. If you decide to go with Insteon or SmartThings, however, you'll find that the basic setup and operation is similar; you'll need to connect the hub to your home network and smartphone app, and then pair individual devices with the hub. Once everything is set up, you can create custom rooms and scenes and such to better automate your abode. The specific instructions may differ, but the general gist of things is pretty much the same.

Setting Things Up

To set up a Wink system in your home, you need a Wink Hub and the Wink smartphone app. You can purchase the former online (www.wink.com) or at your local retail store; you can download the latter from Apple's App Store (for iOS devices) or the Google Play Store (for Android phones). The app is free.

Which Hub?

Wink currently offers two different hubs. The original Wink Hub ($70) may still be available, but the second generation Wink Hub 2 ($100) is a better device, with faster Wi-Fi, improved Bluetooth, and more technological enhancements that make it faster and more reliable. The balance of this chapter focuses on setting up and using the Wink Hub 2.

Connect the Wink Hub 2

Everything you do with Wink is done through the Wink Hub 2. Although all the individual Wink-compatible devices connect to the Hub wirelessly, the Hub itself has to be connected directly to your Wi-Fi router via Ethernet cable.

(1) Connect the Wink Hub into a power source.

(2) Connect one end of the Ethernet cable (supplied) to the LAN jack on the back of the Wink Hub.

(3) Connect the other end of the Ethernet cable to an open port on your Wi-Fi router. The light on the front of the Wink Hub begins to slowly blink (what Wink calls "breathing") while the Hub connects to your home network.

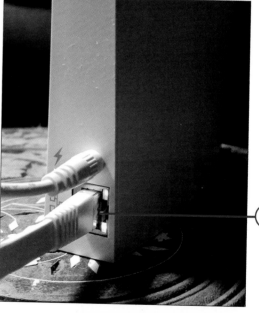

(4) Open the Wink app on your smartphone. Make sure your smartphone is connected to the same network as your Wink Hub.

iOS and Android

The Wink app is available for both iOS (Apple) and Android phones. The step-by-step tasks in this chapter focus on the Android version, but the iOS version looks and works similarly.

(5) The opening screen on the app should announce that your new Wink Hub has been found. Tap **Add to Wink.**

(6) The Hub is added to the Wink app and you are prompted to name this hub. You can accept the default name (Wink Hub 2) or enter a new name into the **Name Your Hub** field.

(7) Tap **Done.**

(8) The Hub needs to install necessary updates. When prompted, tap **OK, Got It.** The light on the front of the Hub should turn green and then blue as it downloads and installs any required updates. This might take several minutes.

Wink

AT&T   🛜 ⊿ 77% 🔋 8:15 PM

New Wink Hub Found!

A new Wink Hub has been detected on your network. Would you like to add it to your Wink account now?

ADD TO WINK

ADD LATER

Cancel   WINK HUB 2   Done

NAME YOUR HUB

Wink Hub 2

Success!

Your Wink Hub has been successfully added. A new Hub update is required and will take a few minutes.

OK, GOT IT

9 When the light turns solid blue, the updates are finished installing. In the Wink app on your smartphone, you see a screen for your newly installed Wink Hub.

Add a New Device via Barcode Scanning

There are two ways to add a new smart device to your Wink system. You can use the Wink smartphone app to scan the new device's barcode (and have Wink automatically recognize the device) or you can add the device manually, through a series of screens on the app. Let's work through the barcode method first.

1 In the Wink app on your smartphone, drag the menu icon to the right to display the main screen.

(2) Tap the **Home** icon to display the Home screen.

(3) Tap **Add a Product.**

(4) Tap **Scan Barcode**, then aim your phone's camera at the barcode on the new device's package.

(5) When your device is identified, tap **Next** and follow the onscreen connections to pair the new device with the Hub. Depending on the type of device, you might be prompted to plug it into a wall socket, screw it into a light socket (for light bulbs), or press a button to turn on or synchronize the device.

Videos
The Wink app includes videos for how to install some specific devices. If a video is available and you want to watch it, tap the **Play** icon.

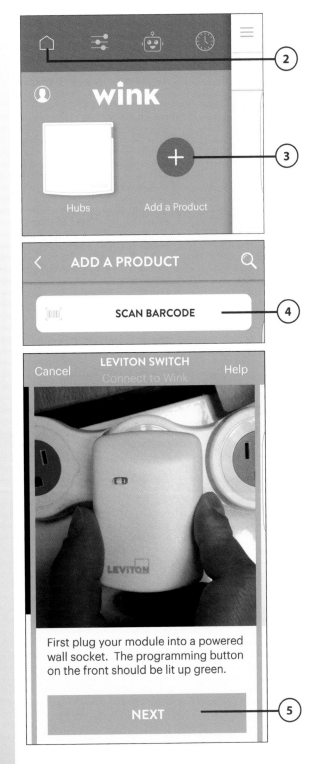

6. When prompted, tap **Connect Now.** The light on the Wink Hub should start blinking blue.

7. The app tells you when the paring is successful. In the Wink app, tap **Name *Device*.**

8. Enter a name for the device into the text box.

9. Tap **Done.**

10. Tap **Get Started** to begin using the new device.

When you're ready, tap Connect Now button. Then wait for your hub to start blinking blue (about 5 seconds).

CONNECT NOW — 6

LEVITON SWITCH
Cancel   Connect to Wink   Help

SUCCESS!

Your Leviton switch is connected to Wink.

NAME LIGHT — 7

GET STARTED

Cancel   **NAME LIGHT**   Done — 9

Floor light — 8

GET STARTED — 10

Manually Add a New Device

Alternatively, you can manually add devices without scanning the device's barcode. All compatible devices are listed in the Wink app; it's a simple matter to select your new device from the list.

1. In the Wink app, drag the menu icon to the right to display the main screen.

2. Tap the **Home** icon to display the Home screen.

3. Tap **Add a Product.**

4. Tap the type of product that you're adding.

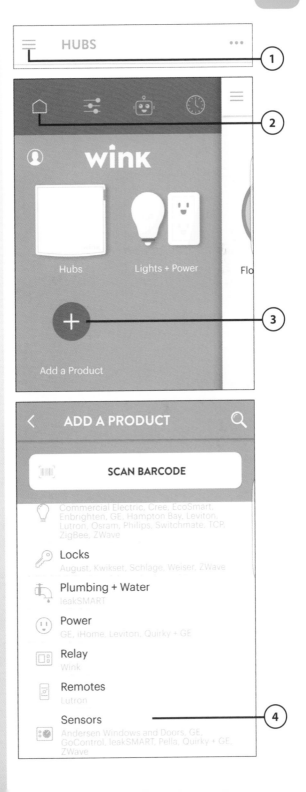

(5) Tap the specific product you're adding.

(6) Follow the onscreen instructions to proceed through the installation. When prompted, tap **Connect Now.**

(7) The app tells you when the paring is successful. In the Wink app, tap **Name *Device*** to rename the new device, or **Get Started** to start using the device now.

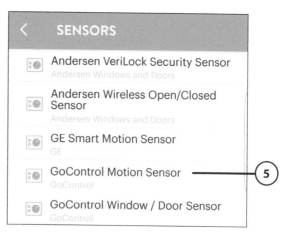

SENSORS

Andersen VeriLock Security Sensor
Andersen Windows and Doors

Andersen Wireless Open/Closed Sensor
Andersen Windows and Doors

GE Smart Motion Sensor
GE

GoControl Motion Sensor ——— (5)
GoControl

GoControl Window / Door Sensor
GoControl

CONNECT NOW ——— (6)

SUCCESS!

✓

Your GoControl Motion Sensor is connected to Wink!

NAME SENSOR

GET STARTED

(7)

>>>*Go Further*

CONTROLLING YOUR HOME WITH THE WINK RELAY

Various companies offer a number of different controllers you can use with the Wink system. Most of these are wall switches to control either individual outlets or devices.

The Wink Relay touchscreen controller

You can go beyond a simple wall switch, however, with the Wink Relay. This is a touchscreen controller that you mount on your wall that lets you control both individual and groups of smart devices. You can program the Wink Relay to activate both shortcuts and more complicated commands (what Wink calls "robots," which are covered later in this chapter). You can even use multiple Wink Relays as a wireless room-to-room intercom system.

You can purchase the Wink Relay directly from the Wink website. A pack of two controllers sells for around $150.

Using the Wink App

Once you've paired your smart devices with the Wink Hub, they appear in the Wink app. This lets you turn on and off your devices from your smartphone—even if you're away from home!

Control from Anywhere

The Wink app on your smartphone enables you to control your smart home devices —and set up shortcuts and robots—from anywhere there's an Internet connection; you don't have to be in the same room to use the app. For example, right now I'm sitting at a coffee shop and turning the lights on and off in my living room. (Of course, if there's anyone in my living room right now, they might think the place is haunted!)

Turn a Device On or Off

Turning an individual device off or on is as easy as tapping an onscreen icon.

(1) Tap to display the **Home** screen.

(2) Tap the type of device you want to work with.

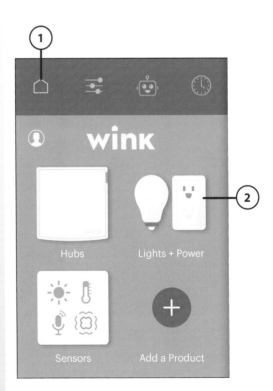

(3) Icons in color represent devices that are currently turned on. Icons that are grayed out are currently turned off. Tap the icon for a device currently turned off to turn it on.

(4) Tap the icon for a device currently turned on to turn it off.

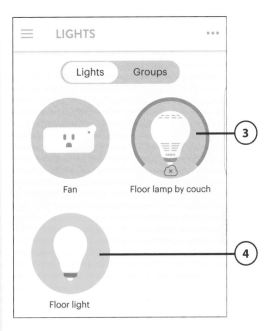

View Information from a Sensor

If you have sensors of any type connected to your Wink system, you can view the current status of a sensor from the Wink app.

(1) Tap to display the **Home** screen.

(2) Tap the **Sensors** icon to display the Sensors screen.

3 Basic information from each sensor is displayed. Tap the icon for a given sensor to view more detailed information.

4 Tap the sensor name to view even more information, if available.

5 View the detailed information.

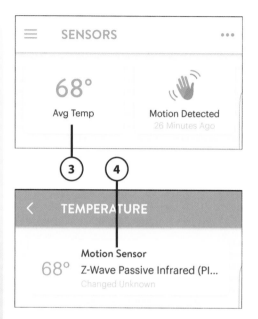

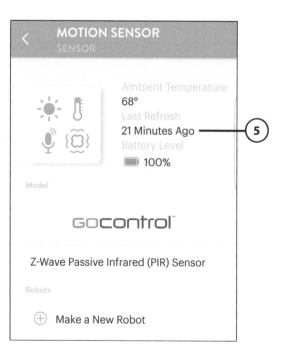

Create a Shortcut

As you've just seen, you can turn on or off individual devices from within the Wink app. It's probably more convenient, however, to group like devices in a given room and control them with a tap of a single icon.

Fortunately, Wink lets you create *shortcuts* that do just this. Create a shortcut with all the lights in your living room, for example, and you can turn them on or off with a single tap.

(1) Tap to display the **Shortcuts** screen.

(2) Tap **Add Shortcut** to display the Create Shortcut screen.

(3) Tap within the **Name** box to enter a name for your shortcut.

(4) Enter a name for your shortcut.

(5) Tap **Save** to return to the Create Shortcut screen.

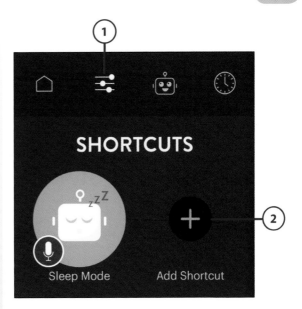

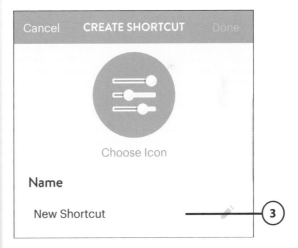

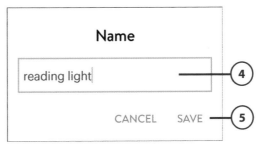

(6) In the Shortcut Action section, tap **Make This Happen.**

(7) Tap the item you want to control.

(8) Tap the action you want for the selected item. For example, if you select a light, you can choose to turn the light off or on, or set the brightness to a certain level.

(9) Tap **Save.**

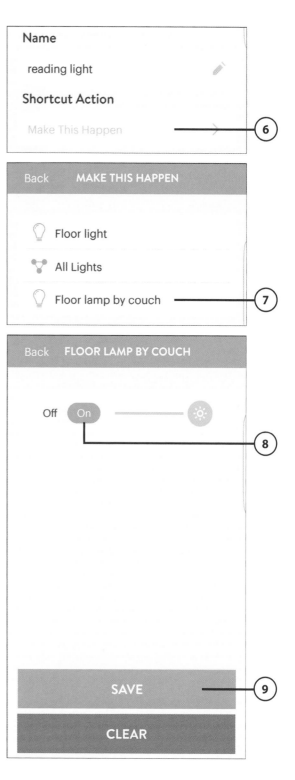

(10) To add another action to this shortcut, tap **Make Something Else Happen** and repeat steps 7 through 9.

(11) To select a different icon for this shortcut, tap **Choose Icon.**

(12) Tap **Done.** The new shortcut is added to the Wink app's Shortcuts screen.

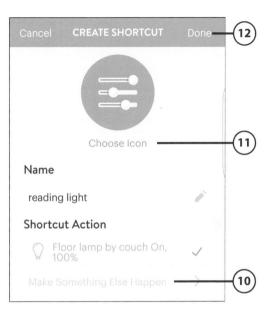

Activate a Shortcut

Activating a shortcut is as simple as tapping that shortcut's icon.

(1) Tap to display the **Shortcuts** screen.

(2) Tap the icon for the shortcut you want to activate.

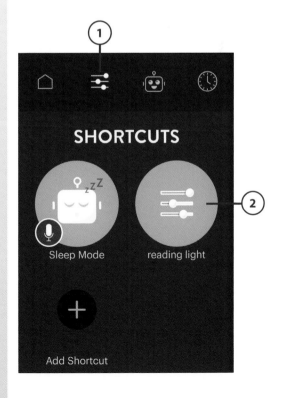

Automating Activities with Robots and Events

A shortcut in Wink is a relatively simple thing. You tap a button and something happens. It's really just a convenient form of manual remote control.

Wink can be smarter than that, however. The app lets you create what Wink calls *robots*, which are multistep routines that happen automatically when some initial condition is met.

For example, you can create a robot to turn on a room's lights when someone walks into the room (based on motion sensed by a motion sensor). Or you can create a robot to send you an alert if the temperature in a room gets too cold—or that turns on a fan or air conditioner if the temperature gets too warm.

It's all a matter of creating strings of commands. If *this* happens then do *that*. It's a lot easier than it sounds, and it really brings the smarts into your smart home.

Create a Robot

1. Tap to display the **Robots** screen.
2. Tap **New Robot** to display the New Robots screen.

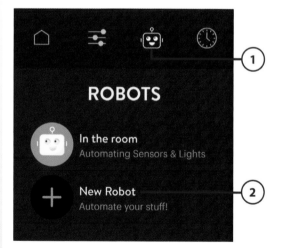

(3) Tap within the **Name** field to enter a name for this new robot.

(4) In the If This Robot Detects section, tap **Something.**

(5) If you want to base this action on something happening in a different location, tap the **Location** field and choose a different location. (My Location—that is, your house or apartment—is selected by default.)

(6) To base this action on something detected by a sensor, tap that sensor.

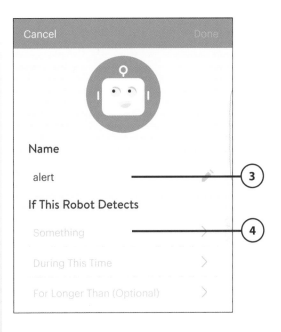

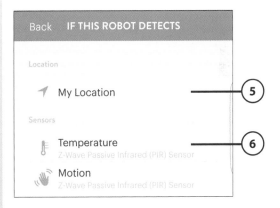

(**7**) Select the condition(s) you want to activate this action. For example, if it's a motion sensor, you select either that it detected or didn't detect motion. If it's a temperature sensor, you could select if the temperature went above or below a specified degree.

(**8**) Tap **Save.**

(**9**) Tap **Anytime** if you want to limit when this action can occur, and then select the desired start and stop time.

(**10**) In the Then section, tap **Make This Happen.**

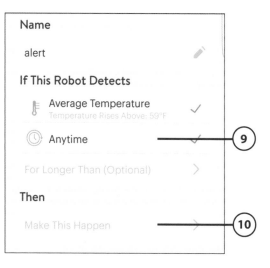

11 Tap to select what you want to have happen when the condition is met. You can choose to receive a notification or email, or to trigger any other device connected to your system.

12 If you want to trigger an additional action, tap **Make Something Else Happen** and repeat step 11.

13 Tap **Done** to create and activate the robot.

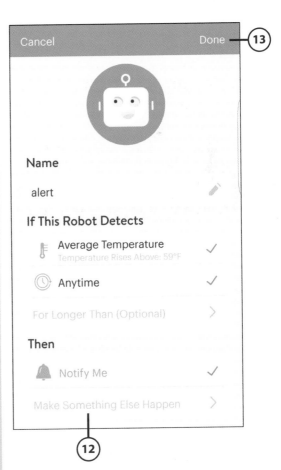

Remove a Robot

Once you've created a robot, you can choose to delete it at any time.

(1) Tap to display the **Robots** screen.

(2) Tap the icon for the robot you want to delete.

(3) To deactivate (but not delete) this robot, scroll to the bottom of the screen and tap "off" the **Enable Robot** switch.

(4) Completely delete the robot by scrolling to the bottom of the screen and tapping **Remove Robot.**

(5) Tap **Remove** in the confirmation box. The robot is deleted.

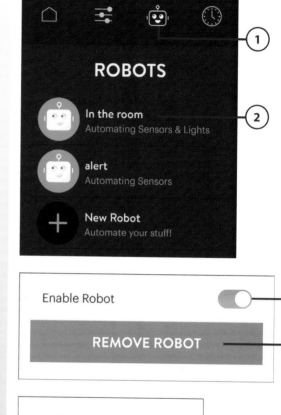

Create an Event

In addition to robots, you can also set schedules to activate specific devices. Wink calls these *events*, and you create them from the Settings screen.

For example, you could create an event that turns on all your bedroom lights at a certain time each morning. Or an event that turns on a connected coffeemaker at a given time. Or an event that turns off all your houselights at a given time. You get the idea.

(1) Tap the **Menu** button.

(2) Tap the **Settings** button.

(3) Tap **Schedule.**

(4) Tap **Week** to display your schedule for an entire week.

(5) Tap **Day** to display a daily schedule.

(6) Tap **List** to display all scheduled events.

(7) Tap + to add a new event.

(8) Tap within the **Name** field to give this event a name.

(9) Tap **Date** to display the Date box.

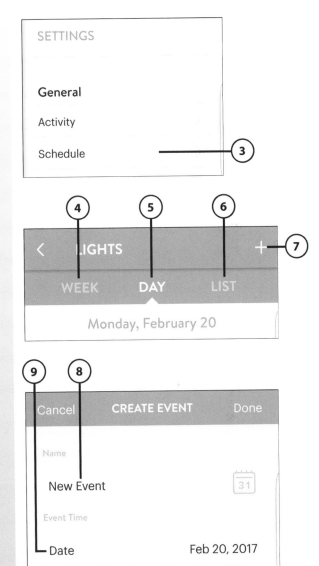

(10) Tap the date controls to set the month, day, and year for this event.

(11) Tap **OK.**

(12) Tap **Time** to display the Time box.

(13) Tap the time controls to set the hour, minute, and AM/PM to start this event. (You can also opt to start the event at sunrise or sunset.)

(14) Tap **Done.**

15 Tap Repeat to make this a recurring event.

16 Tap which days of the week you want this event to recur.

17 Tap **Set.**

18 Tap **Make This Happen.**

19 Tap the device you want to activate.

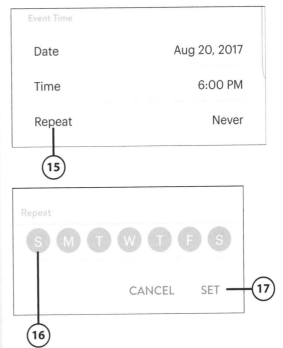

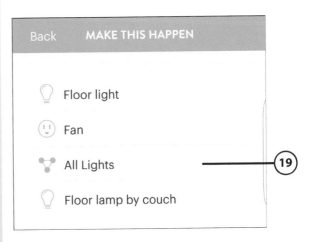

(20) Tap what you want this device to do.

(21) Tap **Save.**

(22) Review your settings, then tap **Done.** The event is now added to your schedules.

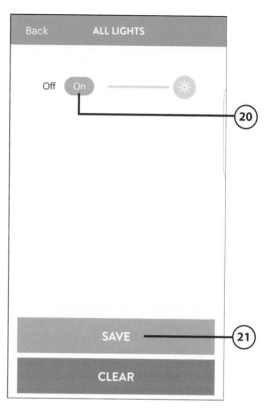

(23) Tap **List** to view all the events scheduled.

(24) Tap "off" the switch next to an event to disable it.

In this chapter, you learn how to use Apple HomeKit and the Home app to control your smart devices.

→ Understanding Apple HomeKit
→ Adding Devices and Rooms
→ Controlling Your Smart Devices
→ Automating Multiple Devices

Controlling Your Smart Home with Apple Home

Today's smart home devices are typically controlled from your smartphone. Every smart device has its own individual mobile app—which means if you have a lot of different smart devices, you have to work with a lot of different mobile apps. Want to control your Nest thermostat? Use the Nest app. Want to turn up your Hue lights? Use the Hue app. Want to turn down your LIFX lights? Use the LIFX app. If you have a dozen smart devices in your home, you need a dozen apps on your smartphone.

Working with all these different apps can be a little confusing, if not downright annoying. Wouldn't it be easier if you had a single app that controlled all the smart devices in your home?

Apple feels your pain and offers a cross-platform solution called HomeKit. This means that all smart devices compatible with Apple's HomeKit can be controlled by a single app—Apple's Home app—on your iPhone or iPad. That's one app instead of many, which is a lot less confusing and a lot easier to use.

In this chapter you find out how to set up compatible smart devices in the Home app and how to use the Home app to control all those devices.

Understanding Apple HomeKit

Apple HomeKit is a system for controlling smart devices from a variety of suppliers with a single app—or with Apple's Siri voice-controlled personal assistant. If a device is compatible with HomeKit (not all are), it's a simple matter to link the device to the Home app on your iPhone or iPad, and control it along with other devices with a tap of your finger.

It's actually kind of a big deal to have centralized control of multiple smart devices with a single app. For one thing, using one app is a lot more convenient than using multiple apps. Beyond convenience, however, HomeKit also lets you centralize control of multiple devices in a single room, as well as create automated sequences, called *scenes,* that control multiple connected devices with a single tap. HomeKit makes possible a lot of combined automation that makes your smart devices work smarter together.

How HomeKit Works

Apple's HomeKit is not a smart home system like Insteon and Wink. Instead, it's a way to control smart devices from a mobile app. Link a device to your HomeKit account and you can control it from Apple's Home app.

That said, HomeKit isn't a smart home system per se; it doesn't operate from a central hub, as do SmartThings, Wink, and similar systems. HomeKit is more like the standalone smart controllers offered by Amazon (Echo) and Google (Home), but it works through a smartphone/tablet app instead of a piece of hardware.

So how does HomeKit work? It all revolves around Apple's Home app, which comes installed with all newer iPhones and iPads.

If a smart device is compatible with the HomeKit standard, it's typically discovered by Apple's Home app when you first power on the device. (If it's not automatically discovered, you can add it manually to the app.) Once a device is linked to the Home app, you specify what room it's in. You can then control the device from the Home app, or via any scenes or automations you create. (Your iPhone or iPad must be connected to your home Wi-Fi network to do this; Home can't control your smart devices remotely.)

What's Compatible with HomeKit

To work with HomeKit, smart devices need to be certified by Apple. This means that it's more likely that newer products will be compatible with HomeKit, as it's easier to get them certified while they're being developed, and less likely that existing products will go back and get certified. I suppose that positions HomeKit as the smart platform of the future, but it leaves out a lot of current devices.

So what's compatible? The list changes daily, but includes big names such as August, Ecobee, iHome, Insteon, and Philips. Missing from the list, unfortunately, are several major smart systems, including Nest, SmartThings by Samsung, WeMo by Belkin, and Wink. That said, Apple continues to work with other companies to gain compatibility with their smart devices. You can check a current compatibility list at www.apple.com/ios/home/accessories/.

>>>*Go Further*

APPLE ONLY

Another limitation to making HomeKit universal is that the Home app is only available for iOS devices. You can't use Home/HomeKit on Android phones or tablets, which excludes at least half of all consumers with mobile devices.

You also can't run the Home app on older Apple devices. You'll need a newer iPhone, iPad, or iPod touch running iOS 10; the app simply isn't available for older versions of iOS. (The app comes as part of the operating system, so you shouldn't need to download it from the App Store.)

HomeKit also works with the Apple TV set-top box. When you link your HomeKit account to your Apple TV box, you turn the Apple TV into a stationary hub for your system. You can then operate the Home app remotely with your mobile device, as the commands you issue go over the Internet to your Apple TV box and then to your smart home devices. (This is the only way to use the Home app remotely; without an Apple TV hub, you're limited to controlling your devices only when your iPad or iPhone is directly connected to your home Wi-Fi network.)

And, if you have an Apple Watch, you can use it to control some basic operations for your smart devices. You can use your Apple Watch to turn devices on or off, as well as turn on or off entire rooms and scenes.

Adding Devices and Rooms

Before you can use the Home app to control your devices, you have to add those devices to the app. You can also assign devices to specific rooms in your home.

iPhone Versus iPad

For the purposes of the examples in this chapter, we're using the Home app on an iPad tablet. The iPhone app is similar, but if you run Home on an iPad, you can also use the iPad to create a Home Hub that enables you to automate various operations. (Learn more about Home Hubs in the "Automating Multiple Devices" section, later in this chapter.)

Add a New Device

Apple calls smart devices "accessories." Compatible accessories are relatively easy to add to the Home app. Just make sure the accessory is powered on and connected to your home's Wi-Fi network—and that your iPhone or iPad is connected to the same network.

1. Launch the Home app on your iPhone or iPad.

2. The first time you open the Home app, you see the Welcome screen; tap **Get Started** to proceed. Each subsequent time you launch the app, you see the Home screen; tap the + button to proceed.

3. Tap **Add Accessory.**

4. Your new device should appear in the Add Accessory panel. Tap it.

5. Look for the HomeKit code on the new device or in the device's documentation. Position the camera of your iPhone or iPad to capture this code.

6. If for some reason step 5 doesn't work, tap **Enter Code Manually** to enter the code with your phone or tablet's onscreen keyboard.

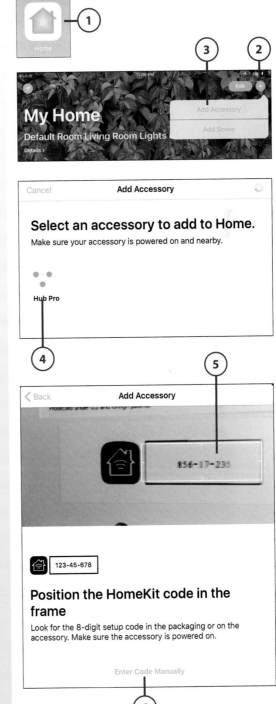

(7) Change the name of this accessory by tapping the current name and then entering a new one. (Siri identifies this device by the name you give it here.)

(8) By default, the new accessory is added to your default room. To add the accessory to a different room, tap **Location** and select another room.

(9) Include this accessory in your favorites on the Home app's home screen by tapping "on" the **Include in Favorites** switch.

(10) Tap **Next.**

(11) If the accessory requires additional setup, tap **View** and follow the onscreen instructions.

(12) Tap **Done** to complete the installation.

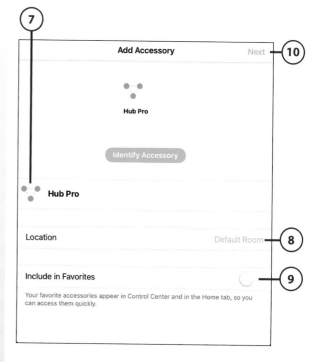

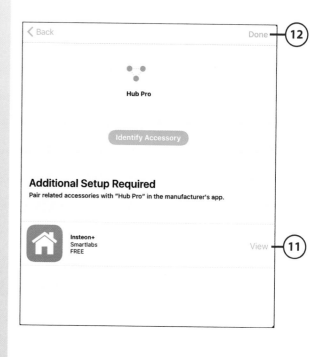

Add a New Room

As noted, when you install a new accessory you assign this device to a given room in your home. You can create additional rooms corresponding to your actual physical rooms.

1. Tap the **Rooms** icon to display the Room screen.

2. Tap the **Menu** button in the upper-left corner of the screen.

3. Tap **Room Settings.**

4. Tap **Add Room.**

5. Enter a name for this room into the **Room Name** field.

6. Change the room's background wallpaper by tapping **Choose from Existing** and then making a selection.

7. Alternatively, you can take a photo of the room to use for the wallpaper. Tap **Take Photo** and proceed from there.

8. Tap **Save.** The room is now added to your room list.

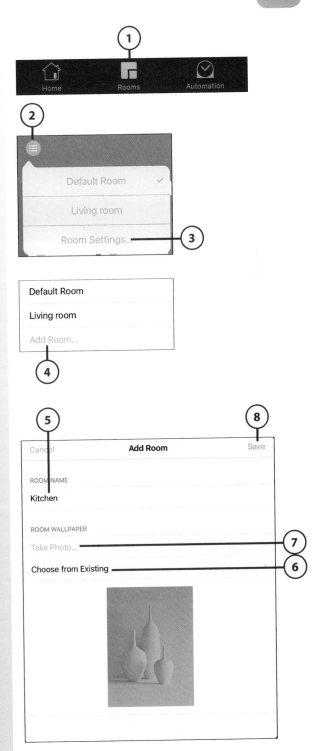

Assign an Accessory Device to a Room

By default, any new accessory/device you install is assigned to the Home app's default room (which is called Default Room). You can, however, assign an accessory to a different room, or move an accessory from one room to another.

One Room per Accessory

Just as it is in the physical world, in the Home app each accessory can be assigned to one room only. You can't assign accessories to multiple rooms.

1. Tap the **Rooms** icon to display the Room screen.

2. Swipe left or right until you get to the room that contains the accessory you want. Alternatively, tap the **Menu** button at the top left and select the room from those listed.

3. Touch and hold the accessory you want to move.

4. Tap **Details.**

5. Tap **Location.**

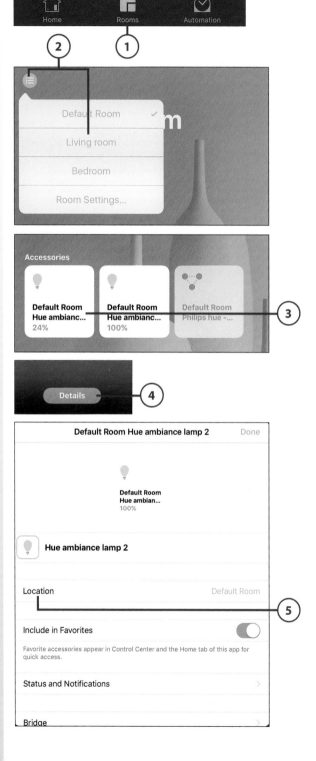

(**6**) Tap to select the room you want to move this accessory to.

(**7**) Tap **Done** to return to the previous screen.

(**8**) Tap **Done.**

(**9**) The accessory is moved to the room you selected.

Create a Scene

Apple Home doesn't limit you to controlling one device at a time. You can control multiple accessories at the same time by creating what Apple calls *scenes*.

For example, you can create a scene called "Good Morning" that turns on the smart lights in your bedroom and turns up your smart thermostat, or one called "Arrive Home" that turns on your living room lights and unlocks the front door. You activate a scene with a single tap from the home or room screen, or via Siri command.

(1) On either the Home or Rooms screen, tap the **+**.

(2) Tap **Add Scene.**

(3) Tap one of the suggested scenes (Arrive Home, Good Morning, Good Night, or Leave Home) or tap **Custom** to create a different scene.

(4) If you chose one of the default scenes for a given room, you see the devices for that room. To include additional devices or to remove one of the current ones, tap **Add or Remove Accessories.**

(1) Edit   +

Add Accessory

Add Scene   (2)

(3)

Cancel   New Scene

SUGGESTED SCENES

Arrive Home   >

Good Morning   >

Good Night   >

Leave Home   >

Custom   >

Accessories

Press and hold to adjust accessories for your "Arrive Home" scene.

DEFAULT ROOM

Default Room Hue ambian... 70%   Default Room Hue ambian... 70%

Test This Scene

Add or Remove Accessories

(4)

(5) Tap those accessories you want to add, or tap to remove those accessories you don't want to include.

(6) Tap **Done.**

(7) Back in the New Scene pane, tap and hold an accessory to adjust its settings.

(8) Tap **Test This Scene** to see if the scene works as you want.

(9) Make sure the **Show in Favorites** switch is "on" to display this scene on the home screen.

(10) Tap **Done** to add this scene.

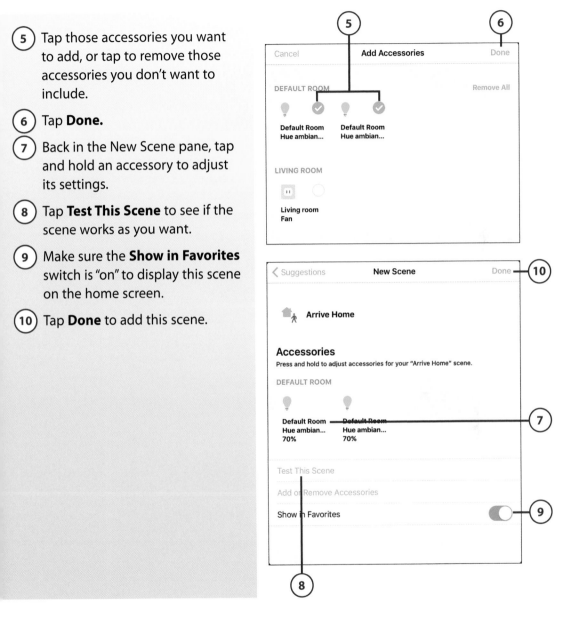

Controlling Your Smart Devices

Once you've installed a device/accessory in the Home app, you can then use your iPhone or iPad to control that app in various ways.

Control a Device or Scene

Turning a device on or off, or activating a scene, is as easy as tapping your phone or tablet's screen. For many devices, additional controls are also available.

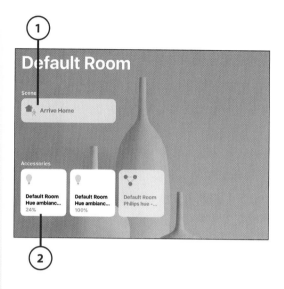

(1) On either the Home or Rooms screen, tap an accessory or scene to turn it on or off. The tile for the accessory or scene dims when the device is turned off; the tile has a white background when the device is turned on.

(2) Tap and hold the tile for an accessory to access additional controls.

(3) For example, with smart lights, you can tap and drag the divider bar to increase or decrease the light's brightness.

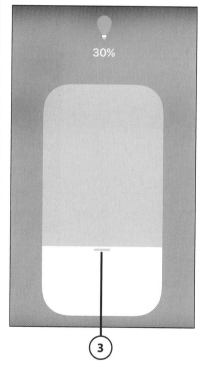

Controlling Devices and Scenes with Siri

The Siri personal digital assistant is part and parcel of iOS devices. If you use an iPhone or iPad, you're probably used to asking Siri to do all manner of things, from looking up information to reading the latest news and weather reports.

Siri can also operate various apps on your iOS device, including the Home app. This means you can use Siri to control your connected smart devices using voice commands. This makes your smart home that much easier to use.

To use Siri to control any devices and scenes you've added to the Home app, all you have to do is speak to your iPhone or iPad. Say "Siri," then speak the desired command.

Obviously, which commands you speak depend on which devices you have installed, and what you want them to do. For example, if you want to turn off the lights in your bedroom, say

Siri, turn off the lights in the bedroom.

Pretty simple. If you want to reduce the brightness for a given light or room, say

Siri, set brightness for the living room lights to 50 percent.

To set your smart thermostat, say

Siri, set the temperature to 70 degrees.

You can even ask questions of Siri regarding your smart devices, like this one:

Siri, did I lock the front door?

If you have scenes created (refer to the "Create a Scene" task earlier in this chapter), you can turn on a scene by saying

Siri, set my relaxing scene.

It's all very common sense. All you have to do is speak to Siri via your iPhone or iPad, and she works within the Home app to do the rest.

Automating Multiple Devices

Until now, you've seen how to use the Home app to directly control individual accessories or groups of accessories in a given room by tapping a tile for a device or scene. You can also use the Home app to automate operations across multiple accessories based on a specified trigger. You can trigger these *automations* when your location changes (when you leave the house, for example), at a specified time of day, or when another accessory does something.

>>>Go Further
SET UP YOUR IPAD AS A HOME HUB

Normal Home commands flow directly from your iPhone or iPad to the device or devices speci-fied. Automations, however, are triggered by other events—a given time, a location change, or a control from another device. For automations to work, then, you need some sort of central control that's active even if your phone is with you across town.

To create and use automations, then, you need to set up what Apple calls a Home Hub. There are two ways to do this.

First, if you have an Apple TV box connected in your home, you can use that as your hub. The Apple TV box is always there and always on, so you can use it to trigger the automations you create.

Second, you can use your iPad (running iOS 10) to do the job. This is probably the option of choice for most users, as you're more likely to have an iPad than an Apple TV Box. Just know that if you choose to use your iPad as a Home Hub, it needs to stay in your home, connected to your home Wi-Fi network, to work.

To set up your iPad as a Home Hub, tap **Settings,** tap **iCloud,** and then sign in with your Apple ID. Make sure iCloud Keychain and Home are both turned on, tap **Settings** again, and then tap **Home.** Tap "on" the **Use This iPad as a Home Hub** switch, and you're ready to go.

Create a Location Automation

A location automation is triggered when your iPhone comes near or leaves a specified location. That location can be your home (to trigger actions for when you leave or arrive home), your office or club, or any place on the map.

(1) Tap the **Automation** icon to display the Automation screen. Any previously created automations are displayed here.

(2) Tap **Create New Automation.**

(3) In the New Automation pane, tap **My Location Changes.**

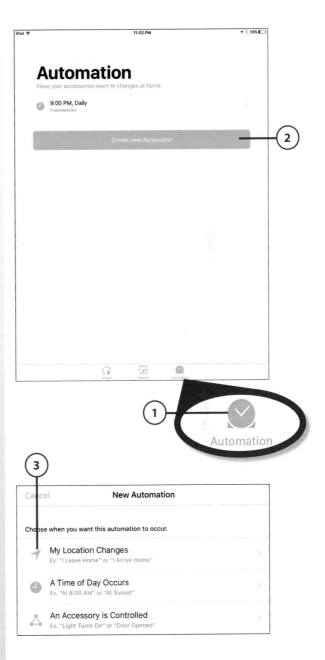

(4) Your home and other nearby locations are listed. Tap to select one of these, or enter a name or address into the search box to search for and select a different location.

(5) Tap **When I Arrive** to trigger the automation when you arrive at the selected location, or tap **When I Leave** to trigger the automation when you leave the location.

(6) Your selected location displays as a red pin on the map at the bottom of the pane. Drag the blue dot to enlarge or shrink the area around the selected location; this will be the range that triggers the action.

(7) Tap **Next.**

(8) Select those scenes and accessories you want to trigger when you arrive at or leave the selected location.

(9) Tap **Next.**

(4) (7)

‹ Back   **Location Automation**   Next

🔍 Home   ⊗

🏠 Home   ✓

📍 Prince of Peace Lutheran Church
   13901 Fairview Dr, Burnsville, MN 55337-5797, United States

📍 Bluff Creek Golf Course
   1025 Creekwood St, Chaska, MN 55318, United States

📍 Golf Zone
   825 Flying Cloud Dr, Chaska, MN 55318, United States

📍 Apple Valley Medical Clinic

When I Arrive   When I Leave

(5)

(6)

‹ Back   **When I Leave Home**   Next → (9)

Select scenes and accessories to automate.

DEFAULT ROOM   Add All

💡 ○ 💡 ○

**Default Room   Default Room
Hue ambian...   Hue ambian...**

LIVING ROOM

⏸ ✓   (8)

**Living room
Fan**

10 Review the automation you've created, and then tap **Done.**

Create a Time Automation

A time automation is triggered at a specific time on a specific day or days. This is kind of like an alarm that triggers the designated accessories or scenes.

1 From the Automation page, tap **Create New Automation.**

2 In the New Automation pane, tap **A Time of Day Occurs.**

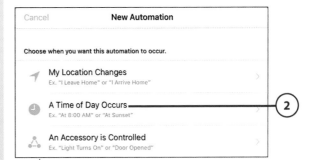

3 Use the **Time of Day** controls to select the hour, minute, and AM/PM you want this automation to run. (Alternatively, you can opt to run the automation at sunrise or sunset.)

4 Tap those days of the week you want this automation to run. You can select one, some, or all days.

5 Tap **Next.**

6 Select those scenes and accessories you want to trigger at the designated time.

7 Tap **Next.**

❮ Back   **Time Automation**   Next — **5**

When:

Sunrise

Sunset

Time of Day   ✓

7	58
8	59 AM
9	00 PM — **3**
10	01
11	02

REPEAT

S   M   T   W   T   F   S

Every Day

4

6   **7**

❮ Back   **9:00 PM, Daily**   Next

Select scenes and accessories to automate.

DEFAULT ROOM   Remove All

Default Room   **Default Room**
Hue ambian...   Hue ambian...

LIVING ROOM

**Living room
Fan**

8 Review the automation you've created, and then tap **Done**.

Create a Controlled Automation

Finally, you can create a controlled automation. This is an automation that is triggered when a designated device is activated. For example, the automation may be triggered when the front door opens.

1 From the Automation page, tap **Create New Automation.**

2 In the New Automation pane, tap **An Accessory Is Controlled**.

3 On the Accessory Automation pane, tap the device that will start this automation.

4 Tap **Next.**

(5) Tap the action that will start this automation.

(6) Tap **Next.**

(7) Tap the scenes or accessories you want to activate when the automation is triggered.

(8) Tap **Next.**

(9) Review your new automation and then tap **Done.**

(5)

‹ Back   **Accessory Automation**   Next ——(6)

When the Default Room Hue ambiance lamp 1...

Turns On   ✓

Turns Off

‹   When the Default Room Hue ambiance lamp 1 Tur...   Next ——(8)

Select scenes and accessories to automate.

DEFAULT ROOM

💡   ◯

Default Room
Hue ambian...

LIVING ROOM

[II]   ✅

Living room
Fan

(7)

(9)

‹   When the Default Room Hue ambiance lamp 1 Tu...   Done

When:

⏦   Default Room Hue ambiance lamp 1 Turns On

Only after sunset   ◖

Accessories:
Press and hold to adjust accessories.

LIVING ROOM

[II]

Living room
Fan
Turn On

In this chapter, you learn how to use the Alexa personal assistant to control smart home devices via Amazon's Echo and Echo Dot devices.

→ Understanding Alexa—and Echo
→ Meet Amazon's Echo Devices
→ Setting Up Your Echo Device
→ Working with Alexa
→ Using the Alexa App
→ Working with Alexa's Skills
→ Using Alexa to Control Your Smart Devices

Controlling Your Smart Home with Amazon Alexa

All the smart home systems and hubs come with their own smartphone apps to control their various smart devices. And, as described in Chapter 10, "Controlling Your Home with Apple Home," there's Apple HomeKit, which lets you control systems from multiple companies from the unified Home app. All of these apps attempt to simplify the operation of what is essentially a set of complex technologies.

But if you really want to make your smart home easy to control, there's nothing easier than using voice commands. That's where Amazon comes in, via its Echo and Echo Dot devices and Alexa personal digital assistant. The Echo/Dot devices connect to all (or most) of your smart hubs and devices via your home's wireless Wi-Fi network, and then you can control those devices via simple voice commands. Just tell Alexa what you want to do, and it controls the devices to do it.

It's far and away the easiest way to control your smart home. (And there's more beyond that, too!)

Chapter 11

Understanding Alexa—and Echo

In spite of the name and the voice, Alexa isn't a person. No, Alexa is just a piece of software, a kind of intelligent digital assistant that interacts with you using voice commands. That is, you talk to Alexa and she (or is it an it?) talks back. There are no keyboards to type or touchscreen to touch; it's all done vocally.

What Alexa Does and How Alexa Works

In many ways, Alexa is similar to Siri on an Apple iPhone or Cortana in Windows 10. You ask Alexa a question or issue a command, and Alexa answers your question or does what you've asked it to do. You speak, Alexa listens. Alexa "speaks," and you get whatever it is you've asked for.

What can you use Alexa to do? Well, you can have Alexa find current information (weather forecast, news headlines, sports scores), find interesting and useful facts, calculate math problems, and retrieve recipes. You can also use Alexa to play music, add items to your calendar or to-do list, and order items online. And, more pertinent to our current interests, you can use Alexa to control various smart devices in your smart home.

For Alexa to do all that she does, she has to connect to the Internet. That's where she gets all the answers to your factual queries, from various news sites, Wikipedia, and the like. When you ask a question, Alexa essentially does an Internet search and comes back with the closest answer, which she then reads to you. It's a little unnerving if you've never dealt with artificial intelligence; close your eyes, and it's as if you're talking to a human servant instead of a digital one. (In fact, it's easy to drift into a conversational mode with Alexa, which doesn't really work that well.)

Using Alexa as a Smart Home Controller

In addition to connecting to the Internet to find pertinent information, Alexa can also connect to various smart devices in your home. When your smart hub has discovered your Echo device, you can then use Alexa to control those connected devices, using similar voice commands.

Just say "Alexa, turn off the living room lights" and, assuming you have everything set up correctly, the lights will turn off. It's a lot easier than using a smartphone app—or turning off your lights by hand!

Meet Amazon's Echo Devices

Alexa is a piece of software. You interface with Alexa via a piece of hardware, a freestanding controller that plugs into the nearest electrical outlet and connects to the Internet via your home's Wi-Fi network.

Amazon currently sells five Alexa-controlled devices, and more are no doubt on the way. All these devices include wireless connectivity, feature built-in speakers, and operate in a similar fashion.

Amazon Echo

The original Alexa controller is the Amazon Echo. Amazon originally sold Echo as a kind of wireless speaker, and its height belies the full-range speaker enclosed within. That speaker is useful when you want to use Alexa to play streaming music from Pandora and Spotify and other streaming music services.

The Amazon Echo

Like all of Amazon's Alexa-controlled devices, the Echo uses far-field voice recognition to hear your commands from across a room, even if it's noisy or there's music playing. The voice recognition works surprisingly well, better than you may be used to with other voice-controlled devices.

The Echo sells for around $180 and is available in both white and black versions. You can order direct from Amazon (www.amazon.com); it's also available at select retailers. (When you order direct from Amazon it ships preprogrammed with your Amazon account details.)

Amazon Echo Dot

If you don't need a full-range speaker, go with the Echo's smaller sibling, the Echo Dot. The Echo Dot does everything the Echo does but is a lot less obtrusive on your living room or bedroom end table. And, because the Dot does include a speaker (just a smaller one), you can still hear Alexa speak and listen to music; it just won't sound quite as good as with the larger Echo. (If you want better sound, you can connect the Dot to external speakers or headphones via Bluetooth or the included 3.5mm audio jack.)

The Echo Dot

You can also save a hunk of money with the Echo Dot, which sells for just $50. That's right—you get all the Alexa functionality of the $180 Echo for less than a third of the price. Unless you really, really need that full-range speaker, that makes the Echo Dot a heck of a bargain. (It's available in both black and white versions, like the original Echo.)

Amazon Echo Show

Amazon's newest Echo is quite a bit different from the others. The Echo Show is an Echo device with a 7-inch touchscreen—or, looking at it another way, a 7-inch touchscreen with Alexa functionality included. It has the same capabilities as the normal Echo (including built-in speakers and microphone), but it adds a built-in display and camera that let you see Alexa's answers and results, as well as engage in two-way audio and video calling with other Alexa users.

The Echo Show

The display can also play back videos, including content from YouTube, Amazon Video, and various news sources (as part of your Flash Briefing). It can also function as a digital picture frame, display lyrics to songs you're playing from Amazon Music, and show live feeds from connected security cameras.

Obviously, the Echo Show is a bigger device than the normal Echo or Echo Dot, and isn't near as unobtrusive as those devices. It's also more expensive, selling for about $230.

Which Echo Is Right for You?

Which device you choose depends on your specific needs. If you want visual feedback, video playback, or the ability to monitor smart security cameras, your only choice is the Echo Show with its touchscreen display. If you want to use the device as a freestanding speaker, then definitely go with the better-sounding Echo. If you want to use the device as a smart home controller, however, and don't care so much about the quality of the music playback, then save some bucks and go with the smaller and less-expensive Echo Dot.

Personally, I use the Echo Dot in my living room (and am considering adding a second one in my bedroom). Its smaller size fits better in my living room, and as I have an existing home audio system, I don't need it to function as a speaker. Considering its low price, the Echo Dot is the right smart home controller for many similar users.

Other Alexa Devices

Amazon currently sells two other Alexa-enabled devices. The Amazon Tap is a battery-powered wireless speaker, and the Amazon Echo Look includes a selfie camera to help you make better fashion decisions. In terms of smart home control, both function similarly to the original Echo and Echo Dot.

>>>Go Further
MULTIPLE DEVICES

You're not limited to a single Echo or Echo Dot in your home. In fact, Amazon encourages you to purchase multiple Echo devices, so you can put one in each room where you have smart devices—in your living room, of course, but also in your bedroom or kitchen.

All Echo devices include Echo Spatial Perception (ESP) technology that ensures only the device closest to you will respond to your commands. This eliminates the possibility of your living room Echo responding to you when you're talking to the one in your bedroom.

Setting Up Your Echo Device

Whichever Echo device you have, setup and operation is identical. When you first unpack your device, you need to connect it to your home Wi-Fi network, download the Alexa app to your smartphone or tablet, and then pair your Echo with the smartphone app. After that, you can configure a handful of settings to make Echo work better for you.

Echo and Echo Dot

Going forward, I refer to both the Echo and Echo Dot as the Echo because their functionality is identical. The figures show the Android version of the Echo app, but it's functionally identical to the iOS (Apple) and Fire OS versions.

Set Up Your Device

Setting up the Echo in your home is a relatively quick and easy process. Just make sure you have a nearby electrical outlet and that your Wi-Fi wireless network is readily accessible. You also need to have the Alexa app installed on your phone or tablet; you can download it (for free) from the Amazon Appstore, Apple App Store, or Google Play Store, depending on what type of phone or tablet you have.

Alexa

(1) Connect one end of the supplied power cable to the Echo, and the other to a nearby power outlet.

(2) Launch the Alexa app on your phone or tablet.

(3) The Alexa app should recognize you from your Amazon account. (If it doesn't, follow the onscreen instructions to sign in to your account.) Tap **Begin Setup.**

Welcome, Michael Miller!

Get started with these easy steps:

- Connect your device to Wi-Fi
- Learn how to use your device

Amazon processes and retains audio and other information in the cloud to provide and improve our services, and may exchange information with third party services to fulfill your requests. Learn more . Alexa also allows purchasing by voice using your default payment and shipping settings. You can require a speakable confirmation code, turn purchasing off, and see product and order details in your Alexa app. Learn more .

By tapping "Begin Setup", you agree to all the terms found here . Your music will be saved to the cloud to protect your purchases.

Begin Setup

④ Tap to select the device you're setting up—**Echo**, **Tap**, or **Echo Dot.**

⑤ On the next screen, select your language (if it isn't English) then tap **Continue.**

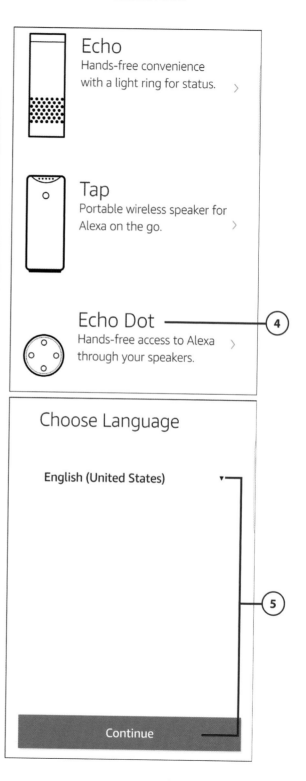

Echo
Hands-free convenience with a light ring for status. >

Tap
Portable wireless speaker for Alexa on the go. >

Echo Dot ———④
Hands-free access to Alexa > through your speakers.

Choose Language

English (United States) ▾

Continue

(6) Make sure your smartphone or tablet is connected to your home Wi-Fi network, and then tap **Connect to Wi-Fi.**

(7) When your Echo is ready to connect, Alexa tells you so and the ring on the top of the device turns orange. When this happens, tap **Continue.**

(8) Your smartphone now tries to pair with your Echo. When the connection is established, tap **Continue.**

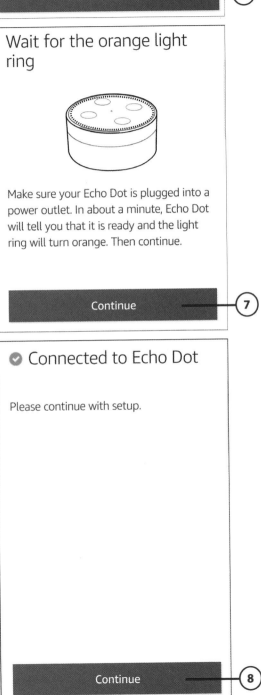

Connect to Wi-Fi — (6)

Wait for the orange light ring

Make sure your Echo Dot is plugged into a power outlet. In about a minute, Echo Dot will tell you that it is ready and the light ring will turn orange. Then continue.

Continue — (7)

✓ Connected to Echo Dot

Please continue with setup.

Continue — (8)

9 You now see a list of available Wi-Fi networks. Tap to select your network from the list. (Make sure the network you choose is the same one to which your smartphone is connected.)

10 Enter the password for your network into the **Password** box.

11 Save this password, so you don't have to enter it every time you launch the app, by tapping **Save Password to Amazon.**

12 Tap **Connect.**

13 Amazon prepares your Echo for initial use. This might take a few minutes and involve downloading the latest updates.

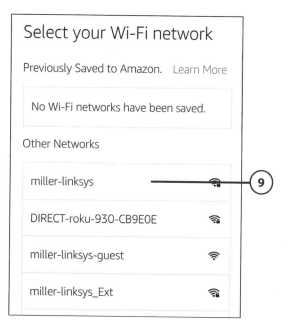

Select your Wi-Fi network

Previously Saved to Amazon.   Learn More

No Wi-Fi networks have been saved.

Other Networks

miller-linksys — **9**

DIRECT-roku-930-CB9E0E

miller-linksys-guest

miller-linksys_Ext

Select your Wi-Fi network

| Network | miller-linksys_Ext |
| Password | Password — HIDE | **10** |

☑ Save password to Amazon
Helps connect other devices. Learn More — **11**

Show advanced options

Connect — **12**

Preparing your Echo Dot — **13**

This may take a few minutes.

14 When the setup is complete, tap **Continue.**

15 If you're connecting an Echo Dot, you're prompted to indicate how you want to use the device—with a Bluetooth speaker, with an external speaker via audio cable, or with no additional speakers. Make your selection. You're prompted to view a short video (if you want), and then you see the Alexa app's home screen.

Amazon Account

Your Echo device needs to be connected to your Amazon account to take advantage of all the information and content in your account. As noted previously, if you purchase your device direct from Amazon, it arrives loaded with your account information. If you purchase the device elsewhere, you need to log in to your Amazon account from the Alexa smartphone app when prompted during the initial setup process.

Setup Complete

Echo Dot is now connected to Wi-Fi.

Continue — **14**

Select how you want to use your Echo Dot

Bluetooth
Pair Echo Dot with your speaker >
using Bluetooth.

Audio Cable
Connect Echo Dot to your speaker >
using an audio cable.

No speakers — **15**
Use Echo Dot as a stand-alone >
device.

Changing the Wake Word

To ask Alexa a question or give her a command, you have to speak a *wake word* to your Echo device. By default, this wake word is "Alexa." So, for example, if you wanted to know today's weather forecast, you would say "Alexa, what's the weather today?" If you don't say the wake word, your Echo doesn't wake up, and Alexa doesn't hear you.

But what if you don't like the wake word "Alexa"? What if your name is Alexa and you get tired of your Echo activating every time someone calls you by name? What if you just want to wake up your Echo with something cooler?

Whatever your reasons, Amazon enables you to change your Echo's wake word. You can choose from four different words:

- Alexa (default)
- Amazon
- Echo
- Computer

That last one is a gift to *Star Trek* fans. Everybody on the starship *Enterprise*, whichever generation, interfaces with the ship's computer by first saying, "Computer." In fact, if you want to have a little fun, ask Alexa "Computer, beam me up" or "Computer, tea, Earl Grey, hot." There are definitely some Trekkies on the Amazon programming team!

Why "Alexa"?

There were two main reasons that Amazon's engineers choose Alexa for the Echo's wake word—and thus gave the digital assistant its name. First, Alexa is a relatively uncommon word; saying most other words might falsely trigger the device. (Imagine if the wake word was "Dave" or "bread" or "mom.") The second reason is that the "x" in "Alexa" is a hard consonant that is recognized with greater precision than other letters.

Change the Wake Word

1. From the Home page of the Alexa app, tap the **Menu** (three-bar) button to display the left navigation pane.

2. Tap **Settings** to display the Settings screen.

3. In the Devices section at the top of the screen, tap your Echo device.

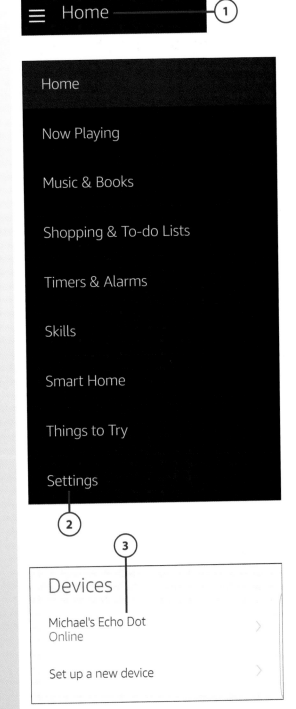

4 Scroll down to the General section and tap **Wake Word Alexa.**

5 Tap the down arrow in the first list box.

6 Tap to select your desired wake word.

7 Tap **Save.** You will now be able to wake your Echo with your new wake word.

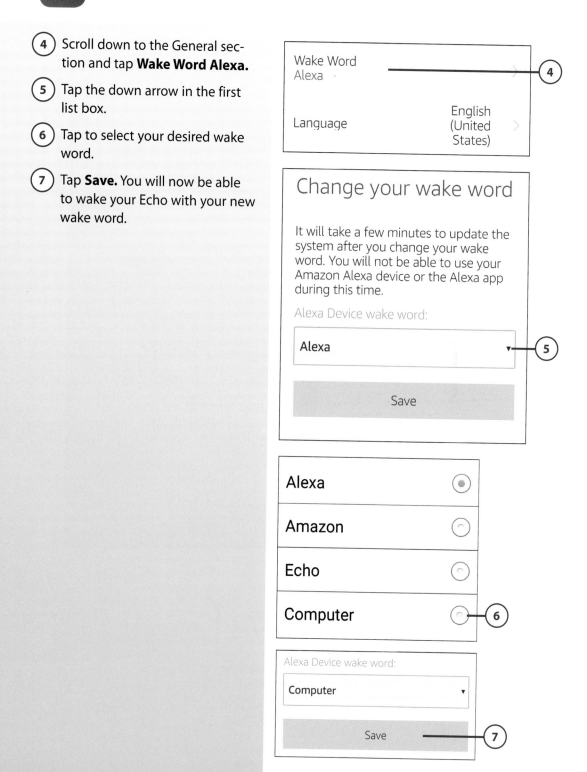

Working with Alexa

Using Alexa is as easy as speaking into your Echo device. Say the wake word ("Alexa," by default), followed by whatever it is you want Alexa to do.

When the Echo hears the wake word, the ring on the top of the device lights blue, with a small cyan area pointing in the direction of whomever spoke. Alexa listens to your request, and then (sometimes after "thinking" about it for a few seconds) voices her response.

The top ring on your Echo lights blue when it's listening to a voice command

Now, Alexa is not all-knowing. There are many questions you can ask of Alexa that she can't answer. If that's the case, she tells you. She also tells you if she just doesn't understand the question; when this happens, try stating the command again, or maybe try saying it a different way.

In most instances, however, Alexa tells you what she knows, or does what you asked her to do.

What, then, can you ask of Alexa? The questions and commands are almost limitless, but the following sections explain some common questions and commands you can try.

Source Data

Alexa obtains its data from multiple sources. Weather forecasts come from AccuWeather; news comes from a variety of media, including the Associated Press, NPR, ESPN, and local radio stations; music comes from the user's Amazon Music account as well as Pandora and Spotify; and factual information comes from Wikipedia.

Employ General Commands

There are a lot of specific commands you can issue, but depending on what you want to do, there are also a handful of general commands that apply across all actions and applications. When you're using Alexa, you can use the general commands shown in Table 11.1.

Table 11.1   General Commands

Alexa command	Does this
Alexa, stop.	Stops the current operation
Alexa, pause.	Pauses the current operation
Alexa, cancel.	Cancels the current operation
Alexa, mute.	Mutes the sound
Alexa, unmute.	Unmutes the sound
Alexa, volume five.	Sets the volume level; use a number between 0 and 10
Alexa, louder or Alexa, turn it up.	Raises the volume
Alexa, softer or Alexa, turn it down.	Lowers the volume
Alexa, repeat.	Repeats what Alexa just said
Alexa, help.	Requests assistance with the current operation

Tell Alexa What to Do

Alexa can perform a wide variety of operations, from retrieving the latest news and weather to reading audiobooks to answering all manner of questions. Here's a short list of what you can ask Alexa to do:

- Read the latest news stories: "Alexa, play my Flash Briefing."

- Read the weather report: "Alexa, what's the weather forecast?"

- Read the latest sports scores and news: "Alexa, play my Sports Update," or "Alexa, what's the score for the [your team] game?"

- Get traffic information: "Alexa, how is traffic?"

- Play music: "Alexa, play [song or album or artist or genre]."

- Read an audiobook: "Alexa, read the book [book name]."

- Find nearby restaurants and businesses: "Alexa, what [type of food] restaurants are nearby?" or "Alexa, where are the nearest [type of business] stores?"

- Set timers and alarms: "Alexa, wake me up at [time]," or "Alexa, set a timer for [duration] minutes."

- Manage your calendar: "Alexa, what's on my calendar today?" or "Alexa, add an event to my calendar."

- Create shopping and to-do lists: "Alexa, what's on my to-do list?" or "Alexa, add [item] to my shopping list."

- Shop online at Amazon.com: "Alexa, order [item]," or "Alexa, add [item] to my shopping cart."

You can also ask Alexa a variety of random questions. If you want to know how far it is to the moon, what is the capital of Brazil, what was the name of Bob Dylan's first album, or what the square root of 42 is, just ask. Alexa probably knows the answer.

Using the Alexa App

Even though Alexa lets you control your Echo device via voice commands, there's also a lot of behind-the-scenes configuration that you can do by voice. That's one of the reasons why Amazon created the Alexa app for your smartphone, to let you configure and control Alexa when necessary.

Tour the Alexa App

The Alexa app is relatively simple and easy to use, and you won't need to use it much. But it's good to know what's there and why and how to use it, if you need to. To that end, here's a short tour.

1. Launch the Alexa app on your smartphone or tablet. (It's available for Android, Apple iOS, and Fire OS devices; the step-by-steps in this chapter use the Android version.)

2. The Home screen displays *cards* that reflect specific commands or activities that Alexa has completed; the most recent is shown first. Scroll down to view additional cards.

3. If you've been playing music on your Echo device, a now playing pane may appear at the bottom of the screen. Tap the **Play** button to resume playback, or tap the **Volume** button to change the volume level.

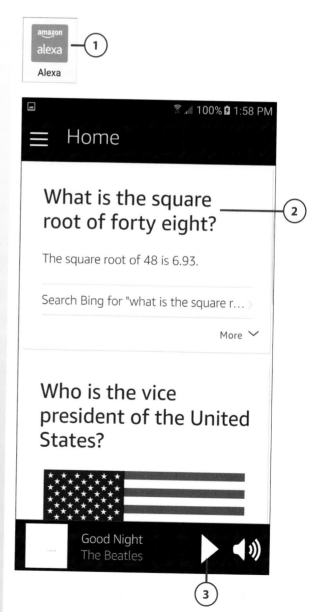

(4) For some cards, Alexa would like to know how well she performed. If Alexa heard you right, tap **Yes.** If Alexa had a problem, tap **No.** Alternatively, tap **Less** to not display this section.

(5) Tap the **Menu** (three-bar) button to display the left navigation panel.

(6) Tap **Now Playing** to display the Now Playing screen. From here you can control playback of items you've played through your Echo; view items in the queue, and view recently played items (History).

(7) Tap **Music & Books** to view details about and control specific music and book services connected to your Alexa account.

(8) Tap **Lists** to view and edit your shopping and to-do lists.

(9) Tap **Timers & Alarms** to manage the timer and alarm volume, and select alarm sounds.

(10) Tap **Skills** to view and add skills to Alexa.

(11) Tap **Smart Home** to view and control smart devices with Alexa.

(12) Tap **Things to Try** to get suggestions of fun and useful things you can do with Alexa.

(13) Tap **Settings** to view and configure additional Alexa settings.

Voice feedback

▶ Alexa heard: "alexa how much snow are we going to get tomorrow"

Did Alexa do what you wanted?

Yes   No

Remove card   Learn more

Less ⌃

(5)   (4)

≡   Home

Home

Now Playing   (6)

Music & Books   (7)

Lists   (8)

Timers & Alarms   (9)

Skills   (10)

Smart Home   (11)

Things to Try   (12)

Settings   (13)

Skills

Learn more about skills in the "Working with Alexa's Skills" section, later in this chapter.

Smart Home

To learn more about Alexa's smart home features, see the "Using Alexa to Control Your Smart Devices" section, later in this chapter.

Link Accounts from Other Services

Alexa gets more powerful when you link her to other services that you use. You can link Alexa to your accounts with streaming music services, online calendars, and online to-do lists.

1. From within the Alexa app, tap the **Menu** button to display the left navigation panel.

2. Tap **Settings** to display the Settings screen.

3. Scroll to the Accounts section and tap **Music & Media.**

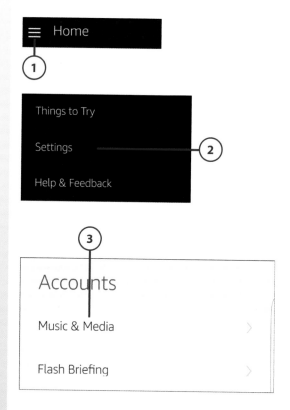

(**4**) Go to the account you want to add to Alexa and then tap **Link Account.**

(**5**) If you already have an account with this service, tap the **Log In** button or link and then follow the onscreen instructions to log in to and link to this account.

(**6**) If you don't yet have an account with this service, tap the **Sign Up** button or link and then follow the onscreen instructions to create a new account.

(**7**) Return to the Settings screen, scroll to the Accounts section, and then tap **Calendar.**

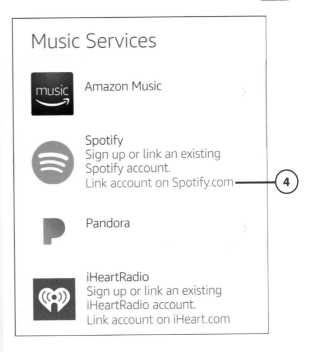

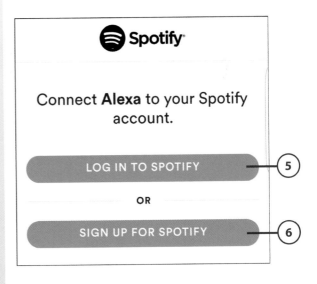

8. Tap the tile for the calendar you'd like to use with Alexa.

9. Tap **Link Your Calendar Account** to link this account, and then follow any additional onscreen instructions to log on to your calendar account and complete the process.

10. If you want to link to a third-party to-do list service, in addition to the lists feature built-into Alexa, return to the Settings screen, scroll to the Accounts section, and then tap **Lists.**

11. Tap **Link** for the to-do list account you want to link to, and then follow the onscreen instructions to complete the process.

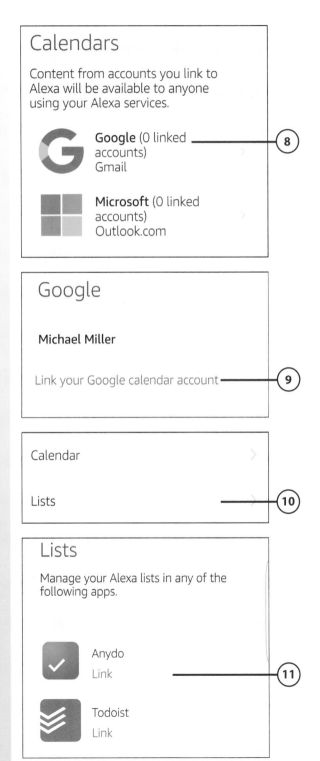

Calendars

Content from accounts you link to Alexa will be available to anyone using your Alexa services.

Google (0 linked accounts) Gmail ⟶ 8

Microsoft (0 linked accounts) Outlook.com

Google

Michael Miller

Link your Google calendar account ⟶ 9

Calendar ›

Lists › ⟶ 10

Lists

Manage your Alexa lists in any of the following apps.

Anydo
Link ⟶ 11

Todoist
Link

Working with Alexa's Skills

Alexa can get a lot smarter and a lot more useful when you add new skills to her repertoire. A *skill* for Alexa is like an app on your smartphone; an application that enables Alexa to perform a specific task based on a given voice command. You install skills when you want Alexa to be able to do more than she does out of the box.

Amazon offers more than 10,000 skills you can add to your Alexa. There are skills for playing soothing nature sounds (**Ambient Noise**), reading children's stories (**Short Bedtime Story**), and playing trivia games (**Test My Trivia**). There are skills that tell you how to prepare various cocktails (**The Bartender**), concoct a recipe from whatever you currently have in the fridge (**Best Recipes**), and order pizza from Domino's (**Domino's Pizza**) or Pizza Hut (**Pizza Hut**). There's even a skill that lets Alexa serve as a personal alert system if you're in trouble (**Ask My Buddy**).

Even more useful are those skills that let Alexa connect to other applications and devices. For example, the **Fitbit** skill connects your Fitbit personal activity tracker to Alexa and lets you query Alexa on various statistics gathered by your Fitbit device. And, not surprisingly, there are a ton of skills available when you connect your smart home devices to Alexa.

Smart Home Skills

Learn more about Alexa's smart home skills in the "Using Alexa to Control Your Smart Devices" section, later in this chapter.

Find a Skill

Finding a new skill is as easy as browsing or searching for it from within the Alexa app.

1. From within the Alexa app on your smartphone, tap the **Menu** button to display the left navigation panel.

2. Tap **Skills** to display the All Skills screen.

(1)

≡ Home

Timers & Alarms

Skills ———————————— **(2)**

Smart Home

③ New and recommended skills are displayed first. Scroll down to view more skills, and scroll left and right through any section to view all the skills of that type.

④ To search for a skill, enter a short description (or the skill's name, if you know it) into the search box at the top of the screen, and then tap the **Search** (magnifying glass) button.

⑤ To browse through skills by category, tap **Categories**.

⑥ Tap the category you want to view.

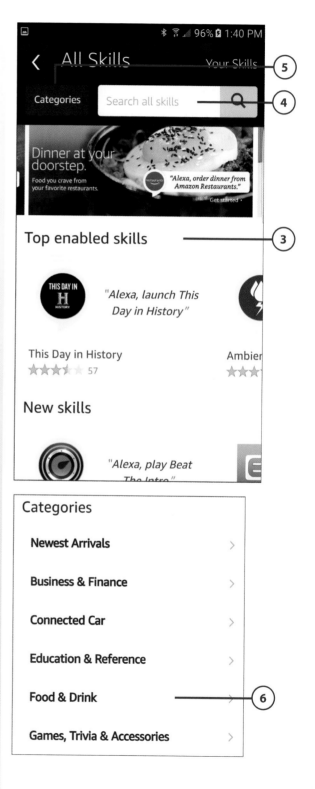

7 Skills within that category are now listed, newest first. Scroll down to view more.

8 To change how skills are displayed, tap the **Sort By** list.

9 Tap to sort by **Relevance, Avg. Customer Rating**, or **Release Date** (the default).

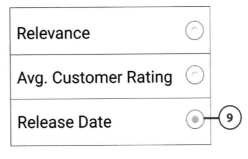

239 Results   Sort by   Release Date — **8**

CookingOil — **7**
AGupta
★★★★★

"Alexa, ask cooking oil to tell me a cooking oil fact"

Tasty Food Thoughts
Christophe Gaboury
★★★★★

"Alexa Open tasty food thoughts"

Beer Buddy
Joseph Yi
★★★★★ 1

Relevance	◌
Avg. Customer Rating	◌
Release Date	◉ — **9**

Add a Skill to Alexa

Adding a skill to Alexa is as easy as tapping a button and then following any additional onscreen instructions. You can add an unlimited number of skills to Alexa—and if you end up not using a skill, it's no big deal.

(1) Use any of the methods discussed in the previous task to find the skill you want to add.

(2) Tap the **Enable** button.

(3) The skill is now enabled. Scroll down to read more about this skill, including suggested voice commands.

More Steps Required

Some skills require additional steps to install. For example, if the skill involves a third-party service or website, you might need to sign in to that service or website to enable the app. Follow the onscreen instructions to complete the installation.

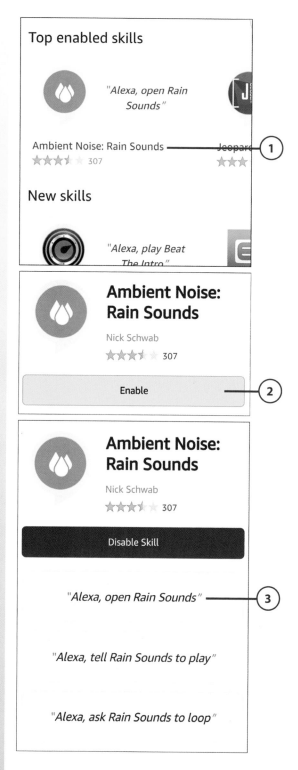

Using Alexa to Control Your Smart Devices

All this talk about Alexa and voice commands and skills leads us to the topic you're probably most interested in—how to use Alexa with your smart home devices.

Here's the good news: Alexa is compatible with the majority of smart home hubs and devices on the market today. That means you can control these devices, individually or collectively, via Alexa voice commands. And that's a very neat thing.

What's Compatible?

What smart home devices does Alexa work with? It's a long list, and includes most major smart home systems and devices, including Insteon, SmartThings, and Wink. You can find a complete list at www.amazon.com/alexa-smart-home/b?node=13575751011.

In addition, many other smart devices work with Alexa when they're connected to an Alexa-compatible hub, such as the Insteon, SmartThings, and Wink hubs. In short, there's not a whole lot that *doesn't* work with Alexa, which is good.

IFTTT

Alexa also supports the If This Than That standard for creating new smart tasks on a variety of smart devices. Learn more in Chapter 14, "Adding More Functionality with IFTTT."

Connect a Smart Device to Alexa

Before you connect any smart device to Alexa, make sure the device is connected to its own smartphone app and to your Wi-Fi network, typically via the device's or system's hub. For example, if you're connecting a Wink-compatible device, make sure it's connected to the Wink Hub; if you're connecting a Philips Hue smart light, make sure it's connected to the Hue Hub. Your Echo device connects to the smart device via the connected hub.

(1) From within the Alexa app on your smartphone, tap the **Menu** button to display the left navigation panel.

(2) Tap **Smart Home**.

(3) Scroll to the Your Smart Home Skills section. Any skills you've previously installed are displayed here. Tap **Get More Smart Home Skills.**

(4) Additional smart home skills are now displayed. Browse or search the list to find the skill for the smart device you want to connect and then tap that skill to open the skill screen.

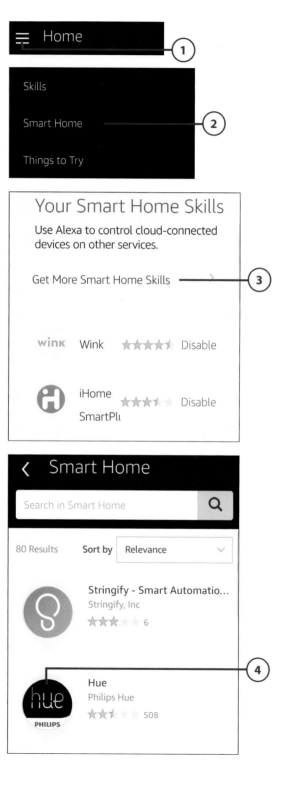

5 Read about the selected skill and tap **Enable.**

6 If you're prompted to sign in to the account for your smart device, do so now.

7 If you're prompted to let Alexa control your smart device, tap **Yes** now.

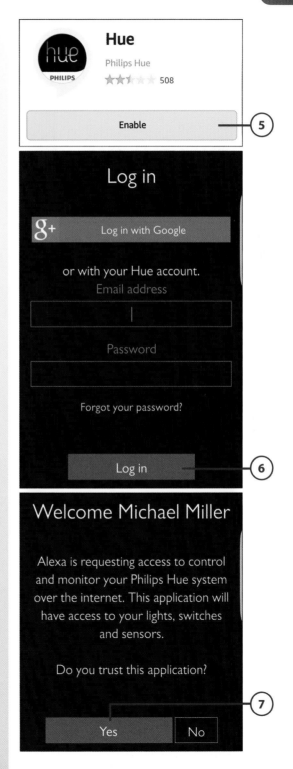

(8) When the connection is complete, tap **Back to the App** to return to the Alexa app.

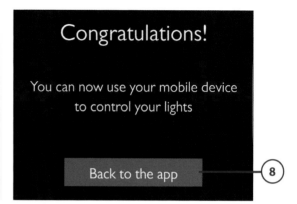

Working with Device Groups

One of the nice things about Alexa is that you can control multiple devices from multiple companies. Now, you can control each device individually with its own unique voice command, but you can also create a single command to control multiple devices at one time. This is useful, for example, for controlling all the lights in a single room, even if those lights come from different manufacturers.

You do this by creating what Alexa calls a *group*. When you add all the lights in your room to a "living room lights" group, for example, you can control all those lights just by telling Alexa to do something to the living room lights, such as, "Alexa, turn off the living room lights." One command takes care of multiple devices when you have them linked together in a group.

Create a Device Group

(1) From the left navigation menu, tap **Smart Home.**

2 In the Your Groups section, tap **Create Group**.

3 Type a name for this group into the **Enter a Group Name** box.

4 Tap to select those devices you want to include in the group.

5 Scroll to the bottom of the page and tap **Save**. Your new group is now saved and ready to use.

Your Groups

Use groups to control multiple devices at a time.

Living room lights
4 Devices   >

Create group ——— **2**

Enter a group name ——————— **3**

Devices in this group

Alexa works best with group names she can understand like "Living Room" or "Upstairs". Names that include numbers, like "Kitchen 1", can be hard for Alexa to understand.

——— **4**

☐ Hue ambiance lamp 1

☐ Concentrate in Living room

☐ Energize in Living room

☐ Floor lamp by couch

Cancel

Save ——— **5**

Controlling a Smart Device with Alexa

After you've connected all your smart devices to Alexa, installed all the pertinent skills, and created groups of devices for easier operations, you can start using Alexa to control those devices. As with anything related to Alexa, all you have to do is say "Alexa," followed by your command.

What you can control depends on the devices you've connected and groups you've created. Some devices only let you perform simple on/off operations with Alexa, like this:

Alexa, turn on the hallway fan.

Other devices let you perform more sophisticated operations, such as dimming lights and such, like this:

Alexa, dim the Hue lights to 50 percent.

Of course, groups have their own commands, like this:

Alexa, turn off the bedroom lights.

And if you've connected a smart thermostat, like the Ecobee or Nest, you can use Alexa to control your temperature, like this:

Alexa, set the house temperature to 70 degrees.

Or this:

Alexa, lower the living room temperature.

You can use Alexa to control all manner of smart devices. For example, both GE and Whirlpool offer appliances that can be voice-controlled by Alexa. Alexa even lets you guide your Roomba vacuum cleaner around the room via voice commands. The sky's the limit!

To learn more about what you can do with a particular device, go the Smart Home screen in the Alexa smartphone app and tap the skill for that device. Most skills have examples of commands you can use.

More to Come

Amazon is continually adding new compatibilities, skills, and features to Alexa. To learn what's new, go to the Home page on the Alexa app; to view the latest skills, go to the app's Skills page.

In this chapter, you learn how to use the Google Assistant on Google Home in your smart home.

→ Understanding Google Home and the Google Assistant
→ Setting Up and Using Google Home
→ Working with the Google Assistant
→ Using Google Home to Control Your Smart Devices

Controlling Your Smart Home with Google Home

Two years ago, Amazon Echo became the first voice-controlled smart home controller (what some call a "smart speaker") on the market. Now, however, Amazon has some real competition in the form of Google Home—a smart controller that taps into the power of Google and its personal digital assistant software, dubbed the Google Assistant.

In and of itself, the Google Assistant is both fun and useful. You can ask the Google Assistant whether it's going to rain today, how far it is to the nearest star, and if there's a good Mexican restaurant nearby. And when you pair the Google Assistant with your various smart devices, you can use Google Home to control your smart home from the comfort of your couch. It's even easier than using a smartphone app!

Understanding Google Home and the Google Assistant

Like Amazon's Echo and Echo Dot, Google Home is a small wireless speaker that you can operate with voice commands. Google Home easily sits on your nearest end table and functions as a wireless speaker and controller for other devices in your smart home.

Also like the Amazon devices, the Google Home device contains a personal digital assistant, dubbed the Google Assistant, of which you can ask all sorts of questions. You can command the Google Assistant to play music from a variety of streaming services, manage your calendar and to-do lists, and even stream movies and TV shows to your living room or bedroom TV. (That later capability comes only if you have a Google Chromecast device connected to your TV.)

Google Home, in a variety of colors

You can also use the Google Assistant to control a variety of smart home devices. Once you've connected a smart device to Google Home, just say "OK Google, turn on the living room lights" or "OK Google, turn up the air conditioner," and the Google Assistant sends the necessary commands to the appropriate smart devices to do your bidding. Google Assistant is compatible with all manner of smart devices, from smart light bulbs to smart kitchen appliances, and just about everything in between.

The Google Assistant differs somewhat from Amazon Alexa in that it uses more advanced artificial intelligence (AI) technology to better interpret and learn from your commands. After you use the Google Assistant for a while, it kind of starts to feel as if you're talking to a real human being. Really.

The Google Assistant is part and parcel of the Google Home device. Google Home is a stylish little gadget that looks a little like a small table lamp or an overgrown air freshener. It connects to a nearby power outlet and (wirelessly) to your home's Wi-Fi network. When you talk to Google Home, a series of colored lights on the top of the unit light up and swirl. It contains a built-in speaker for fairly decent-sounding music playback.

Google Home is available in most electronics stores and online at store.google.com/product/google_home. It sells for around $130, and you can connect multiple units in different rooms in your home.

Change the Color

If you don't like the stock white look of Google Home, you can accessorize the unit with different colored bases. Just slide off one base and replace it with another one that better suits your room's color scheme. Replacement bases come in either fabric or metal in a variety of colors, from violet to copper, and sell for between $20 and $40. They're also available online.

Setting Up and Using Google Home

Google makes it relatively easy to set up and start using a new Google Home device. You'll want to have your own Google account beforehand, and you should download the Google Home app to your handy smartphone. (The Home app is free and available for both Android and iOS devices.)

Essentially, you connect Google Home to the Home app via Wi-Fi and then use the Home app to connect the Home device to your home's Wi-Fi network. Once connected, there are a few settings you can configure and services to connect, but then you're good to go.

Set Up Your Device

Setting up Google Home takes no more than five minutes or so using the Google Home app. Just make sure you have a nearby electrical outlet and that your Wi-Fi wireless network is readily accessible. Your phone needs to be connected to the same Wi-Fi network to which you'll be connecting the Google Home device.

Android Versus iOS

The following instructions—and all the instructions in this chapter—focus on using the Android version of the Google Home app. The iOS (iPhone) version of the Google Home looks a little different but works in a similar fashion.

1. Connect your Google Home device to an electrical outlet and then launch the Google Home app on your smartphone.

2. Tap **Accept** on the Welcome screen.

3. If you're asked to turn on Location Permissions for the app, tap **Turn On Location.** (And if your phone asks permission for the Home app to access your device's location, tap **Allow.**)

4. The Google Home app looks for nearby Google Home devices.

Home ——① 1

Welcome to the Google Home app

Tap "Accept" to agree to the Terms of Service and Privacy Policy

CANCEL   ACCEPT ❯ ——② 2

Turn on Location Permissions for setup

Google Home app requires Location Permissions in order to discover and set up nearby devices

SKIP   TURN ON LOCATION ❯ ——③ 3

Welcome to Google Home

Looking for devices ———④ 4

Looking for devices nearby that are plugged in and ready to use or set up

5 When the app finds your Google Home device, tap **Continue.**

6 The Google Home device creates a temporary Wi-Fi hotspot, and uses that hotspot to connect to your smartphone and the Google Home app. (At this point, your phone is *not* connected to your home network; instead it's connected to the temporary wireless network established by the Google Home device.)

7 Confirm that you're connected to the correct device by tapping **Play Test Sound.**

Google Home found

There are just a few steps to set up and personalize your Google Home

CONTINUE > — **5**

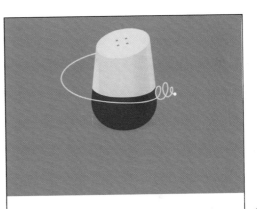

Connecting to Google Home — **6**

Your mobile device will switch to a temporary Wi-Fi hotspot on your Google Home.

Next, your Google Home will play a test sound.

This is to confirm that you've connected to the right Google Home.

PLAY TEST SOUND > — **7**

8. If everything is connected properly, you hear a test sound from the Google Home device. Tap **I Heard It** if you heard it. (Or tap **Try Again** if you didn't.)

9. Select which room your Google Home is in. Tap the down arrow and select the most appropriate choice.

10. If you want to send data about your Google Home usage to Google, leave checked the **Send Google Home Device Usage Data and Crash Reports to Google** option. If you'd rather not share this data, tap to deselect this option.

11. Tap **Continue.**

12. Connect your Google Home device to your home network. Tap the down arrow to view a list of nearby networks, and select your network from the list. (Make sure you select the same network to which your phone is connected.)

13. Tap **OK** to retrieve the network's password from your phone. (This doesn't work on all phones; if your phone doesn't automatically retrieve the password, proceed to step 14.)

14. Manually enter your network password by tapping **No Thanks.**

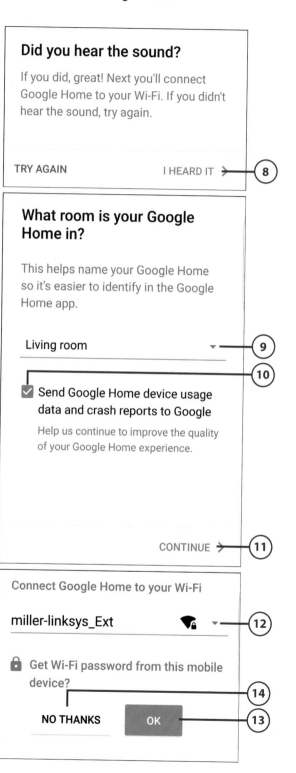

Did you hear the sound?

If you did, great! Next you'll connect Google Home to your Wi-Fi. If you didn't hear the sound, try again.

TRY AGAIN   I HEARD IT →   8

What room is your Google Home in?

This helps name your Google Home so it's easier to identify in the Google Home app.

Living room   ▼   9
                                10

☑ Send Google Home device usage data and crash reports to Google

Help us continue to improve the quality of your Google Home experience.

CONTINUE →   11

Connect Google Home to your Wi-Fi

miller-linksys_Ext   🔒 ▼   12

🔒 Get Wi-Fi password from this mobile device?   14

NO THANKS   OK   13

15. Enter the password for your Wi-Fi network.

16. Tap **Continue.**

17. To get the most out of your Google Home device, you need to be signed in to your Google account. Tap **Sign In.**

18. Tap to select your Google account.

19. Tap **Continue as *Name*.**

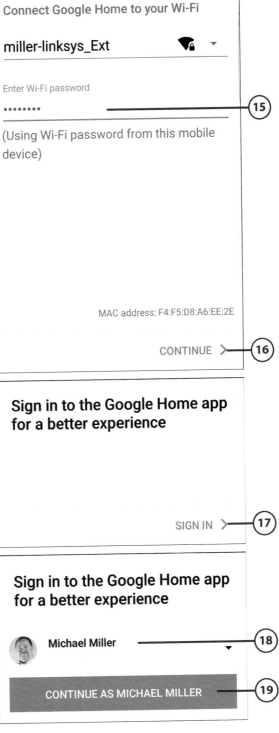

Connect Google Home to your Wi-Fi

miller-linksys_Ext

Enter Wi-Fi password

••••••••

(Using Wi-Fi password from this mobile device)

MAC address: F4:F5:D8:A6:EE:2E

CONTINUE >

Sign in to the Google Home app for a better experience

SIGN IN >

Sign in to the Google Home app for a better experience

Michael Miller

CONTINUE AS MICHAEL MILLER

20 Google wants to access the personal data you enter to enhance your experience. Tap **Allow.**

21 Google automatically enters your home address as the location for your Google Home device. Tap the pencil icon to edit or enter a new address.

22 Tap **Set Location.**

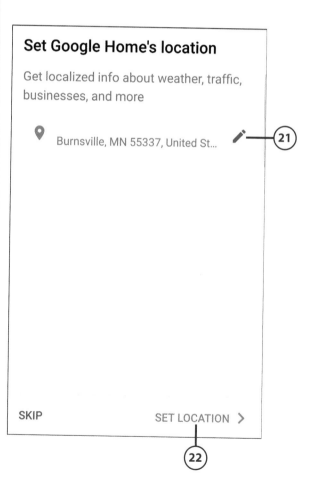

Get personal results

Google Home can use your personal info (e.g., photos and shopping list) to assist you. Anyone in speaking range can access this info.

SKIP   ALLOW > —**20**

Set Google Home's location

Get localized info about weather, traffic, businesses, and more

📍 Burnsville, MN 55337, United St... ✏️ —**21**

SKIP   SET LOCATION >

22

(23) If you want to receive email notifications about new features and offers, tap "on" the **Get E-mail Notifications** switch. If you don't want notifications, tap "off" the switch.

(24) Tap **Continue.**

(25) You are prompted to link one or more music services to your Google Home. If you already have an account with Google Play Music, Pandora, Spotify, or YouTube Music, tap **Link** for that account and follow the onscreen instructions.

(26) If you don't yet have an account with a given music service, tap **Get Free Trial** for that service and follow the onscreen instructions.

(27) Tap to select the music service you want Google Home to use by default.

(28) Tap **Continue.**

Get the most out of your Google Home

Stay up to date on new features, apps, offers, and more for your device and your Google Assistant

Get e-mail notifications **(23)**

CONTINUE **(24)**

Link your music services, then select a default

Google Home works with multiple services. Your default service will be used first when possible. **(27)**

Google Play Music
Free trial available
GET FREE TRIAL

YouTube Music
Free trial available
GET FREE TRIAL **(26)**

Spotify
Premium account required
LINK **(25)**

Pandora

HELP   CONTINUE **(28)**

(29) Your Google Home device is now set up and ready to use. If you want to view a short tutorial about how to use Google Home, tap **Continue.** *Or…*

(30) Tap **Skip Tutorial** to begin using Google Home.

Navigate and Configure the Google Home App

You use the Google Home app to configure and monitor your Google Home device and Google Assistant activity. Let's take a quick tour so you know what's where.

(1) Launch the Google Home app on your smartphone.

(2) There are two tabs at the top of the screen. The Listen tab offers suggestions for listening to music. Tap **Discover** to view cards for the most recent questions you've asked the Google Assistant, as well as suggestions for new things to ask. Scroll down to view more.

(3) Tap the **Activity** icon to view a detailed list of your Google Home activity.

(4) Tap the **Menu** (three bars) button to display the left navigation pane.

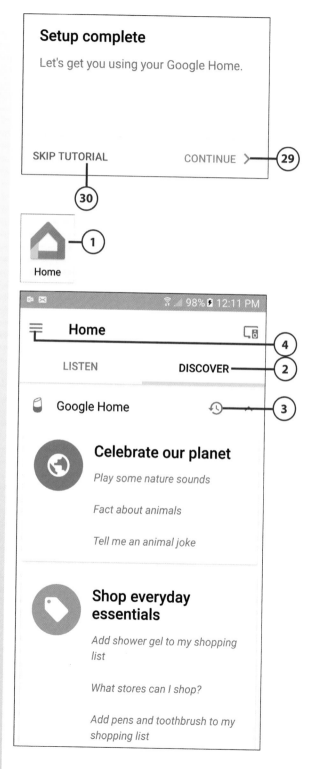

Setup complete

Let's get you using your Google Home.

SKIP TUTORIAL   CONTINUE >

Home

98% 12:11 PM

Home

LISTEN   DISCOVER

Google Home

Celebrate our planet

Play some nature sounds

Fact about animals

Tell me an animal joke

Shop everyday essentials

Add shower gel to my shopping list

What stores can I shop?

Add pens and toothbrush to my shopping list

5 Tap **Cast Screen/Audio** to control a Chromecast device connected to your TV.

6 Tap **Things to Ask** to view suggestions on how to use the Google Assistant.

7 Tap **Music** to connect streaming music accounts (Google Play Music, Pandora, Spotify, and YouTube Music) to the Google Assistant.

8 Tap **Home Control** to connect smart home devices to the Google Assistant.

Smart Devices

Learn more about smart home control in the "Using Google Home to Control Your Smart Devices" section, later in this chapter.

9 Tap **Shopping List** to manage your shopping list.

10 Tap **More Settings** to display additional Google Assistant settings.

11 Tap your name to display the Personal info screen.

12 Tap **Home & Work Locations** to enter or edit your home and work addresses.

13 Tap **Nickname** to tell the Google Assistant what you'd like to be called. (Michael rather than Mike, for example.)

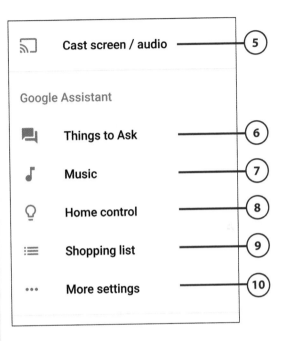

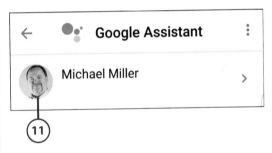

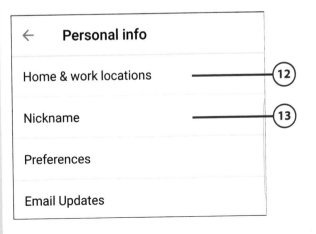

(14) Tap **Preferences** to choose between weather temperature in Celsius or Fahrenheit.

(15) Tap **Email Updates** to choose whether to receive emails relating to Google Home.

(16) Tap the back arrow to return to the Google Assistant screen.

(17) Tap **Home Control** to set up your smart home devices.

(18) Tap **News** to determine which news sources you hear when you tell the Google Assistant, "Listen to the news."

(19) Tap **My Day** to determine what you hear when you say to the Google Assistant, "Tell me about my day." You can choose to hear your local weather forecast, work commute information, your next meeting on Google Calendar, reminders, news, and more.

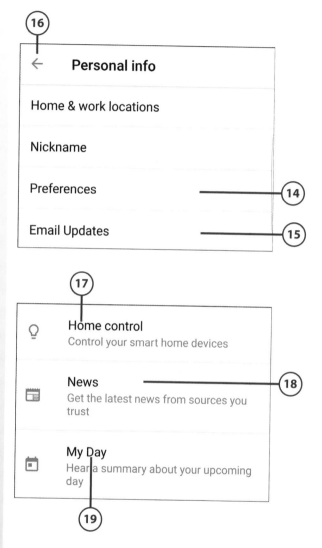

(16)

← **Personal info**

Home & work locations

Nickname

Preferences —————— (14)

Email Updates —————— (15)

(17)

Home control
Control your smart home devices

News —————— (18)
Get the latest news from sources you trust

My Day
Hear a summary about your upcoming day

(19)

20) Tap **TVs and Speakers** to control music and video playback on your Google Home and Chromecast devices.

21) Tap **Shopping List** to manage your shopping list.

22) Tap **Services** to add third-party services and apps to the Google Assistant.

23) Tap **Videos and Photos** to set up photo viewing and Netflix and YouTube video streaming between Google Home and a Chromecast device.

24) Tap **Shared devices** to set up Google Home to recognize the voices of additional users and use their individual Google accounts.

25) Scroll down the screen to view additional settings.

26) Tap the back arrow to return to the navigation pane.

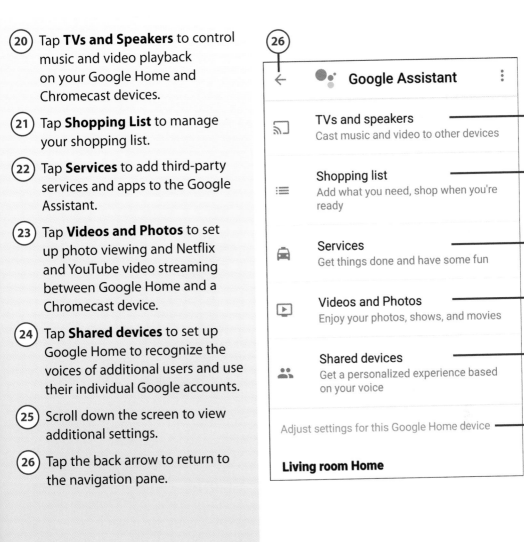

26)

← ●: **Google Assistant** ⋮

TVs and speakers — 20)
Cast music and video to other devices

Shopping list — 21)
Add what you need, shop when you're ready

Services — 22)
Get things done and have some fun

Videos and Photos — 23)
Enjoy your photos, shows, and movies

Shared devices — 24)
Get a personalized experience based on your voice

Adjust settings for this Google Home device — 25)

Living room Home

>>>*Go Further*
CHROMECAST

Google Chromecast is a small device that connects to the HDMI port on your living room or bedroom TV and lets you stream photos and videos. You can use Chromecast to watch Netflix and YouTube videos, or view pictures from Google Photos.

A Google Chromecast device

You can also use Chromecast to stream media from your Google Home device—and use Google Home to control playback from your Chromecast device. Just connect your Chromecast to your Google Home app, and then speak commands to the Google Assistant. You can then tell the Google Assistant to "Play [*movie or TV show name*] on my TV" or "Play [*name of song or artist*] on my TV." (You can purchase Chromecast devices at most electronics stores or online at www.google.com/chromecast; the basic unit costs about $35.)

Working with the Google Assistant

Using the Google Assistant on Google Home is as easy as talking to it. You speak a wake word, which wakes up the device, followed by your question or command. When the Google Assistant hears the wake word, four colored lights on the top of the Google Home unit light up. The device searches for the answer, the lights whirl in a circle, and then the Google Assistant speaks the answer or executes the command.

Wake Words

What are the Google Assistant's wake words? Well, they're more accurately wake *phrases*, and there are three of them you can use:

- Hey Google
- OK Google
- OK Boo Boo

So a typical command might be "Hey Google, what's the weather today?" or "OK Google, how far is it to Albuquerque?" (You don't have to choose just one to use; you can use "Hey Google," "OK Google," or "OK Boo Boo" interchangeably with the Google Assistant on Google Home.)

Not surprisingly, the Google Assistant taps into Google's rich variety of resources on the Web. Depending on what you ask, Google might consult Google Search, Google Calendar, Google Flights (airline information), or Google Maps (maps and directions). It also pulls information from and links to a variety of relevant websites and services, including OpenTable, Uber, Wikipedia, and the like.

More important, the Google Assistant taps into Google's almost two decades of search expertise. Google knows a lot about what people search for and how, and the company has applied that knowledge to the AI behind the Google Assistant. Your queries don't have to be precise; the Google Assistant does a really good job of figuring out what you're trying to say. Just talk to Google Home as you would a family member or friend. How it responds is uncanny.

So what kinds of things can you ask of the Google Assistant? The following sections detail some of the more common uses.

Employ General Commands

General commands (like those in Table 12.1) work across just about anything you're doing with the Google Assistant. Remember to precede each command with either "Hey Google," "OK Google," or "OK Boo Boo."

Table 12.1   General Commands

Command	Does this
Stop	Stops the current operation
Be quiet	Stops the current action
Pause	Pauses the current operation
Resume	Resumes the current operation
Cancel	Cancels the current operation
Repeat that	Repeats the last answer
Volume [five]	Sets the volume level; use a number between 0 and 10
Louder *or* turn it up	Raises the volume
Softer *or* turn it down	Lowers the volume
Flip a coin	Flips a virtual coin
Roll a die	Rolls a virtual die
Help	Requests assistance with the current operation

Tell the Google Assistant What to Do

There's a lot you do with the Google Assistant on your Google Home device. Here's a short list:

- Read the latest news stories: "OK Google, what's today's news?"
- Read a personalized My Day summary: "OK Google, tell me about my day."
- Read the weather report: "OK Google, what's the weather forecast?"
- Find the latest sports scores: "OK Google, what's the score for the [*your team*] game?"
- Get traffic information: "OK Google, how's my commute?"
- Play music: "OK Google, play [*song* or *album* or *artist* or *genre*]."
- Find nearby restaurants and businesses: "OK Google, what [*type of food*] restaurants are nearby?" or "OK Google, where are the nearest [*type of business*] stores?"

- Set timers and alarms: "OK Google, wake me up at [*time*]" or "OK Google, set the timer for [*duration*] minutes."

- Manage your Google calendar: "OK Google, what's on my calendar?"

- Create shopping lists: "OK Google, what's on my shopping list?" or "OK Google, add [*item*] to my shopping list."

You can also ask the Google Assistant the types of general questions you're used to querying with the web-based Google Search. You can ask how far it is New York City, what's the capital of New Zealand, why is the sky blue, how many ounces are in a gallon, how do you say "hello" in Chinese, or what is 72 divided by 9. Google almost always has the answer.

Using Google Home to Control Your Smart Devices

There are lots of different ways to control and monitor the smart devices in your smart home. You can use the device's proprietary smartphone app. You can (often) use a smart system's hub and smartphone app. (I'm talking Insteon, SmartThings, and Wink here.) You use your iPhone and Apple's Home app to control multiple devices. And you can also use Google Home and the Google Assistant to do the controlling for you.

Controlling your smart devices with voice commands is incredibly easy; if you're tired or incapacitated or don't want to or can't get up from the couch, just tell the Google Assistant what you want your smart devices to do. You don't even have to deal with lifting and working a complicated remote control or smartphone app; controlling everything via voice puts you in control even if you're physically challenged in any way.

What Does Google Home Control?

Google Home is compatible with a large and growing number of smart home devices, including SmartThings and Wink hubs and devices. (Not Insteon, however.) See a complete list of compatible devices at madeby.google.com/home/services/, and expect even more compatibility in the future.

IFTTT

Google Home also works with IFTTT (If This Then That), the standard that lets you create rules that let multiple smart devices trigger one another under specified conditions. Learn more about IFTTT in Chapter 14, "Adding More Functionality with IFTTT."

Pair a Device with the Google Assistant

To control a smart device via the Google Assistant on Google Home, you first have to pair that device with the Google Home app. Once paired, you can then use the appropriate voice commands to control that device.

1. Tap the **Menu** (three bars) button to display the left navigation pane.

2. Tap **Home Control.**

3. Make sure the **Devices** tab is selected. Any devices you've previously added are displayed here.

4. Tap the **+** to add a new device.

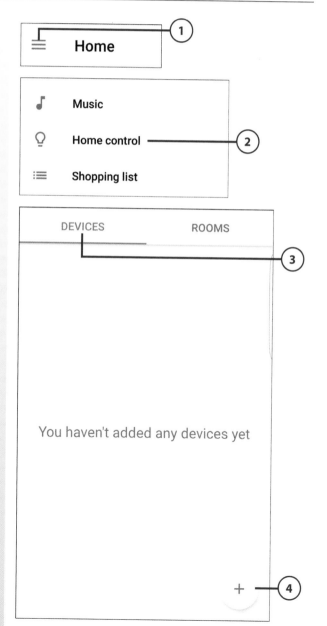

(5) Tap the device you want to add.

(6) Follow the onscreen instructions
to pair the device. You might
have to press a button on the
device, or tap the **Pair** link in the
Google Home app.

Add new

Honeywell

Insignia Connect

Iris

LIFX

Lutron Caséta Wireless

Nest

OSRAM LIGHTIFY (US)

Philips Hue ————————— (5)

SmartThings

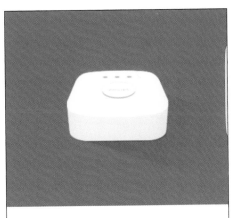

Connect Hue Bridge to Google

To connect your Google Home to the Hue
Bridge, Tap "PAIR" below. Then press the link
button on the Hue Bridge.

PAIR ———— (6)

7 When the pairing is complete, you may be prompted to assign this device to a specific room. Tap **Assign Rooms.**

8 Tap the **Edit** (pencil) icon for the device you want to assign.

9 Tap the room to which you want to assign this device. (Or, to create a new room, tap **Add a Room** and enter the desired name, like "Mike's Bedroom.")

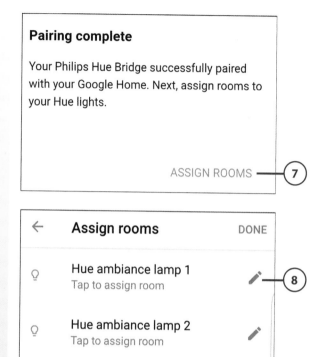

Pairing complete

Your Philips Hue Bridge successfully paired with your Google Home. Next, assign rooms to your Hue lights.

ASSIGN ROOMS —— **7**

← **Assign rooms** DONE

Hue ambiance lamp 1
Tap to assign room —— **8**

Hue ambiance lamp 2
Tap to assign room

← **Rooms**

Add a room

○ Attic

○ Backyard

○ Basement

○ Bathroom

○ Bedroom —— **9**

○ Deck

○ Den

⑩ Tap **Done.**

←	**Assign rooms**	DONE ⑩
♀	Hue ambiance lamp 1 Bedroom	✎
♀	Hue ambiance lamp 2 Tap to assign room	✎

Use the Google Assistant to Control Your Smart Devices

After you've paired all your devices with the Google Home app, controlling those devices is as easy as issuing a vocal command to the Google Home Device. What command you issue depends on the specific device and what you want to do.

For example, if you're working with smart lights, simply tell Google something like the following:

Hey Google, dim the bedroom lights.
Hey Google, set the living room lights to 50 percent.
Hey Google, turn on the living room lights.
Hey Google, turn off all the lights.
Hey Google, are the lights on in Bobbie's bedroom?

If you're controlling a smart switch or plug, and it's assigned to a given appliance, you can tell Google

Hey Google, turn off the hallway fan.
Hey Google, turn on the coffee maker.

Got a smart thermostat connected to your system? Then tell Google

Hey Google, turn up the heat.
Hey Google, set the thermostat to 70 degrees.
Hey Google, what's the temperature inside?

It's really that simple. The Google Assistant does a great job of figuring out what you want to do with a given device. And if you're not sure which commands work, look them up on a given device's website, or just experiment. Chances are, the Google Assistant will know what you're asking.

In this chapter, you learn how to use smart technology to enhance your independence— and the independence of loved ones.

→ Making Daily Living Easier
→ Keeping You and Your Loved Ones Safer
→ Embracing In-Home Care

Using Smart Technology for Independent Living

Most people want to stay in their homes and live independently for as long as possible. Ambient assisted living (AAL) lets them do that. AAL is defined as "the use of information and communication technologies (ICT) in a person's daily living and working environment to enable them to stay active longer, remain socially connected and live independently into old age."

This fancy definition really boils down to using various technologies— including but not limited to smart home technologies—to enable more independent living. Making your life easier on a day-to-day basis is what smart home technology is all about, and it's especially useful when you're dealing with physical or mental challenges.

What types of technology and devices are useful for ambient assisted living? The AAL movement embraces anything and everything that makes people safer and more in control of their daily activities. We're talking everything from voice-activated controllers and smart lighting systems to GPS trackers and connected security cameras. This chapter discusses them all.

Making Daily Living Easier

Smart technology can make life easier for people of any age. Depending on your physical condition, the simple act of getting up to turn on the lights or answer the doorbell can sometimes be difficult. The more things you can automate or control from the comfort of your bed or living room couch, the easier it is for you to continue living independently in your family home.

Use a Voice-Controlled Personal Assistant

Arguably the most useful bit of smart technology for independent living is voice control. If you can't get up from your couch or bed, or even find operating a remote control or smartphone problematic, speaking questions and commands into a central device lets you do many things you couldn't otherwise.

There are two such voice-controlled devices on the market today: Amazon's Echo (and smaller Echo Dot) and Google Home. Both the Amazon and Google controllers work with a variety of smart devices; just make sure the devices you have are compatible with the controller you choose.

The key here, after you've purchased and set up your Echo or Google Home device, is to connect it (via the Alexa or Google Home smartphone app) to whatever smart devices you have in your home. Then you can control those devices—turn down the lights, turn up the thermostat, lock the front door, and so on—just by talking to your Echo or Google Home device and its built-in personal assistant, either Alexa or the Google Assistant. Whether you find it difficult to get around or if you're essentially bedridden, being able to use voice commands makes it a lot easier to do basic day-to-day activities.

Of course, an Echo or Google Home device can do a lot more than control your smart lighting and other smart devices. You can use the device's personal assistant assistant to read you the latest news and weather forecast, put together a shopping list, find information about local events and businesses, set alarms and timers, and a lot more—all via convenient voice commands. Essentially, your Echo or Google Home can replace your clock radio, newspaper, encyclopedia, and more.

All of this makes the Echo or Google Home ideal for those with fading eyesight or other physical challenges. Just let Alexa or the Google Assistant read you whatever it is you want to know!

Amazon Echo and Google Home

Learn more about the Amazon Echo device and Alexa personal assistant in Chapter 11, "Controlling Your Smart Home with Amazon Alexa." Learn more about Google Home and the Google Assistant in Chapter 12, "Controlling Your Smart Home with Google Home."

Install Smart Lighting Systems

If you're trying to ensure independent living for yourself or a loved one, what things in your home do you need to connect to your Echo or Google Home voice controller? For most people, the first thing they automate is their home lighting—if for no other reason than it's probably the easiest thing to accomplish.

Smart Lighting

Learn more about the Philips Hue system and other smart lighting in Chapter 3, "Automating Your Home Lighting."

The benefits of smart lighting for independent living are many. When you connect your smart lights to your Echo or Google Home device, you can use Alexa or the Google Assistant to control all your lights (turning them on or off, dimming or brightening them, even changing color temperature) via simple voice commands, without having to lift a finger. You can even automate your lights to turn on or off in a given room at a specified time each day. It sounds like a little thing to control your lights this way, but it really makes a big difference when you have trouble getting around—or remembering to turn off the lights when you go to bed!

There are lots of smart lighting systems to choose from, especially if you want to link your lights to a smart hub, like the Wink Hub. The one I think is easiest to install and use in this situation, however, is the Philips Hue system. Philips makes Hue lights in a variety of sizes and configurations, and they're all easily controlled from the Hue smartphone app or from your Amazon Echo or Google Home device. There's also the added benefit of all these lights being LED lights—which means they'll last a good long time before you have to replace them.

Employ a Smart Doorbell

Whether you expect a ton of visitors or not, installing a smart doorbell can be a smart decision for your independent living. A smart doorbell lets you see who's at the door so you can decide whether to answer, without having to get up off the couch. You can even talk to the person at the door without having to open the door, via the doorbell's smartphone app. It's convenient, it reduces your physical stress, and it increases your security.

There are many smart doorbells out there, and they all do a decent job. My preference is the Ring smart doorbell, simply because installation is so easy. You can connect it to the same wires as an existing doorbell (nice if you're in a house) or just hang it outside your door without having to connect any wires (nice if you're in an apartment). This one's a snap for either you or your designated installer.

Smart Doorbells

Learn more about Ring and other smart doorbells in Chapter 5, "Automating Home Security."

Install a Smart Door Lock

If you want to go one step further from the smart doorbell, consider installing a smart door lock. If someone rings your smart doorbell and you decide to let her in, having a smart door lock means you don't have to get up off the couch and walk across the room to do so. You can control your smart door lock via voice command to your Amazon Echo or Google Home device, or from the door lock's smartphone app. For those people who visit often, you can even give them access via smart lock apps on their own phones. Like all the solutions here, this one just makes your life a little easier.

As to which smart door lock to go with, there are a few good choices. For ease of installation, however, I recommend the August smart lock. Unlike other smart locks that require the complete replacement of your existing deadbolt lock, this one only requires the replacement of the little thumb latch on the inside of your door, which is relatively easy to do.

Smart Door Locks

Learn more about smart door locks in Chapter 5.

Consider a Smart Thermostat

If you get up and down a lot to fiddle the with the thermostat in your house or apartment, a smart thermostat might be worth the investment. On the other hand, if you're more of a set-it-and-forget-it person, then it might not warrant the expense.

A smart thermostat makes your life easier in a couple of different ways. First, it learns your routine—when you turn up the heat, when you turn down the air, and so on—and automatically creates heating/cooling schedules. And second, you can control the thermostat via remote control, using the device's smartphone app or the Amazon Echo or Google Home device, so you can stay comfortable on your couch or bed when you're feeling a little warm or cold.

The most popular smart thermostats today come from Ecobee and Nest, and both work well with most other smart devices and the Echo and Google Home controllers. Know, however, that similar functionality is available from other thermostats from other companies; if in doubt, check with your heating/cooling installer for advice or installation.

Smart Thermostats

Learn more about the Nest and other smart thermostats in Chapter 4, "Automating Heating and Cooling."

>>>Go Further

MEDICATION DISPENSERS

While it's possible to program Alexa or Google Assistant to remind you when it's time to take your meds, you may be better off with a dedicated pill dispenser device. There are many different types available that range from simple low-tech day-grouping dispensers to more sophisticated electronic models that dispense your medication at the push of a button and alert loved ones (via a smartphone app) that you've taken your pills.

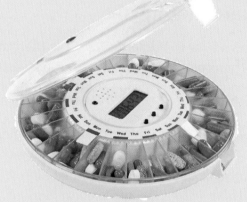

The GMS Med-e-lert Automatic Pill Dispenser

Some of the more popular pill organizers and dispensers include the following:

- GMS Med-e-lert Automatic Pill Dispenser (www.medelert.net)
- HERO (www.herohealth.com)
- MedCenter (www.medcentersystems.com)
- MedMinder (www.medminder.com)
- MedReady (www.medreadyinc.net)
- PillPack (www.pillpack.com)
- Tab Time Medelert (www.tabtime.com)

The goal is to make it harder to forget to take necessary medications. Sometimes even a little reminder—along with some forced organization—will do the job!

Keeping You and Your Loved Ones Safer

Smart home technology can also make it safer for those adults who need more constant supervision. In the past, when a mentally or memory challenged adult developed an inability to take care of himself or a propensity to wander off unassisted, the only solution was to move that person into an assisted care facility—even if remaining in the family home was preferred. Smart home technology, however, can duplicate some of the oversight and care you can get in an assisted-care facility, without having to move that person into a new home.

Smart Home Security

Learn more about home security systems in Chapter 5.

Whether it's you who's having memory lapses or difficulty doing things yourself, or an older family member with the same evolving challenges, you can employ existing smart home technology in creative ways to put off the decision about moving into assisted care.

Install a Smart Door Lock

We talked earlier about how a smart door lock can make day-to-day living a little easier. Well, a smart door lock can also help you keep track of individuals who might want to wander away when they should be safe at home.

How is this? Simple. Although a smart door lock can't keep someone inside against their will, it can keep track of their comings and goings—and alert you or other responsible individuals if that person opens the door when she shouldn't. You can set up most smart door locks to issue alerts (via email, text, or in-app messages) when the door is unlocked during specified hours. If your family member decides to take a stroll at 2:00 in the morning, you'll know about it as soon as the door is unlocked.

In addition, you can control whether the door is locked or not, from the comfort of your own home. Just use the smart door lock app to either set a lock/unlock schedule in advance or manually lock/unlock the door. You essentially take control of the door lock away from the person in the room and instead control it all from your smartphone.

Employ Smart Door and Window Sensors

If you'd rather not install an expensive smart lock, you can go with cheaper door and window sensors to let you know when your family member has opened a door or window. You won't be able to lock the doors remotely, but you'll at least receive an alert on your smartphone when something gets opened.

There are lots of smart door and window sensors out there. Samsung has a SmartThings Home Monitoring Kit targeted at this type of home security use, complete with SmartThings Hub, two multipurpose sensors (for doors and windows), and a motion sensor. That'll do the job for a typical apartment; you can add more multipurpose sensors to cover more doors and windows.

You can also piece together a similar system from the Insteon and Wink hubs. Wink is an especially good choice, as it's compatible with window and door sensors from a variety of third parties.

Add Smart Cameras

You can augment your smart home system (Insteon, SmartThings, or Wink) with smart add-on or freestanding security cams. Position multiple cameras throughout the house, connect them to your system's hub or use their own smartphone apps, and trigger them with their built-in or auxiliary motion sensors. This way the camera will capture video whenever your family member walks into that room. You can then configure the security cam so that you see the captured images on an app on your smartphone.

This type of monitoring system isn't quite as sophisticated as what whole-house-monitoring companies offer, but it'll get the job done for many families. You don't want to be too intrusive (so maybe you don't put a cam in the bathroom), but it does let you keep track of your loved ones from a distance.

Monitoring different rooms in your house with the Arlo smartphone app and cameras

There are several smart cams out there that can connect to an Insteon, SmartThings, or Wink system. Netgear, for example, sells a variety of indoor and outdoor Arlo cameras that you can position around your home. The accompanying app lets you watch up to a half-dozen different cams from anywhere you are, via your smartphone.

Use a Personal GPS Tracker

Another way to keep track of loved ones is to equip each one with a personal GPS tracker. This type of device is small enough to fit on a keychain or clip on a belt, and then it tracks the person's position via GPS and relays that information to a remote smartphone app. Most of these devices also include emergency alert buttons, too.

There are several of these small GPS trackers on the market, targeted variously at older people and children. Some of the more popular devices include:

- LifeAlert (www.lifealert.com)
- Lively Mobile (www.greatcall.com)
- MobileHelp (www.mobilehelp.com)
- PocketFinder+ (www.pocketfinder.com)

For example, the PocketFinder+ lets you live monitor the device's position via smartphone app or receive alerts when the device moves out of a designated zone. It's a good use of technology to track anyone who might potentially wander from their house or apartment.

Employ a Personal Safety Device

If you don't want to go the complete GPS tracking route, you can still ensure your loved ones' safety with a personal safety device. This is a small wearable with a big button that your loved one can press if she falls, gets hurt, or just feels threatened.

Several companies offer their own version of the personal safety device, including

- Athena (www.roarforgood.com)
- React Sidekick (www.reactmobile.com)
- Revolar (www.revolar.com)
- V.ALRT Personal Alert Button (www.vsnmobil.com)

The Revolar personal safety device

Let's examine the Revolar device as an example. It's small enough to tuck in a pocket or on a belt loop and consists pretty much of a single big button. When your loved one presses the button, a message is sent to a list of designated contacts. (And you can send multiple levels of alerts; press once to check in with contact, press twice for a yellow alert, or press three times for a red alert.)

Allen Band

More expensive—but also more useful—is the Allen Band (www.theallenband.com). This $350 device is a wrist band that can detect when you fall. If you don't press the button on the band in time after a fall, it automatically contacts family members or caregivers on your contact list.

There are also more sophisticated medical alert systems, typically accompanied by 24/7 on-call services. These systems employ devices that not only serve as panic buttons but also are capable of detecting falls and other potentially dangerous situations. When something bad is detected, the device automatically calls into the system's call center and alerts appropriate authorities and family members.

Some of the more popular of these services include the following :

- Bay Alarm Medical Alert System (www.bayalarmmedical.com)
- LifeFone (www.lifefone.com)
- LifeStation (www.lifestation.com)
- Lively (www.mylively.com)
- Medical Guardian (www.medicalguardian.com)
- MobileHelp (www.mobilehelp.com)
- Philips Lifeline (www.lifeline.philips.com)

Obviously, these services aren't a one-time purchase. Instead, you sign up for a monthly subscription. Prices vary according to services offered.

>>>*Go Further*

TRACK LOST ITEMS

Losing a thing isn't as dire as losing a person but can still be disconcerting. Ever lost track of your cell phone, TV remote control, reading glasses, or the like? Well, now there's technology that can help you find the things you lose.

The TrackR Bravo in a variety of colors

Case in point is the TrackR Bravo (www.thetrackr.com), a small and relatively inexpensive little circle thing. Attach a TrackR to whatever item is important to you, then sync that TrackR to the company's smartphone app. If the item goes missing, use the app to locate the item's TrackR in your house—or make the TrackR "ring" to help you find it. You can even program the app to notify you if the TrackR (and its item) get too far away from your phone. You can also use Amazon Alexa to find TrackR devices via voice command, which is doubly useful.

Embracing In-Home Care

All of the devices mentioned in the previous section are simple off-the-shelf consumer solutions to the growing challenge of assisting and monitoring loved ones who are living independently. And, to be honest, most of these solutions can be circumvented by a smart and motivated individual. (Hint: Just turn off the home's Wi-Fi router!)

When the challenge becomes too great, it may be time to evaluate companies that offer more extensive in-home care. These services go well beyond what you can do on your own, even as they employ similar smart technology.

The goal here is for you or your loved one to live at home as long as possible; it's what industry professionals call "aging in place." Yes, there may come a time where your only option is to move into an assisted living facility, but a combination of smart home technology and personalized care can help you stay where you are for as long as is feasible.

A quick Google search will reveal many qualified caregivers and caregiver services in your area. You can also search for caregivers using the following websites:

- Care.com (www.care.com)
- CareLinx (www.carelinx.com)
- Visiting Angels (www.visitingangels.com)

Obviously, you need to interview any potential caregiver in which you may be interested. In addition to asking about services and prices, ask about their familiarity with smart home technology. If you have smart devices in your house or apartment, you might want to add your caregiver as a contact or user. This way the caregiver can continue to monitor you or your loved one when the caregiver isn't physically present.

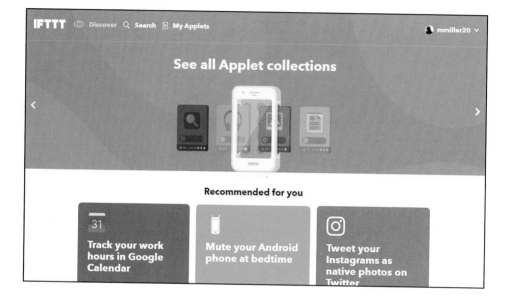

IFTTT ⊙ Discover 🔍 Search 📋 My Applets   👤 mmiller20 ⌄

See all Applet collections

<

>

Recommended for you

Track your work hours in Google Calendar

Mute your Android phone at bedtime

Tweet your Instagrams as native photos on Twitter

Adding More Functionality with IFTTT

As you've learned, all the available smart home devices, hubs, and controllers let you do quite a lot of automating of your day-to-day household tasks. There's more you can do, however, if you learn how to make all those various controllers and devices interact with each other—automatically.

Think of a potential task that involves more than one device. Suppose, for example, you want your porch light to come on if someone approaches your front door. This task would involve the motion sensor in your smart doorbell and the smart light on your porch; when the motion sensor senses motion, it triggers the smart light to turn on.

Now, you can't do that with either the smart doorbell or smart light individually. But you *can* do that with a special web-based service called If This Then That (IFTTT). With IFTTT, you can program the following sequence of events:

IF your smart doorbell senses motion, THEN turn on the porch light

It seems pretty simple, and it is—if you know how it all works.

Understanding IFTTT

If This Then That is a kind of web-based programming language. You create a series of conditional statements (IF THIS happens, THEN THAT happens) that are then linked to the smart devices in your home. When the condition you specify is met then the rest of the actions take place. In this fashion you can have IFTTT control multiple smart devices in your home—even devices that would not otherwise work together.

Technical Stuff Ahead!

Using IFTTT is a little more technical than the information we've presented previously in this book. If you're into a little basic computer programming then IFTTT is right up your alley. If, however, you're not comfortable with this technical stuff then bypass this chapter—or turn your IFTTT programming over to a friend who is more familiar with this sort of thing!

How Does IFTTT Work?

The IFTTT statements you create are called *applets*. An applet includes a single trigger and its resulting action. It's actually quite simple.

You can choose to employ applets created by others or create your own applets. You can browse existing applets and create your own on the IFTTT website (www.ifttt.com).

Before you turn on an applet, you have to link the appropriate device accounts to your IFTTT account. So if you have Philips Hue lights, a Ring doorbell, and an Amazon Echo, for example, you have to link those three accounts to your account on the IFTTT website.

After you create or choose an applet, it communicates with the appropriate devices via the Internet using the accounts you've linked. So, for example, if you activate an applet that operates a Hue light, the IFTTT website sends the appropriate command to the light via your Hue account online. (This also means that IFTTT applets don't work if your Internet is down.)

Why Would You Want to Use IFTTT?

Put simply, IFTTT lets your smart devices do more than they would do otherwise. IFTTT facilitates multi-device operations and helps automate many activities that you just couldn't otherwise. In short, IFTTT really powers up your smart home!

What are some of the things you can do with IFTTT and the appropriate smart devices? Here's just a sampling, in no certain order:

- Close your smart blinds if the outside temperature rises above a set level
- Display a notification on your TV (via your cable box) when Alexa plays a certain song—or when your smart smoke detector detects smoke
- Flash your smart lights when a door or window is opened
- Flash your smart lights when someone rings your smart doorbell or sets off the doorbell's motion sensor
- Have Alexa find your smartphone
- Have your smart lights blink on and off when your Alexa timer goes off
- Tell Alexa to play music on your smartphone
- Tell Alexa to turn on or off your smart oven
- Turn a smart light a different color if the door to your smart refrigerator is open too long
- Turn on smart lights or other devices when motion is sensed in a room
- Turn on your smart lights when your Fitbit senses you're awake
- Turn on your smart lights and set your thermostat to a given temperature when your connected car gets close to home

And that's just a sampling. The sky is quite literally the limit when it comes to creating IF…THEN statements that let your various smart devices work together.

>>>*Go Further*

CONNECT TO WEB-BASED SERVICES

IFTTT isn't just for smart devices. You can also link your IFTTT account to and activate IFTTT applets based on various web-based services. So you can connect to web-based email accounts (Gmail, etc.), social media (Facebook, Twitter, etc.), online storage services (Dropbox, Google Drive, OneDrive, etc.), instant messaging services (Skype, etc.), and more.

The possibilities here get interesting. For example, you can have IFTTT

- Create and update a spreadsheet of all the songs you play with Google Home

- Have Alexa text or email you your shopping list

- Have your smart lights flash when you receive an email or text message

- Save all the songs you play with Alexa to a Spotify playlist

- Schedule events in Google Calendar that automatically arm your smart security system

- Switch on your smart lights when a given weather service says it's started to rain.

Of course, all those web-based services can talk to each other, too. You need to check out the entire IFTTT website to see all the various applets that are available. You might find a few you want to use, all smart devices aside!

What Does IFTTT Work With?

Perhaps the better question is, what *doesn't* IFTTT work with? IFTTT works with smart devices from A (Amazon Alexa) to Z (Z-Ware). About the only big system missing from the list is Insteon, for whatever reason.

To see all the devices and services that work with IFTTT, go to www.ifttt.com/search/services. They're all listed there.

Using IFTTT Applets

To employ IFTTT, you must create an IFTTT account. This is free, and you can do so from the IFTTT website (www.ifttt.com) or smartphone app (available for both iOS and Android in either the Apple App Store or Google Play Store).

Link a Device or Service to IFTTT

Before you can turn on an app, all the devices or services used by that app have to be linked to your IFTTT account. All you need is your username (typically your email address) and password for that device's account, and you can then get going.

(For the purposes of the examples in this chapter, we're focusing on the IFTTT website. You can perform most of the same operations from the smartphone app, however.)

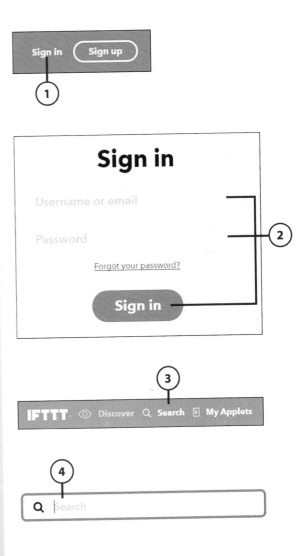

1. From within your web browser, go to www.ifttt.com and then click **Sign In.** (If you do not yet have an IFTTT account, instead click **Sign Up** and follow the on-screen instructions.)

2. Type your username or email in the first box, type your password into the second box, and then click **Sign In.**

3. The next page displays recommended applets. Ignore these for the moment and click **Search** to display the search page.

4. You can browse for devices and services by type, but with so many available choices it's quicker and easier to search for the specific one you want. Enter the name of the smart device or service you want to link into the **Search** box and press **Enter.** You see a list of services (devices) and applets that match your query.

5 In the Services section, click the device you want to link.

6 Click **Connect**.

7 When prompted, enter the email address or username and password for your device's account, then click **Log In.**

8 If prompted to allow IFTTT to access and control your device, click **Yes.**

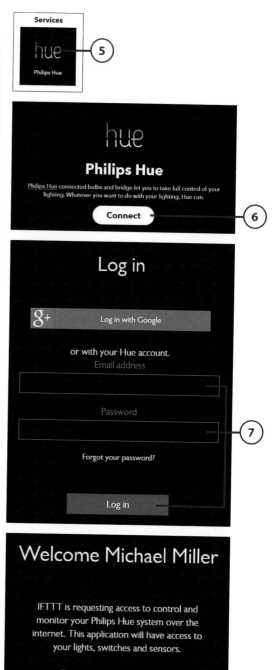

9 Your accounts are now linked and you're returned to the IFTTT page for that device.

Find and Activate an Applet

There are tens of thousands of applets available on the IFTTT site. You can browse or search for applets that work with your smart home devices.

1 Click **Search** to display the search page.

2 Browse for apps by category by tapping one of the categories beneath the Search box.

3 At the top of the category page you see all the devices or services within this category. Click a tile to view all applets for that device.

4 Scroll down the category page to view all the applets in this category.

5 To search for applets, return to the Search page and enter the name of your device or the type of action you want to include into the **Search** box and then press **Enter.**

6 You see tiles for all relevant applets. Each tile displays the name of the applet, the name of the user who created the applet, how many people have downloaded the applet, and which devices are required. Click a tile to view more information.

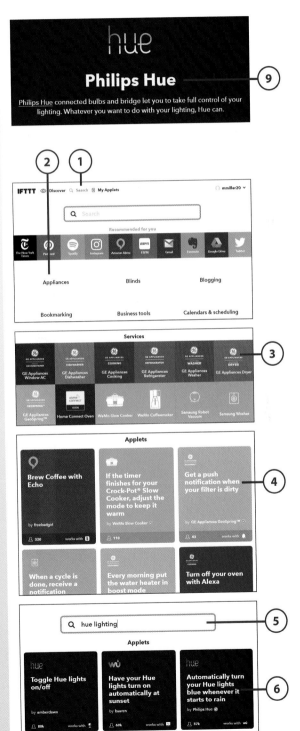

7 Click "on" the applet. (With some touchscreen devices, you need to slide the control to the "on" position.) If you've not yet linked a given device to your IFTTT account, you're prompted to do so.

8 Some applets require you to configure certain settings. Make the appropriate choices and then click **Save.**

hue

Automatically turn your Hue lights blue whenever it starts to rain

Match your mood lighting to the weather! When the current conditions turn to rain, your Philips Hue lights will follow suite.

by **Philips Hue** ✓

Turn on ———— 7

👤 **57k**   works with **wu**

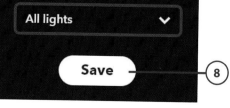

hue **Change color**

This Action will change the color of your hue lights. NOTE: Accepts color names and CSS hex color values. Defaults to white if no color match is found. NOTE: not compatible with hue lux bulbs.

Lights

| **All lights** ⌄ |

Save ———— 8

Manage Your Applets

After a time you might find that you've activated some applets that you don't want or need anymore. You can easily turn on or off individual applets from the IFTTT website.

1. Click **My Applets** at the top of the IFTTT home page.

2. All your applets are displayed on the Applets tab. Tap any applet to view more information or to turn the applet off.

3. Tap the Activity tab to view the activity for all your applets.

Creating Your Own Applets

You're not limited to the applets available on the IFTTT site. You can create your own applets based on the devices you own and your own personal needs.

Understanding the Parts of an Applet

Creating an applet is as simple as writing a simple IF…THEN statement. There are three elements to a typical applet:

- **Service.** This is the device or service used within the applet.

- **Trigger.** This is the action that activates the applet. In essence, the trigger is the "if this" part of the IF…THEN statement.

- **Action.** This is what happens when the trigger is triggered. In essence, the action is the "then that" part of the IF…THEN statement.

You specify the trigger and the related service, then you specify the resulting action and its related service. IFTTT does the rest.

Create a New Applet

You put together these elements by clicking through the prompts on the IFTTT site. Click IF to enter the trigger and related service, and then click THEN to enter the action and related service. You don't need to write any code; IFTTT does it all for you.

This example shows you how to create an applet that flashes your Hue smart lights when the Ring smart doorbell senses motion outside your front door.

1. Click **My Applets** at the top of the IFTTT home page.

2. Click **New Applet** to display the New Applet page.

3. Click the blue **This.**

4. Search or browse for the service/device you want to use for the trigger and then click it.

5. You now see available triggers for this device. Click the trigger you want to use.

6. Make any necessary configurations for this device and trigger and then click **Create Trigger.**

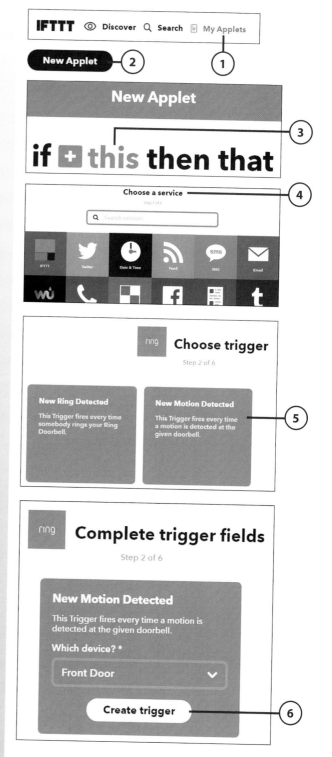

7. Click the blue **That.**

8. Search or browse for the service/device you want to use for the action.

9. You see available actions for this device. Click the action you want to use.

10. Make any necessary selections for this device and trigger. Click **Create Action.**

(11) Review the IF...THEN statement for this applet.

(12) If you want to receive notifications when this applet runs, click "on" the green switch; click it "off" if you don't want to receive notifications.

(13) Click **Finish** to activate the new applet.

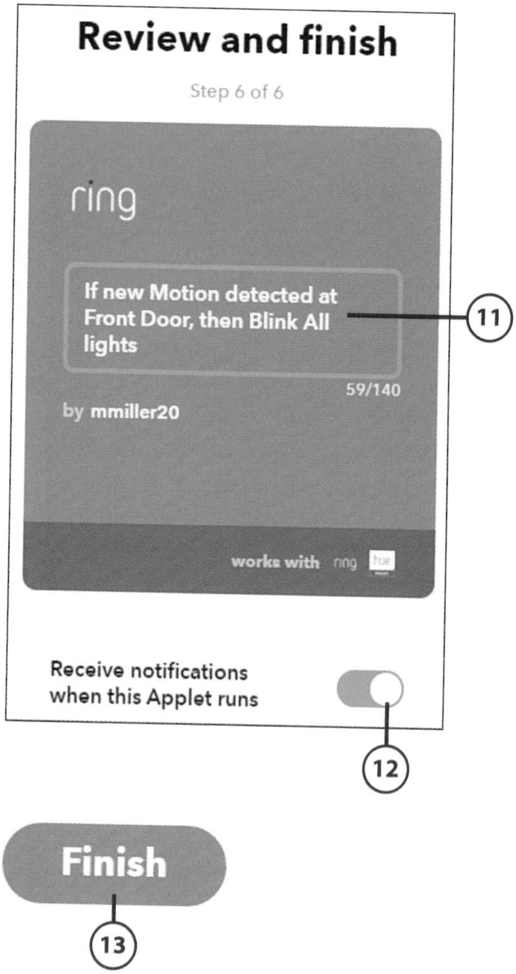

Review and finish

Step 6 of 6

ring

If new Motion detected at Front Door, then Blink All lights — (11)

59/140

by **mmiller20**

works with nng hue

Receive notifications when this Applet runs

(12)

Finish

(13)

Gateway > Connection > WiFi

Gateway
- At a Glance
- Connection
  - Status
  - XFINITY Network
  - Local IP Network
  - Wi-Fi
  - Firewall
  - Software
- Hardware
  - Wizard
- Connected Devices
- Parental Control
- Advanced
- Troubleshooting

TIP: View technical information specific to your WiFi connection. Click Add WiFi Protected Setup (WPS) Client to add additional WiFi clients to your network.

Private WiFi Network

Name		Protocols	Security Mode	
miller-linksys		G,N	WPAWPA2-PSK (TKIP/AES)	EDIT

ADD WIFI PROTECTED SETUP (WPS) CLIENT

Mac Filter Setting

The TC8305C can allow the wireless client stations to connect to your TC8305C in any of these ways:

SSID: miller-linksys ▼

MAC Filtering Mode: Allow-All ▼

Wireless Control List (up to 16 items)

#	Device Name	MAC Address

Auto-Learned Wireless Devices

Device Name	MAC Address	
Roku Stick - 630	08:05:81:E5:8B:D3	ADD
Unknown	54:8C:A0:2A:97:DC	ADD
HarmonyHub	16:91:82:54:73:0E	ADD

In this chapter, you learn the potential privacy and security risks of smart home technology—and how to make your smart home safer and more secure.

→ Privacy Concerns
→ Security Issues
→ What Can You Do?

15

Evaluating Privacy and Security Concerns

Turning your home into a smart home is certainly appealing. There's a lot to gain from automating much of the humdrum daily operations, and even more benefit when you connect multiple devices together to do things you never thought of before.

Alas, all good things come with some risk, and it is such with the technology behind the smart home. When you delve down beneath the surface, you'll find that there are multiple privacy and security concerns with today's smart devices—concerns enough that might cause you to abandon this new technology completely.

How safe is today's smart home? That's a great question, and you'll have to read on to answer that question for yourself.

Privacy Concerns

One of the most pressing concerns with smart home technology concerns privacy—your privacy. All those smart devices and sensors collect a lot of information about you. To perform all their tricks and automate their operations, they need to know what you do, where you do it, and when you do it. We're talking about knowing when you leave the house and when you return, which rooms you stay in the most, when you go to bed and when you wake up, even what kinds of foods you cook (in your smart oven, of course). Your smart devices know what temperature you like your home, when you water your lawn, even how much water and electricity you use and when—not to mention whether your front door is locked.

It's a lot of data, when you think about it. And it's all personal.

What Do They Really Know About You?

On the one hand, having your smart devices collect all this data can be quite useful. If your smart home knows that you're likely to be in a given room at a given time, you can save energy by turning off the lights and turning down the heat in all the other rooms. If your smart fridge (of the future) knows you like eggs for breakfast but it only counts a single egg in the bin then it can notify you that you need to buy more eggs. If your smart security system knows you're out of town for the week, it can make sure all the windows are closed and the doors are locked.

That's a good use of collected data.

On the other hand, what if all this data gets into the wrong hands? If a given smart device (like a smart hub or thermostat) collects useful data over time, what's to stop that device from transmitting that data back to the manufacturer?

After all, just about any data about you can be useful to many different types of companies. The company that manufactures a smart device might find your data useful for fine-tuning their existing services or designing new devices. They might also benefit (financially) from selling that data to other parties who can then use your data to target you for advertising, promotions, and other schemes.

Now, many of the companies offering smart devices say they'll sell only aggregated anonymized data—that is, the numbers from many customers all added up—not the specific details about you or other individuals. Even if that is true (and not all companies are saying they'll do this), there's still the possibility, if not the likelihood, that individual details can and will be extracted from the whole.

It gets even scarier when you realize that data from multiple devices can be combined and analyzed to reveal a variety of intimate details about what you do during the day, where you go, your interaction with others, your medical needs, your personal habits. You might be comfortable with all this information being available to strangers; many others may not.

How bad can it be? Let's look at a few examples.

Consider a smart thermostat like the Nest Learning Thermostat. This little hockey puck collects a huge amount of data that could be of interest to various parties. Yes, it learns your heating and cooling preferences, but that information isn't terribly interesting. What's more interesting is the data that other devices share with the Nest. When the thermostat is connected to your garage door opener or car, for example, it knows when you've left the house, so it can enter Away mode. Who might want to know when you've just locked the door and driven out of the driveway? Burglars, of course. Or maybe bill collectors who want to grab that expensive lawn mower on which you're three months behind on payments. Or even an ex- or soon-to-be ex-spouse who wants to build a case about your supposedly philandering ways.

Some uses of this collected data aren't quite as nefarious but could prove equally annoying. Your smart TV knows every program you watch; there are lots of companies that would like to have that information—the better to feed you advertisements based on your viewing habits. Shopping data is equally interesting to these parties, as is data that can infer other leisure activities. Or maybe a home goods company buys your personal data from your smart hub company and uses it to pitch you heavier blankets in the wintertime. It's not criminal, but it is insidious.

And that's the *good* use of this type of collected data. There's always the possibility of data theft—not from you, but from the companies collecting and storing your data. Even if a company that collects your data doesn't do anything untoward with it, a hacker breaking into the company's database will find data that he can personally use or sell to another criminal party. Just having the data out there is a big risk.

Alexa and the Google Assistant

Here's a scary thing. The voice-activated controllers from Amazon and Google store voice recordings on their servers to improve their voice recognition technology and services. That's a lot of data that, while undoubtedly well protected by the companies involved, still could be hacked. Remember, Amazon and Google are listening!

How Much Privacy Do You Need?

Data collection of this sort isn't something new to the world of smart home technology. For ages credit card companies, online retailers, and more have been collecting data about your spending habits—how much money you spend and on what. Websites use "cookie" technology to capture data about what pages you visit, and use that to serve up personalized online ads. And online streaming services know what you've watched or listened to so that they can offer "recommendations" based on your past viewing/listening habits.

On the surface, not all of this is bad—in fact, the slight loss of privacy provides a more customized experience online, and even in the real world. One can argue that that's an acceptable tradeoff. In today's electronic age—and tomorrow's world of the smart home—privacy simply isn't part of the equation. In order to benefit from the interconnectivity of smart devices, privacy is willingly abandoned.

Others, privacy advocates especially, believe that smart technology companies should not collect this data, even anonymously. Privacy advocates want transparency, too—they want manufacturers of smart devices to be perfectly clear about what data they collect and for what purposes. Consumers should have the option of turning off the data flow or deciding who gets access to that data.

The problem with turning off the data flow from smart devices is that it turns smart devices back into dumb ones. It's exactly that interconnected flow of data that makes the smart home so smart; if the data isn't flowing, all you have is a collection of isolated sensors, switches, and light bulbs.

There are no easy answers to this one, other than to recognize that there are tradeoffs involved. If you want total privacy, you might want to shy away from smart home devices and technology. And if you want all the benefits that come from smart devices, you might have to sacrifice some of your privacy.

Privacy Organizations

If you're at all concerned about your online privacy, look into the work being done on your behalf by The Electronic Privacy Information Center (www.epic.org) and the Privacy Rights Clearing House (www.privacyrights.org).

Security Issues

Related to the privacy concerns of smart technology are issues that have to do with security. Can unwanted intruders hack into your smart home devices—and what happens if they do?

Spyware and Botnets

Some attackers have even more malice in mind than just stealing a bunch of digital data. Think of the problems that could ensue if hackers gained control of the smart devices in your home, car, or city.

The dangers of someone hacking into your smart home in some ways resemble those of third-parties hacking into your home computer system. Computer hackers have been around for decades, and we know exactly what they like to do.

One of the most popular things hackers do is place spyware on your system. This is malicious software—dubbed *malware*—that tracks what you're doing on a given device and feeds that information back to the hacker. On a computer, spyware most often feeds information about the websites you visit to a central source that then uses that info to feed intrusive advertising back to your PC. When you're looking at smart devices, spyware might be employed to feed usage information back to a central source. I don't know what a third party might do with information gleaned from your smart thermostat or hub, but it likely wouldn't be good.

The other thing that hackers like to do is to take control of hacked devices and use them to perform other types of activities. In the computer world, hijacking a computer in this way turns it into what is called a *zombie computer*, and when you put together a network of thousands or millions of these hijacked devices, you create a *botnet* that can be used to attack other computers and websites.

Botnet attacks from compromised computers have been around for decades. Only recently, however, have smart devices been remote controlled in this fashion.

On October 21, 2016, the Internet experienced a massive outage when a rogue botnet attacked the computers at Dyn, a company that directs Internet traffic along the east coast of the United States. Dyn received tens of millions of malicious requests, which overloaded its system and brought the Internet to its knees.

DDOS Attack

The type of attack directed at Dyn is technically known as a Distributed Denial of Service attack, or DDoS for short. In a DDoS attack, multiple compromised devices are used to target a single server, system, or website by overloading it with multiple and repeated address requests.

What was unique about this attack is that it didn't come from zombie computers. Instead, this botnet was thought to have been comprised of smart devices—smart thermostats and smart hubs and such—all of them compromised by a specific type of malware. That's right, the Internet was attacked by a network of rogue smart devices.

Are the smart devices in your home vulnerable to this sort of hijacking? In short, probably—and especially if you are using easily guessed or hacked usernames and passwords for each of your devices and accounts. If you think about it, every smart device in your home is another potential entry point for malicious hackers. You need to be even more diligent about protecting your smart home system than you are protecting your home computer from attack.

>>>*Go Further*

SMART HOME SECURITY—NOT SO SMART?

Computer manufacturers and software developers learned a long time ago that bad guys want to get into your system, and the good guys need to protect against that. That's why you see a constant barrage of security updates if you own a Windows computer, and are under constant advice to install anti-malware software from McAfee, Norton, and others to protect your system. That's a good thing.

Unfortunately, many of the companies that manufacture smart devices are not as security conscious. Many of these companies do not come from the world of personal computing, and simply don't have the experience or knowledge to adequately prepare for or even be aware of hacking and malicious intrusion. In short, they don't provide adequate security protections because they don't know any better.

Now, that isn't a good excuse, but it's the reality of smart devices today. While some companies, especially those with a background in personal computing, pay attention to these security concerns, many others don't—at least not yet. Unfortunately, their ignorance puts you and your home at risk.

And that's a scary thought.

Seizing Control

We know that hackers can gain control of your smart devices to attack other parties. But what about hackers that might want to gain control of your system to attack you personally?

We're talking cyberterrorists who break into individual smart home systems or groups of systems with the sole purpose of gaining control of important systems and operations. When the smart devices in your home are no longer under your control, mayhem can result.

Admittedly, some of these scenarios might sound comical. A cyberterrorist gaining access to your home's smart lighting system could turn your lights on and off at random. Someone hacking into your smart TV could feed you unwanted commercials or propaganda broadcasts. A bad guy hacking into a smart toilet might make it flush repeatedly and force the lid to keep going up and down.

Okay, not too scary. But there are more ominous scenarios. How about a hacker breaking into your smart lighting and security system to douse all your lights and alarms and unlock all your smart doors in preparation for a robbery or home invasion? Or a cyber voyeur hacking into your smart security system to spy on you via your smart cameras? Or someone with even more malicious intent turning a company's smart heating/cooling system against them by cutting off air flow or inducing dangerous gasses into the system?

Spy Cams

There are already numerous instances of hackers taking over Web-based baby monitors and webcams to spy on unsuspecting homeowners.

It gets worse when you consider the larger city-, state-, and nationwide smart systems under development. Consider the potential chaos that would ensue if cyberterrorists decided to attack your friendly neighborhood power plant? Or tried to take control of your local water company? Or the nation's arsenal of nuclear weapons?

The more things inside and outside the home we connect via smart technology, the more things that malicious individuals or organizations can try to damage or control. It may sound nice to have virtually every device in the world connected via smart technology, but it makes for a very scary situation security-wise.

What's the solution? More and better security, as always. Some of this is on you, the consumer, but most is on those companies collecting, transmitting, and managing the data generated by smart devices. Every point in the network needs to be secure, which is a daunting task. The network of connected smart homes, as large as it likely will become, will only be as strong as its weakest link—that is, the least-protected smart device.

What Can You Do?

Given the potential privacy and security risks associated with smart devices, how concerned should you be? Are the risks big enough to scare you away from smart homes completely? Or are there things you can do to minimize the risks?

Making Your Smart Home Safer

There are a number of things you can do to improve the security of your smart home devices. Most of these are similar to how you protect your home and work computers.

First, you need to beef up the security on your wireless network. That means going into your router's configuration screen and changing the default network name and password. (See your router's instruction manual for details on how to do this.) You want a network name that's not directly identifiable; in fact, you may want to make your router private rather than publicly visible. With a private router name someone trying to hack into your wireless network would need to know the name in advance, which they probably wouldn't.

SSID

Your router name is technically known as a Service Set Identifier, or SSID. An SSID can be publicly visible, in which case it appears to any device looking for nearby wireless networks, or private, in which case its name is not broadcast and thus hidden unless you know it in advance. Obviously, a private SSID is safer from hacking than a public one.

You also want to protect your router by using a high level of wireless encryption. Most wireless routers today employ WPA and WPA2 encryption; you need to enable one of these (on your router's configuration screen) to make sure your wireless communications are harder for hackers to intercept.

In terms of your wireless password, the longer and more complex it is, the better. Obviously, changing the password from the router's default (which is often just "password") is a good idea. But go longer and more convoluted, and include upper- and lowercase letters, numbers, special characters, you name it. Make sure it can't be easily guessed, and you're less likely to have uninvited guests.

The same goes with all the usernames and passwords you use to sign into your smart devices and associated online accounts. Come up with complex and unique names and passwords for each account and device; if you use the same password for every device, then guessing the password of one gives hackers the passwords for all. I know, it's a pain in the posterior to come up with and remember lots of different passwords, but that's how you keep your system more secure. You want every potential access point into your network to be as uniquely secure as possible.

Finally, if you use smart devices from a company that experiences any sort of data or security breach, consider removing those devices from your home network. You might not be able to deal with unknown and unforeseen problems, but you can certainly do what you can about problems you do know about.

>>>Go Further
VIRTUAL PRIVATE NETWORKS

Some security experts recommend that you create a virtual private network (VPN) to isolate your in-home smart communications from the Internet as a whole. A VPN essentially creates a private network that you can access from anywhere but can't be accessed by anyone else without the proper passwords. It also serves to separate your smart devices from anything else connected to your home wireless network.

The main downside to a VPN is that it's difficult to install and manage for people who don't have the necessary technical training. So I can't recommend that the average user set up a VPN, although if you have a techie nearby or want to engage the services of a tech support firm for this purpose, it's not a bad idea.

Is It Safe Enough?

Even if you take all the safety precautions you can, there is still an inherent risk in using smart devices in your home. Companies are going to collect data from your devices, and that data could be compromised due to theft or unwanted use. In addition, even the safest home networks and the strongest passwords can't stop really dedicated hackers; if they want to hack into your smart home, they can.

For these reasons, people strongly concerned about security may be best advised to stay away from smart home technology, at least for the time being. There are no guarantees as to safety and security, and smart technology definitely is a little loose around the edges. If you want to stay completely safe, don't connect.

(That goes for any online connection, of course. If you want to be entirely safe and secure, you won't have an Internet connection in your home at all.)

That said, today's smart home devices are probably safe enough for the average person. It's unlikely that some nefarious person is going to hack into your personal home network and turn down the heat on your smart thermostat or turn off your hallway lights. There's not much benefit to that, other than annoying you. It's more likely that hackers will concentrate on the public grid and other city- or region-wide resources. Let's face it, you're just too small a target to the bad guys.

That doesn't mean you can ignore potential privacy and security threats. Keep abreast of the latest trends and make sure you install the latest software and firmware releases for all your smart devices. Over time, the smart technology companies will get smarter about security, too, and you'll benefit from that.

Glossary

Amazon Alexa   Amazon's voice-controlled virtual personal assistant, deployed on the Echo, Echo Dot, and Tap devices.

Amazon Echo   Amazon's wireless speaker/controller that uses Alexa voice-control technology.

Amazon Echo Dot   A smaller version of the Echo wireless speaker/controller.

Amazon Echo Look   A voice-controlled camera with Alexa technology.

Amazon Echo Show   Amazon's Alexa-based controller with a 7-inch touchscreen display.

Amazon Tap   A portable version of the Echo wireless speaker/controller with Alexa technology.

ambient assisted living   The use of technology to support seniors and others who need help living independently.

Android   The operating system, created by Google, used in most non-Apple mobile devices.

app   A mobile application running on a smartphone or tablet.

Apple HomeKit   Apple's smart home initiative. HomeKit-compatible devices work with the Home app on Apple mobile devices.

Apple TV   Apple's set-top box that enables streaming video and audio playback.

applet   Control statements created with IFTTT.

Bluetooth   Wireless technology designed to connect two devices.

botnet   A network of individual computers and/or devices infected with malware and hijacked by a third party without the owners' knowledge.

cloud storage   File storage on Internet-based servers.

Ethernet   A wired network connection.

Google Assistant   Google's voice-controlled virtual assistant, deployed on the Google Home device.

Google Home   Google's voice-controlled wireless speaker/controller.

Harmony Hub   Logitech's centralized hub that controls both smart devices and home electronics.

home automation   Automatic control of household devices and operations.

IFTTT   If This Then That, a free Internet-based service that lets you create chains of commands to operate smart home and other devices.

Insteon   (1) One of the most popular smart home systems, using its proprietary wireless technology to connect compatible smart devices. (2) A wireless protocol that connects compatible smart devices.

Internet of Things   A network that connects and enables communication between devices, sensors, and controllers.

iOS   The operating system used by iPad and Apple's other mobile devices.

iPad   Apple's tablet computer.

iPhone   Apple's smartphone.

malware   Short for malicious software—viruses, spyware, and other files that can damage a computer or mobile device.

motion sensor   A sensor that detects motion in a defined area.

Nest   The company, now part of Google, that created the Nest Learning Thermostat, Nest Protect smoke detector, and Nest Cam security cameras.

network   A system that connects computers and other electronic devices.

night vision   Technology that enhances viewing in low-light or nighttime conditions.

protocol   A set of rules that defines how a given technology works.

Roku   The company that created and sells the line of Roku stream media set-top boxes.

Siri   Apple's voice-controlled virtual assistant, deployed in its line of smartphones and tablets.

skill   For Amazon Alexa, a set of commands that enables specific functionality.

smart controller   A device or app used to control multiple smart devices.

smart device   A device of any sort that wirelessly connects to other such devices and controllers.

smart door lock   A door lock that can be operated remotely or via smartphone app.

smart doorbell   A doorbell, typically with built-in security camera, that can be monitored remotely via smartphone app.

smart grid   An electrical power network that employs smart technology to detect and react to changes of usage in real time.

smart home   A dwelling that uses smart technology to automate basic tasks.

smart hub   A central device that wirelessly connects multiple smart devices.

smart lighting   Light bulbs and fixtures that can be controlled remotely and automatically via smart technology.

smart plug   An AC power plug that can be controlled remotely and automatically via smart technology.

smart security camera   A small video camera that can be controlled remotely and automatically via smart technology.

smart smoke detector   A device that detects smoke and other adverse conditions and can be monitored via smartphone app.

smart switch   A wall switch that can be controlled remotely and automatically via smart technology.

smart technology   Technology that can sense what's happening around a particular sensor or device and act autonomously based on the information it collects.

smart thermostat   A programmable thermostat that can be monitored and controlled via smartphone app.

smart TV   A television set with built-in Internet connectivity and the ability to play content from various streaming media services.

smartphone   A mobile phone with built-in touchscreen, Internet connectivity, and the ability to run freestanding apps.

SmartThings   Samsung's smart home system, compatible with the ZigBee and Z-Wave protocols.

spyware   Malicious software designed to transmit information about a device's use to a third party.

streaming media   Music and video that are transmitted in real time over the Internet to a connected device.

touchscreen   A device display that can be operated by touch gestures.

virtual personal assistant   An application, such as Amazon Alexa and Google Assistant, that lets people ask questions and control devices by speaking natural-language commands.

Wemo   Belkin's smart home system, based on Wi-Fi wireless technology.

Wi-Fi   Short for wireless fidelity, the wireless networking standard used by most computers and connected devices today.

Wink   One of the most popular smart home systems, compatible with both the ZigBee and Z-Wave protocols.

X10   An older home automation technology.

ZigBee   A wireless protocol used to connect compatible smart devices.

Z-Wave   A wireless protocol used to connect compatible smart devices.

Index

Q-R

X-Y-Z

Answers to Your Technology Questions

My Windows 10 Computer for Seniors
Michael Miller

My iPad for Seniors
FOURTH EDITION
Michael Miller

My iPhone for Seniors
THIRD EDITION
Brad Miser

My Samsung Galaxy S6 for Seniors
Michael Miller

My Samsung Galaxy S7 for Seniors
Michael Miller

Mokena Community Public Library District

My Health Technology for Seniors
Lonzell Watson

My Digital Entertainment for Seniors
Jason R. Rich

My Internet for Seniors
Michael Miller

My Smart Home for Seniors
Michael Miller

My Social Media for Seniors
SECOND EDITION — Available August 2017
Michael Miller

My Digital Photography for Seniors
Jason R. Rich

My Digital Travel for Seniors
Jason R. Rich

My Facebook for Seniors
THIRD EDITION
Michael Miller

The **My...For Seniors Series** is a collection of how-to guide books from AARP and Que that respect your smarts without assuming you are a techie. Each book in the series features:

- Large, full-color photos
- Step-by-step instructions
- Helpful tips and tricks

For more information about these titles, and for more specialized titles, visit

quepublishing.com

Pearson

Que